SOCIAL STIGMA OF OCCUPATIONS

Social Stigma of Occupations

The Lower Grade Worker in Service Organisations

CONRAD SAUNDERS

Middlesex Polytechnic

Gower

Published by
Gower Publishing Company Limited,
Westmead, Farnborough, Hants., England

ISBN 0 566 00334 1

Printed in Great Britain by Biddles Ltd, Guildford, Surrey

Contents

VISUAL PRESENTATION

Preface

One's early life experiences leave their mark. When, as a boy in Vienna
I kicked a ball around in the local park in preference to getting on
with homework, my mother threatened I would end up as a sewage worker -
the one occupation symbolising in most European countries the definition
of a less successful life. Strong public consciousness of occupational
status was an accepted norm of the times, despite the prevailing unemployment during the 'thirties, and rare was the mother whose son
wasn't to become a doctor. My memories also extend to the subject of
food, which has always held a culturally signficant place in Central
Europe and which presented a frequent topic of conversation in the home
to reach the alert ears of a child. But it was mainly from my years in
an orphanage (Children's hotel?) that I had my first contact with the
institutional side of catering and a taste of learner-plongeuring when
helping in the kitchen.

From an interest in food, it is only a short step to an interest in the
occupations connected with food, and this continued interest matured
during my University studies in Manchester when my curiosity in hotel
and catering occupations and the feelings of the incumbents was further
aroused by the writings of Prof. William Foote Whyte on human relations
in the restaurant industry in America. My vacation work during that
time in the kitchens of holiday camps, mingling with a fascinating
motley of human types among the porters, kitchen hands, waitresses,
cooks and chefs, increased my interest and I resolved to research the
subject in depth if ever I were to find someone to take on the job of
supervision. It was not until three years later that I found such a
man in George Paton at the University of Aston, who has had considerable
research experience in the comparatively new field of the sociology of
occupations, and who for the hard years of my part-time research became
my enthusiastic mentor in the face of predictions by those who had researched this industry that a study of kitchen porters could never
succeed. They were proved wrong. My thanks go to him for his encouragement, academic guidance, counsel when researching in the field and for
the occasional hospitality of his home, where we discussed matters
sociological in the kitchen while George exercised his own culinary
skills to sustain us.

Most social writers on occupations are agreed that the empirical material still outweighs the theoretical substance. Even so, it might be
considered ironical that researchers have concentrated more on high-
prestige occupations while the atypical groups at the bottom of the heap
have never been looked at. It is my hope that I am helping to redress
the balance by my pioneering efforts to add, as another theoretical
dimension the conceptualisation and (by the surveys and profiles of
some ten occupations at the low end of the prestige scales in society)op-
erationalisation of occupational stigma, to the body of knowledge in
the sociology of occupations. In addition; the focus of this research
interest necessitated that I become acquainted with the works of Prof.
Everett Cherrington Hughes, and I take this opportunity to acknowledge
here my intellectual debt in admiration for his perceptive gifts of
describing the world of work and occupations.

It is hoped that several groups of readers will find this book useful. It aims to add another (the social) dimension to the many functional and pragmatic ones generally found in management texts; it aims by means of a dose of carefully researched case studies of socially undervalued occupations, as seen from different perspectives, to convey the next best thing to those people in management positions who have never personally experienced what it is like to do this kind of work; it aims further to share with the readers the author's endeavours to throw a little more light on and contribute something to the intricacies appendant in the explanation of occupational stigma; it aims also to illuminate the history, over the centuries, of two specific occupations and to show how, out of the decline of one, an entirely new industry arose; the book deals with social aspects of hotel and kitchen organisation and offers suggestions to all grades of management of ways and means to reduce transience among lower-grade workers of all types in exchange for greater stability and savings in cost.

Thus, the book should interest Personnel Managers in the Hotel and Catering and other Service Industries, People in Management Positions in industries where low-prestige occupations prevail and those teaching in hotel and catering in its various aspects on the innumerable courses in this country. It is hoped also that the book would interest not only Occupational Sociologists in Universities and Polytechnics, but also perhaps those engaged in the teaching of Management Studies in the sectors of Manpower and Industrial Relations in Higher Education. Since work is still so central in all our lives, a certain curiosity might also be aroused about this stigma in work phenomenon among social historians as well as a more general readership, who are concerned with such social effects as arise from the status and prestige of occupations and the feelings of those who fill the positions in less attractive work; and indeed, the effects of the changing occupational structure in the present, of many people perplexed by the contemporary industrial climate.

High on the list of additional acknowledgements are those organisations and individuals who helped with the problems of the survey and the empirical side of the research in the many hotels. The financial support of the SSRC, without which the extensive survey might have been difficult to complete, and to Helen Curtis, my research assistant, who travelled to do the bulk of the interviews; the heads and staff of the Catering and Hotel Studies Department of the Polytechnics in Wolverhampton and Middlesex, for allowing me to pester them with questions; the Director of the Catering Education Research Institute, for helping with the categorisation, coding and punching of the survey results; and the London University Computer Centre for advising on the use of the SPSS and for persuading their computer to co-operate with me. I thank the managers of the hotels for their interest and the respondents for their willing co-operation and patience in my endeavours; the HCITB, the Offices of the Population Census, the Departments of Employment and Health, and earlier in my work, the Birmingham Branch of the TGWU - all helped willingly and often at short notice to supply the information needed.

More recently, during the process of exhausting revision and conversion
of the thesis into a readable manuscript, the Seminars of the Centre for
Occupational and Community Research at the Middlesex Polytechnic furnished me with some stimulating ideas, as did some colleagues on the
Behavioural Science side. The Polytechnic's Cartographic Section's expert assistance with the presentation of the visual matter was more than
welcome and my special gratitude must also go to Carol Davis for her
effective and interested typing. Most of all, I acknowledge with appreciation George Paton's help with the reading of the manuscript and for
making suggestions for its improvement. The responsibility for any sins
of commission or omission is, of course, entirely mine.

1 Introduction — the social meaning of work

The very mention of such unsatisfactory occupational designations as Assistants, Operatives, Attendants, Hands, Labourers, Service Workers and indeed Porters, at once places for a job holder upon the public mind a discrediting label. This tends to project a social image of diminished competence, inferior intelligence, minimal if any training, the lowest level of skill and a reduced capacity to make a useful and telling contribution to the overall wealth of society. Added to this, to reinforce stigmatisation, are the apparent characteristics of the limited educational requirements, the heavy physical, dirty or socially demeaning work, unpleasant working conditions and, not untypically, casual or low income.

This book deals with such matters as are not often found in management texts or syllabuses in discussing the work patterns and occupational experiences of the less skilled, the less educated, the less paid, the intermittent, the casual, the alienated grades. It hopes to offer a new perspective on old problems associated with work and industry. Its prime objective is to add an extra dimension to the normally functional approaches in management literature and give the social side of work some added attention. The book contains much about the human shape of work to interest the general reader who desires to know how those in the lower regions of work activity perceive their particular involvement and why some occupations enjoy a lower societal evaluation than others. Attention has been given also to some of the changing industries in which such work people make their living, while the kitchen porter in the hotel industry has been singled out for an investigation in depth (by using in an earlier chapter the occupational history method as an analytical perspective), to trace the evolution of this work over a period of some 800 years.

Those in executive, managerial or supervisory positions who aim to understand their workforce, wish to improve the stability of the under-taking in terms of manpower, and indeed feel some compassion for staff at the lower levels of the enterprise, probably experience some curiosity about the historical development of certain of these occupations. Such background information will undoubtedly provide an extended horizon and a broader understanding of how members of the occupations under review experienced their work through the ages in the social climate in which they found themselves. Occupations such as Janitor, Nightwatchman, Hospital Porter, Catering Worker, Dustman, Car Parking Attendant, Kitchen Porter, Building Operative, Garment Worker and Domestic Service Worker, all appear in various parts of the book to display their occupational roles to the reader.

The first chapter deals in outline with the social meaning of work, its function and centrality in our lives, its evolutionary perspectives, its subjective evaluation and purpose. Chapter Two contains a number of carefully researched case studies, while Chapter Three delves theoretic-ally into the mysteries of occupational stigmatisation to plant the seeds for possible further research. It is slightly more demanding of concentration on the part of the reader in its attempt to analyse the stigma concept in terms of its origin, its anatomy and its general social effects upon incumbents who are contaminated by it. Chapter Four discusses in depth two service industries and their workers and, in context, traces the occupational history of the kitchen porter from the 11th Century to the present day. It also elaborates on historical aspects of the domestic service industry and shows how it was transformed into the hotel and catering industry of our time. Chapter Five looks at hotel organisation, by way of the influence of such matters as tradition, institutional personality, ethos and character, customs and behaviour patterns of a hotel. Another part of the same chapter discusses the hierarchy and status of occupations in the kitchen, and how the menu structure determines the social organisation there. Chapter Six is wholly taken up by our survey in 70 hotels, spread over eleven towns and cities of the West Midlands. The research method we adopted here relates a lowly-assigned occupational category to a whole range of social features (variables) which cover job holders' total profile and identity within the work environment and outside. Chapter Seven turns from the subjective experiences of the work group investigated to objective analysis at macro-level and inter-relates the stigma effect across personal, occupational and industrial boundaries. Chapter Eight, the concluding chapter, and an important one for employers and managers, presents a summary of the survey findings together with some unexpected conclusions; a discussion of how occupation and person interact in relation to the stigma; a critical review of the managerial perception of a low-level worker stereotype; a framework for the interpretation of and an adjustment to occupational stigma; and, finally, proposals towards a re-orientation for management as to how the work role of the lower-grade employee might be differently perceived. The chapter ends the concluding evaluation with a number of points that are thought to have contributed something to new knowledge in this particular field of research.

THE SOCIAL MEANING OF WORK

Many important and interesting questions are closely bound up with the role of work in our lives. At least until the birth of the 'silicon chip', Western industrial society had regarded a man's work role as central to his life and personality. While the economic function of work has long been taken for granted, its social purposes have received scant attention in the literature that deals with the management of people. There is a story of a pragmatic business executive whose limited response to the environment was his obsession with labour costs. When he died and his spiritualist widow managed at long last to make contact with him, he promptly reproached the woman for employing six coffin bearers at the funeral when four could have done the job. Wage costs are undoubtedly a concern, but frequently this hides more deep-seated problems associated with work in employment because work is in some respects a measurable activity. To perceive one's work activity exclusively in this way tends to ignore the profound impact it has on a person, the social effects, and generally gives a distorted view of society.

In the economic sense, the housewife does not work. But if the total of housewives engaged in their multiple tasks around the home had to be paid, our Gross National Product would be amply enlarged by that amount.

Similarly, the housewife who undertook the care of the children of others would be deemed to be 'working'. Another conceptual distortion is the equation of pay with the worth of a person, in this way presenting the unemployed as worthless and the lower-paid as contributing little that society values. Had history been kinder to the kitchen porter, say, than to the physician in the allocation of rewards, the contribution of the former in terms of hygiene and the prevention of disease might have been more highly rated by society.

The definition of, and the problems associated with, the work function are, therefore, more complex than a crude economic approach would indicate and worthy of a deeper consideration by an aspiring incumbent of responsibility in an organisation. Work, as such, had interested philosophers long before the birth of classical sociology, although one of the most prominent founding fathers (Max Weber, 1864-1920) (1) lends it relevance by suggesting that our everyday experiences with others consist largely of unexciting routines, but importantly provide a social fabric that endures over time. Our diagramatic presentation (see Fig.1) of the historical evaluation of work, its centrality, subjective meanings and purposes, should help the reader in placing the various issues with which this book will later be concerned in some rational context of occupational differentiation. Clearly, on a more personal level, the crucial psychological rôle of work in terms of status, competence, achievement, meaningful activity, self-esteem, identity, sense of order in one's life and, not least, how others in society rate one's contribution, can hardly be overestimated.

This raises two questions at the present time: one is that by translating work into occupation, one must immediately take account of new attitudes of job holders towards particular kinds of work; and the other concerns the situation that will be created in the future by the emergence of a new technology for those who feel work to be such an essential activity in their lives that they are demanding a share of it. These two questions are bound up with two considerations, one relating to the coming of the so-called leisure society, still very much a prognostic, if not speculative, theme which perhaps concerns us less in this discussion. The other consideration, i.e., how work is experienced by incumbents as members of particular occupations, is much more the area to which it is intended our treatment should relate.

A recent 'Observer' review of the passing decade compared 'history' with a salami, sliceable thick or thin, where a period of years might be a convenient enough cut to chew without losing the flavour or producing indigestion. Clearly, the coming decades signal structural and technological changes in production (2) and service industries (3) which, for management and work people will require new attitudes to meet the needs for innovation, adaptation and adjustment. Hence, it might be more appropriate to refer to completely new flavours to chew, which while benefiting some will quite feasibly produce indigestion for many others.

If we are to experience the emergence of a spate of new occupations and the demise of others, the continuing centrality of work itself and the specific activities in a number of enduring service occupations - and indeed the feelings of those engaged in them - appear to be of more than just peripheral import. Certainly, the rise of the service economy is a key aspect of modern industrial societies, where increasing technological sophistication requires fewer and fewer people to participate in direct productive activities. At the same time, our advancing standards of affluence (of course still denied to some social groups) have created a demand for the generation of a variety of services into which more and more of the labour force has been and will be diverted.

In addition to the impact of technology on the proliferation of various kinds of work, other characteristics will influence the shape of the occupational structure. The increasing economic involvement of women in service occupations and the expansion of the Tourist Industry are just two examples of this. Recent press reports of acute shortages of staff in hotels in London and the South East (Evening News, 18/9/79), and official publications making reference to the hotel and catering industry needs for large numbers of unskilled older people willing to readjust and to top up the two million already employed there (Department of Employment News, October/November, 1979), are further indications that some of the manpower reservoirs of the less-skilled are being increasingly tapped.

However, the pool among the low-skilled is substantial and fluid due to intermittent, irregular and seasonal employment. This may (or may not) offset the shortages in lowly-esteemed jobs such as dustmen, to which must now be added the predicted enlargements through redundancies, the flow of women workers into the labour market and the projected increase in the population of working age to 28 million by 1991. (4). Given this diversion of large numbers of the personal and other service industries, there will still be an ever-increasing reservoir of people available who are insisting on a share of the available work. For many others, the need will be to avoid widespread aimlessness or to learn how to use free time.

If this reasoning is accepted, we might see a social reappraisal and perhaps a modification of the currently perceived work ethic. Speculations along these lines raise some (presently unanswerable) sociological questions, e.g., whether the social status of even the lowly-regarded occupations might then transcend that of those whom the working world rejects altogether; and whether new cultural norms will have removed the stigma of worklessness from those who no longer experience personal shame on account of being unemployed. There is the thought that by studying the meaninglessness of work so apparent in low-status occupations, the taken-for-granted aspects of meaningful work and job satisfaction are often highlighted also. But, it is now the likely work ethic of the future and how it might embrace the lower-grade service worker that should receive some brief attention.

If the work ethic is seen on an historical continuum, we might pick from our diagramatic presentation (see Fig.1) the times when the worker's muscle power moved the simple conveyances or tools and he was regarded as inferior to a machine because he was subject to fatigue. Towards the mid-20th century, the concept of the 'rational man', who works only for financial advantage, was replaced by the 'psychological man', who while still responding to the carrot and the stick, has feelings and needs and reacts to stimuli from the environment. In the eyes of management, doses of 'welfare' would make him produce. The philosphy suffered a demise by the time of the Second World War, when 'social man' began to receive credence and the worker was viewed as a member of a group where work itself was seen as an activity of the team. We are now in the era of the 'participating man', whose work-setting relates to a stage of important and complex change, directly linking us with post-industrialism and an expanding service sector.

Literary people and philosophers have commented on the 'place' of work in people's lives from Greek to Roman times. For the Greeks, work was regarded as the proper activity of slaves while free men philosophised and engaged in politics, debate and art. In contrast, the Calvinist ethic pronounced work as exalting, self-disciplinary and as a token of grace, while the modern identification is clearly with conscious creativity. Women were excluded from earlier analysis altogether until the Protestant Ethic changed that. Thus, work was regarded as central and a necessity for most, but also for many a curse and to be avoided if possible. The important parts of man's existence were religion, war, politics and play until the craftsman of the Middle Ages took his creative pleasures from a 'job well done'.

THE DIMINISHED ROLE OF WORK

This ethic has now come to be questioned. Futurologists have taken a hand to tell us of the diminished role of work as a consequence of automation and the coming of 'creative leisure'. Such an idea could help to explain a possible relationship between a transient work population and occupational stigma if such sections of the community do not believe in the social necessity of regulated work, nor regard leisure merely as a rhetorical tool and adhere to a culture of leisure far in advance of our time. Lower status occupations may well appear to them not worthy of lengthy occupancy, and turnover in such occupations seen as one of the indicators of the stigma effect. Alternatively, there may be large numbers of persons who, by their mode of life, can be taken as protesting against the domination of work in the way they spend their time. The hobo, the tramp and those whom we call the vagrant, may regard leisure as a source of self-identity, distinguishing it from the ethic of free time, which is simply the antonym of work. It has been argued that the significance of work is a transient phenomenon which, in the prevailing social climate, has changed and may change again.

Many people now work compulsively, are often engaged in trivial tasks and tend to treat work as an end in itself, where it is highly rewarded. Indeed, it is open to doubt whether even the artisan of the past was really the 'free spirit' whose labour expressed his true, inner self, or whether he just produced the goods for the traditional market to survive. Performers of the more menial jobs have never been deluded that such work is unmitigated pleasure, although those in work managed to draw the community's respect and esteem, as has long been the norm, to signify participation in society. To the badly remunerated, work is a painful necessity and when not done at all can endow the affected with guilt or sin. All these conflicting influences have tended to survive together in our culture today.

Such cultural contradictions can splinter the social structure and make it increasingly difficult for the citizen to make up his mind what values he should believe in, what he should want and what he should do. On the one hand, the suggestion is that man's purpose in life is to demonstrate his worth through work, to build for himself, family and future; but man is also told to live well and accept the promise of greater leisure and prosperity. There are many areas which advanced machine technology does not help to solve. The irony is that machines make us produce more in a given time than yield more leisure, and they cannot do without human attention from their very creation. The paradox is that in the most industrialised societies, the percentage of attenders of machines has not increased by as much as the percentage of workers whose task it is to help people through service in other ways.

This brings us right back to the present. A recent, penetrating analysis on the individual and social meaning of work by the American sociologist, Alvin Gouldner (5) raises the debate altogether onto a higher plane by his perceptive interpretation of the different dimensions involved. His case is this: the quality of work in industrial society is insufficiently understood. It is on the one hand a 'familiar world of mundane menaings and routine encounters' - tools, assembly, fixed hours, money, production and consumption, but there is also another world entangled within the accepted shell of industrial power and affluence, the inner world. Complex division of labour and its conflicting occupational specialism make the worker responsible not for any whole object, but only a fraction of it. The orientation towards the production of these objects is firstly utilitarian, while other considerations as design, decoration, appearance, are of secondary importance. The affluent industrial society does not want the man himself, but merely the exercise of his skills; and if that is not needed, then the man is not needed. If the machine can perform the job economically better, the man is discarded.

Gouldner identifies two implications that arise out of this situation: firstly, that opportunity for social participation in the industrial sector is contingent upon a man's imputed usefulness, so that in order to gain admission to it - and the rewards it brings - people must submit to an education and to socialisation that early validates and cultivates only selected parts of themselves, that is those that are expected to have subsequent utility. Secondly, once admitted to participation in the industrial sector, men are appraised and rewarded in terms of their utility and are advanced or are removed in accordance with their utility as compared with that of other men. The common consequence these two processes have is the operation of a mechanism that admits some individual talents or faculties whilst at the same time excluding others as the criterion of division in the usefulness to industrial society. The not useful are the unemployed, the unemployable, the aged, the unreliable or intractable. In the case of individual persons, useless qualities remain at first unrewarded or later punished, should they intrude upon the utilisation of skill. Thus, the system suppresses the expression of talents deemed useless, and in this way moulds the individual personality and the self.

The Standards of Utility (and the excluded self)

Gouldner's argument then proceeds as follows: the individual has to adapt when he learns which parts of himself are not required and not worthy. His personality will be so organised that he conforms to the standards of utility and cuts his losses. In short, 'vast parts of any personality must be suppressed or repressed in the course of playing a role in industrial society'. Since all that a man is, that which is not useful must not be allowed to intrude; in this way, a man becomes alienated or at least estranged from a large part of his own needs, interests and capacities. There is then an 'unemployed self'. Sometimes, as Gouldner puts it, the excluded self takes its revenge upon its betrayer with a sad, poetic justice, as happened in the personal life of the ascetic prophet of time and motion study, F.W. Taylor (known as the 'Speedy Taylor' of scientific management), who spent his days creating a hellish efficiency and his nights propped up in bed, perpetually stricken with insomnia and nightmares.

The English industrial sociologists, Alan Fox (6), in his somewhat clinical, but no less important, analysis produced a logical framework which can help us to understand in what sense the individual may learn to adapt to a work situation and what kind of attitudes may keep him sane in spite of the unemployed self. Intrinsic, extrinsic and instrumental values on the part of the worker are identified to signify a liking of the job itself, a preference for money or simply accepting the need to work as a means to an end. The individual is also subject to qualitative and quantitative dimensions by a decision-making process inside and outside the work organisation, depending whether aspirations are substantive or procedural, that is, improvement, security, more challenging tasks in the case of the former; and a participation in the decision-making process in the latter. Fox also considers the crucial importance of practical priorities when aspirations may be high or low, according to whether they are subject to active endeavour and hope of attainment or held with less conviction, beyond the hope of realisation, or both.

Gouldner's perception of the role and function of work in industrial society today is less explicit in terms of a systematical perspective than that of Fox but he suggests an important new dimension to which perhaps insufficient attention in research has so far been given. He makes us aware of some parts of the self that are wasting away and so also waste away the lives of those engaged in particular types of work. If work in different occupations transforms the environment and so produces the society we live in, society also produces our work, defines and directs it in accord with a delineated purpose, and rewards it. To ask the purpose of work is to ask what purpose society assigns to it and the closer look we are about to take at the work experiences in some occupations will enable us to see whether the new industrial revolution has, by means of human-relations engineering, resolved Marx's criticism of the affluent industrial society: that work is not a satisfaction of need but instead only a means to satisfy needs outside work.

What is widely agreed cross-culturally and supported by empirical research is that society not only assigns work but tends to grade and evaluate it by its own cultural standards. Moreover, it stigmatises certain types of work, diminishes the reward factor by such debasement and thus adds to the frustration already suffered through the nature of the work itself. Stigma, therefore, affects society on a wide scale in a variety of ways. Certain occupations are particularly subject to social discrimination and the question whether human uselessness generated by the performance of certain work contributes in any way to such devaluation in the determination of the causes for the itinerant mode of life of large numbers of employees, is an important one. The kitchen porter, for example, has been called 'the untouchable' of modern times. Social anthropologists have long been concerned with the studies of contemporary cultures, particularly of the social behaviour of castes in India, which is of special

FIGURE 1.

MAKING SENSE OF THE SOCIAL MEANING OF WORK.

Functions and Centrality of Work	Evolutionary Perspectives	Subjective Meaning - (Beneficial)	Subjective Meaning- (detrimental or harmful)	Purpose of and Approaches to Work
Hunting and Gathering Societies: specialization only by personal skills; nomadic way of life. Agricultural Societies: more efficient use of technology, rule of customer, or organic place of work universal. Industrial Societies: mechanization, division of labour and mass production. Centrality of Work: allows a stable base for life; gives an identity and status; shapes the cycle of non-work activities; is for many a centre for social interaction; offers scope for involvement, challenge and interest; provides money for sustenance; produces the goods and services needed by society.	Ancient Greeks: Work is a curse. The Romans: Sentiments similar to Greek - let slaves do the work, pleasure and contemplation more important. The Hebrews: Work is a drudgery, an atonement for sin, but one can attain spiritual dignity from it. The Early Christians: Work for profit offensive; otherwise it is a natural right and duty. The Middle Ages: Work is appropriate for all; it is a means of spiritual purification. The Reformers: Work is the only way to serve God; it must be done to the best of one's ability. The Calvinist Doctrine: Religious sanction is given to worldly wealth and achievement. The Protestant Ethic: Hard work is an expression of one's piety; to be successful a sign of spiritual excellence. Karl Marx Period: If work were freed from capitalist exploitation, it would become a joy as workers improve their material environment around them.	Self-esteem: consisting of the two elements of competence and mastering the environment. Sense of Identity: with one's occupation and/or organization. Sense of Order: one has a fulfilling ordered life and is able to plan ahead. Creativity: producing something that is valued by others. Other Subjective Criteria: Offers a challenge; Occupies time; Enhances one's social estimate; Giving a service; Applying skill and craftsmanship; Making the grade to one-self; Living up to one's expectations; Proving one's personal capacity; Exercising one's judgement; Achieving concrete and specific results; Gives one a measure of sanity, sense of pride, confidence, responsibility, self-appraisal and purpose in life; Relates reality to the inner perception of reality.	May be fragmented; May be subject to continuous supervision; May be exposed to authoritarian treatment; May offer nothing but monetary rewards; May be sentenced to monotony; May be unable to control the pace of the work; May have to perform robot-like tasks; The work may be oppressive and dehumanising; Tasks may be too rigidified; Range of skills may be reduced by the job; Routinization may be increased; Autonomy may be lost; There may be no voice or say in decision-making; The job may be degrading; The work may not be respected by society; The work may be dirty or dangerous.	Purpose: Economic Social Psychological Political Approaches: Classical Industrial Occupational Structural Socio-psychological Ideological Predictive: Temporariness Taskforce Pattern Impermanent Jobs Second Careers Out-of-work Periods Less Work available Indirect Subsidies Re-design of Jobs Worker Participation Education for Leisure Reduced Work-Life Cycle Preservation of the Work Role and its Centrality, at least in the Short Run Policies for dealing with an increasing work force surplus to economic requirements.

8

interest in the context of stigma. On the sociological side, low-level work has attracted attention from researchers in such areas as occupational demography, careers, role relations, mobility, status, managerial philosophies and conflict, among others. There have been many surveys to facilitate the creation of useful conceptual frameworks for occupational sociology. We have tried also to meet an additional need, that of offering a social historical or diachronic perspective, to indicate the origins of occupational stigmatisation in an occupational history setting, as in our Chapter 4.

The aim, in the discussion of the cases to follow, is to penetrate more deeply into the personal and social drama of the work and work environment of occupations such as janitors, hospital porters, nightwatchmen, kitchen porters, car-parking attendants and dustmen, and in later chapters also domestic service, in order to learn of the social devices used to make work tolerable. In drawing attention to this need and abstracting it in terms of the 'other self', however, Gouldner and other writers leave some doubt as to what exactly constitutes the meaning of such need. Hence, the object of comparing these occupational experiences may fulfil the threefold purpose of, shedding some light on this 'need' concept; unfolding the peculiaries and special characteristics of these occupations; and helping to determine to what extent some of the ideas expressed here may require further empirical validation.

NOTES TO CHAPTER 1

1.   Weber, Max (1965), The Protestant Ethic and the Spirit of Capitalism, translated by Talcott Parons, Unwin University Books, London. See particularly Foreword by R.M. Tawney and the author's Introduction on Pages 1-31.

2.   Handy, Charles (1980), Through the Organisational Looking Glass, Havard Business Review, January/February, pp.115-121.

3.   Kumar, Krishnan (1978), Prophecy and Progress, The Sociology of Industrial and Post-Industrial Society, Pelican Sociology, London, pp. 200-219.

4.   Evans, Alistair (1979), What Next at Work, a New Challenge for Managers, Institute of Personnel Management, July, pp. 34-44.

5.   Gouldner, Alvin (1970), The Unemployed Self, in Fraser, Ronald (Ed.), Work,Vol.2, Pelican Books, London. The whole chapter relates.

6.   Fox, Alan (1971), A Sociology of Work in Industry, Collier-Macmillan, New York, Chapter 1.

2   Occupational profiles from the service sector

This introduction paints a preliminary picture of the occupation of
kitchen porter and shows how, in one particular industrial setting,
(e.g., the Hotel and Catering Industry), co-workers, management and
the incumbent himself, may all be instrumental in the construction
of an adversely-projected public image of an occupation and its members.

THE KITCHEN PORTER SEEN AS A STEREOTYPE

In anticipation of more precise statistical details left for later
presentation, we estimate the number of kitchen porters, kitchen hands
and plongeurs in this country at something like 100,000. We base this
figure on estimates published by management consultants of the numbers
of establishments in the industry. Licensed hotels then 12,000;
unlicensed hotels, guest, boarding houses and holiday camps, between
60,000 and 80,000. If we also include hospitals and the great variety
of establishments where institutional catering takes place, and the
vast number of non-residential establishments, consisting mainly of
restaurants, estimated at 35,000, the figure of kitchen porters may
be considerably above the 100,000. (We must also allow for a large
floating population, drifting in and out of the industry). A rough-and-
ready calculation shows this low-status, stigmatised occupation to be
no less than ½% of our total working population, approximately double
the number of doctors in the country, who reside near the top of the
occupational status scale; and forty times that of university profess-
ors, also holding top position in the scale. The kitchen porters are
variously described in the 'trade' as vagrants, unemployables, scum,
crooks, dodgers and alcoholics and similar, and form, therefore, one
section of a large, stigmatised work force much deserving of attention
and research.

THE HOTEL AND CATERING INDUSTRY IMAGE OF THE KITCHEN PORTER

Catering industry executives, chefs, cooks, apprentices and almost
every member of the estimated two hundred different occupations in this
industry will have his own story to tell of the kitchen porter he has
met. In this part of our discussion, we intend to paint a representative picture of the kitchen porter image as reflected in the 'trade',
and to this end quote from opinions, interviews and articles describing
this stereotype. These descriptions confirm, in the main, the observations made in a recent essay by a London College Catering Officer,
from which we may glean a realistic image, as it has existed for many
years, and certainly long before Orwell's time, as our historical observations will show.

   Still sadly true today, it used to be a popular derision in the kitchens of larger London hotels in the war period to ask what has an I.Q.
of 144, to which the standard answer was 'a gross of kitchen porters'.
Traditional catering still exists in the majority of undertakings and
requires the performance of many unpleasant tasks, without which the
provision of hospitality and food would lack essential support. Scour-

ing small and large pots, removing swill, cleaning drains and lavat-
ories, scrubbing floors, are but some of the many distasteful, unpleasant, badly remunerated tasks that today's 'untouchables' have to perform, important as such work may be (were it not done by someone) to
complement a viable business unit. Small, in referring to porters,
cleaners and general skivvies, calls them the 'forgotten legions of the
trade', ignored by theorists and regarded as a necessary evil by employers and 'the subject of slick sneers by everyone from apprentices
to managers':-

> ... your typical kitchen porter arrives flat broke
> and seeking a sub, stays for a few months of spasm-
> odic attendance, but is never at work the day after
> payday, and eventually walks out owing money to any
> other employee fool enough to have lent him any ...(1)

The kitchen porters, of whom a large number are said to have been
guests of Her Majesty, are described as a constant source of worry to
managers and head chefs, not only because of absenteeism disrupting the
smooth running of the kitchen, but also because of the quality of their
work. Small puts it this way:-

> 'All they are fit for but not good at', may seem
> a defeatist and cynical but accurate description
> of the professional kitchen porters, but can you
> deny that it is true of a high percentage of those
> unshaven men in greasy raincoats sent up by the
> labour exchange, ... I suppose that part of the
> definition of a typical professional kitchen porter
> is that he has no fixed home, but moves from one
> seedy lodging house to another (usually owing
> rent). It must be a strange and horrible existence
> in this Dickensian sub-strata of our modern civil-
> isation. Imagine, if you can, what it would be
> like to wash greasy pots in tepid water all day
> long (with occasional spells at spud-bashing for
> light relief) and then to have nowhere to go after
> work but a sordid doss-house, smelling of cabbage
> and socks. Under these circumstances, it is very
> likely that a pub would take most of your meagre
> wage, and as your shoes wore out the price of a
> new pair would not compete in value with a couple
> of evenings on the beer.

We have conducted provisional but unrecorded tests by questioning
hotel and restaurant managers, catering and staff officers, managers
of employment exchanges, chefs, cooks, uniformed hotel staff, waiters
and trainee cooks. In substance, this view prevails within the trade
and most can recall incidents of eccentricity which often support the
image of the kitchen porter stereotype. Once again, we are reminded
of the interacting influences that bear upon an incumbent by reason of
his work and the valuation society places upon it, his basic material
and psychological needs, and his own orientation towards a way of life
which may run counter to expected norms.

We shall now fill in some further gaps in the projected image, relating to the area of rewards for the work performed; but the completion of the picture must be deferred until we look at the operating kitchen as a social system and consider the duties and role relationships of incumbents. Small maintains that, although the kitchen porter belongs to the lowest-paid staff, the problem is not entirely one of extrinsic rewards. In his view, higher pay would still not draw good employees to this sort of work in any regularity and, in many cases, kitchen porters are not worth the rate of pay they actually receive. He adds: 'The general staff situation being what it is, aggravates the kitchen porter shortage. If a porter is clean, bright and reliable, he is soon promoted by staff-hungry management to assistant cook or breakfast and vegetable cook; and anyone remaining a kitchen porter must be pretty hopeless'. We note that Small is foxed by the contradiction of a kitchen porter shortage in times of unemployment and that he associates the type of work performed with a person's character and psychological make-up; but that he accords the kitchen porter the title of a profession. We fear that Small, a catering officer himself, appears to be blissfully unaware of the symptoms that bring about such situations as he describes. In our view, it is not so much a question of mal-socialisation, or that of a business paying 'what a man is worth'. We have already mentioned societal values relative to stigmatised occupations. In a macro-orientation, we must also seek our answers within a static and dynamic climate in the division of labour and specialisation, and the presence or absence of technological shifts as this affects occupational titles. It is a secret to no one that the kitchen porter does his best to live up to the image expected of him. Small does not discuss the need for training of such role incumbents as the kitchen porter; presumably, it is implied that no training is needed for such work. Finally, in micro terms, it will be a question of the resources organisations are prepared to allocate to work behind the scenes that improves the environment for the lower-grade kind but essential work. Indeed, we may remember that the hotel and catering industry is still a wages council industry where regulations regard the practice of living-in as an addition to earnings. Small's experience with kitchen porters living-in is considered fairly typical in the trade. In conceding that kitchen porters have no worthwhile home life in comparison with part-time kitchen maids, who are said to be used to washing pots and cleaning stoves, he argues that kitchen porters have, therefore, no real reason for working. Small goes on to say this about accommodation for kitchen porters:-

> 'Those employers able to offer accommodation for
> their porters do not, strange to say, keep them
> that much longer; but they do acquire a whole new
> set of problems. I shall never forget going round
> the staff wing of an hotel when helping in the
> search of missing silver. It was not an experience
> I would want to repeat too often, for I saw (and
> smelt!) enough dirty underwear, empty bottles and
> soiled china on that occasion to last ... (We
> didn't find the silver, incidentally, but we did
> discover that one of the kitchen porters was
> keeping a greyhound in his bedroom)'.

This general 'give a dog a bad name' attitude in the industry should give cause for concern; and it highlights the need and urgency for further investigating this social problem. Serving this end, we shall have to look upon the kitchen as a social organism within which inter- acting structural elements are represented as holding certain statuses and carrying out certain roles. This has been done in Chapter 5, while Chapter 4 investigates whether, in evolutionary terms, the social groups from which kitchen workers are recruited can be identified, and whether any possible variations in the role and status of this occupat- ional category can be traced over time. Chapter 6 then presents a pro- file of the kitchen porter as he really is, from the findings of our in-depth survey, covering some 70 West Midland hotels. Readers will find the shorter case studies of the six researched lowly-evaluated occupations in this Chapter equally revealing in terms of the work functions involved and how these affect the individuals performing in these jobs.

THE APARTMENT BUILDING JANITOR

Raymond L. Gold, a disciple of Everett C. Hughes (Father of Occupat- ional Sociology), has made a close study of the janitor's work routines in residential buildings in Chicago (2). In terms of intrinsic satis- faction (liking the work for itself), the janitor's work causes him many frustrations. He cannot hide the fact that he makes his living by doing other people's dirty work. Although, like most other occupat- ions, this one consists of various activities but when questioned janitors were bitterly frank about their work. In answer to what they consider- ed the toughest part of their job, they said almost to a man: 'Garbage! The stuff is often sloppy and smelly and almost kills you when you first start. The tenants don't co-operate; you ask them today and tomorrow there is the same mess of garbage over again by the incinerat- or; it is the most miserable thing to sort it out.' Thus, the physical disgust is not only between the janitor and the garbage, but involves also the relationship with tenants. As Prof. Hughes says, when he discussed work and the self, the dirty work of an occupation may be dirty in several ways. It may be simply physically disgusting; it may be a symbol of degradation, something that wounds one's dignity; but, it may also in some way go counter to the more heroic or our moral conceptions. In most occupations, some tasks at least create situat- ions where the role to be played causes the incumbent to feel a little shamed. It is because members of many other occupations do not speak so freely about their work, and may even conceal the infra dignitate, that we get false notions of the problems or overlook them entirely. We therefore also, comments Hughes, get a false notion of the possible psychological and social by-products of the solutions which are devel- oped for the problem of disgust. (3)

There are further conditions within the janitor's work that contrib- ute to intrinsic dissatisfaction and add tension and insecurity. Neither the public nor tenants accord the janitor high work status and he struggles to find ways to reconcile this influence with his self- conception. The other relationship which presents a problem to the janitor is that revolving around his occupational and personal aspirat- ions. Both relationships entail human and moral tensions with which he has to come to terms. Let us look at the interaction with tenants first.

13

The janitor's tasks, as the only permanent employee to give service to tenants in residential buildings, include looking after the heating and water systems, cleaning and maintenance within and outside the building and the less demanding repairs. Part of the work routine is determined by the weather and season - shovelling snow, coal or cutting grass - and the working day is long, although there may be only intermittent heavy duties. The janitor gets some free time during the day, but he must be available lest there is an emergency. He finds ways to escape from the monotony, but his leisure activities are restricted, narrow and confined. When he does 'get away from it for a while', no matter what arrangements he makes, he suffers from anxiety lest there may be a fire, boiler explosion or flooding. The tenant, however, is the one who interferes most with the daily activities of the janitor's life and work; but for a broken window, regular Sunday cleaning could have been done on time; but for a clogged pipe, he would not have been ignominiously called away from a meal with his family and his wife's critical relations,to whom he just explained the importance of his work. Inside the work environment, the tenant can cause a janitor great status pains, by the way he treats him, whilst at the same time being careless by 'dirtying' the place up. And not only that; the tenant-public feels that its individual demands must be catered for at once, thus - in the words of one janitor - 'having to please some fifty bosses at once.' Many janitors do not passively absorb the abuses of 'bad' tenants, but try to change them by 'training'. This means that the janitor uses various sanctions to get the offending tenant to conform to his way of thinking. Friction and countless frustrations do, however, arise when, in the case of 'untrainables', remedial effectiveness is not achieved. Then, the janitor's self-conception is undermined until he manages to come to terms, for example, as janitor-psychologist diagnosing mental instability or illness on the part of a tenant. According to the work concepts of Fox, it will be noted that although janitors are sensitive to intrinsic rewards, they do, in most cases, come to terms with the day-to-day frustrations, aspirations being of either low priority when tenants are beyond training or of high priority when tenant relationships are at a satisfactory level. (4)

Practical priorities also come into the reckoning if we look at the janitor's outside relationships with significant others; that is, role-set members including fellow janitors, superiors and union officials. If the janitor has substantive aspirations, that is if his endeavour is an extending of the nature of the work itself as well as on an extrinsic emphasis, we may then observe a telling social interaction of two kinds: firstly, colleague-animosity and secondly, janitor-boss paternalism. The janitor has some contact with colleagues although Gold has been able to observe only little group feeling. He is conscious of the lowly social image of his occupation in the community at the same time as his personal or self-image approximates more to middle-class values. To reconcile these two images, the janitor's attitude is to affirm the community evaluation, but at the same time not thinking of himself as unprincipled, disorderly and irresponsible, as is the stigma placed upon other janitors. There is not to be found any spirit of true colleagueship among janitors, but the work situation demands some co-operation if there are to be any free evenings. This leads to informal agreements on 'building-switching'. The danger here is that the 'deputy' may neglect unfamiliar tasks which can cost the

14

employed janitor his job. There is also a certain reluctance for janitors to discuss their work, even when they meet socially in the liquor
store. The reason is that they fear each other; fear that certain dis-
closed information may lead to a loss of job. Building-switching is,
therefore, mainly a utilitarian arrangement. Another practice, referred
among janitors as 'cut-throating' is largely responsible for the social
distance. This may be defined as an act that enables a janitor to
steal another janitor's building. This occurs when one janitor per-
suades another janitor's boss that he is the better man to look after
the building; or he might - perhaps as deputy - let unchecked water run
into the boiler of the desired building and get the incumbent into
trouble; a third method is 'stool-pigeoning', for example, disclosing a
breach of union rules when a janitor's wife is known to help him with
his duties. Other, more subtle forms of cut-throating also exist when
a janitor exceeds his level of effort and so forms a threat to the security and livelihood of other janitors in the locality. Since the janitor normally works alone, participation in a decision-making process
has less relevance in this occupation. A dependency relationship may,
however, be valued for its own sake if the incumbent defers to a pater-
nalistic boss or father figure or idolises the boss.

If decision-making be of smaller significance to him, an element of
protection is important to the janitor. He needs to achieve greater
security without becoming completely isolated from social activity.
There are union rules and the landlord will expect no more in the way
of work than conforms to these rules. Yet, janitors feel obliged to do
extra work, for if they do not, they are exposed to cut-throating and
that leaves only the landlords to turn to. Hence, it is the motto of
some janitors that 'a janitor should work in the interest of the owner'.
We have here an additional influence to those propounded by Fox, a high
priority aspiration of an instrumental kind for the removal of fear and
insecurity, under which substantive participation is made difficult
because the janitor is anything but free from the grace and favour of
his boss, who may use the cut-throating practice to further minimise
intrinsic work satisfaction without, at the same time, increasing extrinsic rewards. The janitor's position is, therefore, one of power-
lessness and fear that permeates the entire occupation and forms a
barrier to greater group solidarity and more intimate colleague relationships. The ironic situation seems to be that janitors, to gain security, play up to those against whom they are organised, in order to
obtain protection against those with whom they are organised.

Fox explains that priorities can also change over time. In this context, janitors operate two kinds of mechanism that aid them in their
quest to lessen insecurity. Firstly, Gold discovered no evidence that
any janitor ever aspired to this career; and a wide variety of reasons
were given to account for entry. But, once in this occupation, incumbents formulate a philosophy of success which has, as its base, the kind
of social skills that are to be regarded as even more significant than
technical proficiency, considered by janitors fairly routine. Secondly, in the absence of a threat to his economic security, the janitor's
main concern is his status. This is especially important to him as far
as tenants are concerned, who hold him in low esteem and often treat
him accordingly. The janitor tries to change this by the means demonstrated earlier, and to see himself as a success only if he has 'good'
tenants. The importance of his prestige and dignity factor in the

image of the tenant and the public seems to override that of income, as evidenced by statements of interviewed janitors. Additionally to the janitor's security-prestige motive, many janitors regarded retirement as a means of ending distasteful work. Substantive aspirations are therefore sought through terminal preference for eventual participation, not as a member of a team, but as a boss-man himself. The occupational goal seems to be retirement, but is rarely ever to be reached because, in the first place, the union allows the janitor to serve only as many buildings as he can cope with - which limits his income; and, in the second, saving is difficult when a little luxury status symbol, such as a car, may reduce him to subsistence level. Wealth is equated with security in retirement. Wealthy janitors are few, but they are the subject of envy, gossip and legend. Such values serve to justify modest existence, although great sacrifice has enabled some janitors to profit from property deals. The retirement goal helps janitors to bear the burdens of work; but it is, in fact, an occupational myth, unless it occurs that an apartment owner in a case of a really good relationship will lend the janitor money to invest, an occurrence which bewilders other janitors, who cannot fathom how the money was come by. From this picture of the janitor's work, we have seen that he enjoys a modest degree of independence in day-to-day decision-making, which goes some small way towards satisfying the need of the 'other self'. The position may differ, however, in occupations where such independence is completely absent. We shall look at such occupations next.

THE NIGHTWATCHMAN

In this work experience, we have an illustration of how the controlled pace at which a job holder may have to work plays upon the self and kills the feeling of doing something worthwhile; and how the imposition of tight control, and the removal of any kind of initiative can add to the frustrations of the incumbent. The changing nature of business structures has contributed to the removal of the faithful, ageing or handicapped servant of the firm, drowsing the night away beside his fire. Today, the growing scale of property requires more sophisticated organisation against the increasing volume of crime. Large corporations may be able to carry the loss, but the insurance world demands efficient measures of protection of property for evident reasons. In the words of Tom Nairn, on whom this description of the life of a nightwatchman is based:-

> 'This new protection is complex. A rationalised
> surveillance invades the night, organising nothing-
> ness into a quasi-military discipline of uniforms
> and signals, making sleep at noon a permanent way
> of life for thousands. The most marginal of tasks
> has swollen into a growth-trade, a hive of men
> guarding the sleep of a capital. Producing no-
> thing, this labour exists to make nothing happen,
> its aim is emptiness. Its abstract and solitary
> structure, like a negative image of day-time work,
> reverses the diurnal beast of life and betrays the
> meaning of labour, creating a new, pure, objectless
> estrangement of lasting from every twilight until
> long after dawn'. (5)

The nights, says Tom Nairn - who before becoming an author was a night-watchman himself - are slow torture and the strangest thing is the silence. Nightworkers go to work in the evening, which for them then ceases to exist as a cushion normal workers use for leisure and recreation from the stresses of the day. The evening is really a function of civilisation; a mirage of afterwork; a kind of collective dream of later on, concealing the artificiality of what has been accepted as an institution only through the day/night rotation. Not so to night-men. They have to fit in with the routines of others, entering the tensions of activity just beginning when transport and people go the other way, relaxed and expectant homewards. Nightworkers feel regret, resignation or indifference on the journey to work, depending on how deeply the life of silence has penetrated their being, to follow the rhythm of returning to work every evening at eight.

The work place consists of a large tobacco warehouse in Britain. Except for a few workrooms and offices, the six storey building is made up of partitioned space with a mass of heavy cartons filled with tobacco and cigarettes worth £5m. Night-men are the guards, controlled by a hierarchy of rank in the order of sergeants, inspectors, chief inspectors and commanders. Guards are issued with padlocked bags containing clocks with key-holes below the dial. The keys are fixed to the wall at various parts of the building. One turn will stamp the time and the key number on a paper tape inside the bag and connected to the clock. Thus, time is carried with one as a symbol of the work environment, a watchman's clock-machine, representing a deeper, more intimate penetration into one's being. Padlocked away in the bag, it was as inaccessible as time itself, embodying time's estrangement and compulsive manner, almost like a live companion, demanding attention every few minutes of the working night. The repetitive, solitary circuits constitute the work-action and the clock registers the point-to-point transfer of the body. The complete record of one's labour could be traced by opening the bag and unwinding the tape. Missing out keys is fatal in consequence and six minutes are allowed to get to the next key. The manager, since the big robbery, is a frightened man, says Tom Nairn. The first thing he does in the mornings is to get the tapes from the bags and study them for hours. One wrong time or number missed and he is on the 'phone to headquarters, which brings the inspectors checking on the work routine for a whole week.

Nairn then goes on to describe the subjective experience of a night-patrol man in this way:-

> 'A forced stroll, whose pace can never be altered,
> is exhausting beyond belief... the very ease of the
> actions transforms itself into most utter nausea, a
> lead-like feeling from which no escape is possible...
> one feels packed with staleness, a fatigue coming
> not from exertion but out of systematized rationing
> of exertion... the endless half-tension forces a
> craving for real tension - any violent movement.
> At the end of the patrol, there is a renewed prom-
> ise of liberation, like a short-cut to regaining
> possession of oneself, the self work had taken away
> ... this dream-like, monotonous existence is not
> creative dreaming, the relaxed search of the mind
> for a needed idea or feeling; one emerges empty,

confronting the void with no further resources...
it is the sensation of being turned into an object,
a labouring material thing, that we all are...
where else has civilisation distilled its own
roots in quite this refined fashion, to give such
an undiluted taste of its underlying secret... in
this job, there is no skill, no part of oneself,
no set of dispositions developed as the valuable
thing sold in the transaction with the employer,
and the very vacancy of the task has this as its
corollary; but in turn, paradoxically, this lack
swallowed one completely... demanding no part of
oneself, the job in fact demanded everything. It
consisted of doing nothing... like an endless
vortex, into which one was compelled to fall head-
long, touching nothing, towards nothing, an invad-
ing silence, more deafening than the loudest machine'.

Not every nightwatchman may be able to transmit his feelings in this
articulate manner, but we now get a clearer idea of how (Gouldner's)
'other self' reacts if little or nothing is demanded from it by the
nature of the work in certain types of occupation. One feels that for
this man at least, the absence of intrinsic satisfaction predominates
over everything else and greater extrinsic rewards might not make any
appreciable difference to his suffering.

Prospects of advancement for the ordinary night security guard are
not good, and a number try for a transfer to day jobs within the company, guarding wages or bullion in armoured cars. Very few see the work
as a career. The rest, Tom Nairn informs us, make up an odd collection
of exiles from living, rather more removed from the everyday realities
than the ordinary Soho or Notting Hill prototypes of non-conformity,
putting up a laboured pretence of normality. Many had no family life
at all. The population is made up of divorcees or men separated from
their wives and families, those who had failed in a previous occupation
and were either too old or lacked the courage to try anything new.
Thus, a solitude already established in daylight-living was the usual
condition which enabled the men to bear the loneliness of the night.

We have considered the subjective experience of this kind of work,
looked at the work location and work routine, and career prospects,
later to be compared with the other occupations. In some respects,
like the janitor, the nightwatchman is an isolate. The only human
interaction derives from colleagues who congregate in the warehouse
recreation room after return from patrol. Tom Nairn found in his noct-
urnal labour the social bonds more stunted than he had ever previously
experienced.

Certain symbols, transparent only to fellow watchmen - perhaps only
an exchange of glances beyond what labour demanded - existed as a language of the workplace, which was regarded merely as a means of easier
acceptance of the work's ritual and alienation. The first light at
dawn was the most dreaded moment of the twelve hours. It came at
Nairn's turn to reach the building's roof, which he regarded as the
real end-product of the job; too early, however, to free him from fatigue, and leaving hours of watching still to be filled. The places

where one could collapse for a few minutes out of sight were all known but never mentioned. Finally, at home, sleep was always difficult in spite of the extreme tiredness this work brought. Sleeplessness and an absolute revulsion against the work eventually drove Tom Nairn from the job, as he says:-

> 'I had entered far deeper than ever before into work's estrangement... I picked up the 'phone and told headquarters I was ill and wanted to quit... they were quite used to rapid turnover of the labour force... I sent my uniform and other things in a huge brown paper parcel to headquarters and then did nothing for a whole month.'

HOTEL AND CATERING WORKERS

For reasons to be determined at a later stage in this investigation, social scientists appear to have neglected the hotel and catering industry as a most fertile field for research. During the last twenty-five years, only William F. Whyte (6), a sociologist from Cornell, is known to have made an action-research attempt at gaining some insight into labour relations in the year 1943 and illuminated certain chronic problems as a result of an agreement between the University of Chicago and the National Restaurant Association in the U.S.A. The eventual report was in 1948, published as a book, and will here form a useful source in the discussion of problems peculiar to this industry as seen from a sociological perspective. *

Wherever cooked food is served to customers, one finds that the production and service functions have to be combined. The product is geared to immediate consumption and the whole enterprise directed to this end. Two kinds of activities take place: firstly, those which involve customer contact in the front part of the establishment, and secondly, the work behind the scenes, in kitchen, service pantry, scullery and stores. The tasks of these departments may be differentiated in the actual meal production and the performance of ancillary services as well as in role relationship, the incidental of which will later be the subject of a more detailed investigation. These latter services make the rapid provision of customer's orders possible and our interest is here confined to the kitchen work environment, where low-status actors perform to please primarily the next-higher status incumbent in the occupational hierarchy, rather than the out-of-sight audience out front. Where work takes place in small groups, status assumes considerable internal importance (additional to any external image an occupation may have) and is closely correlated to intrinsic work values.

With the passing of the old French-style cooking of the inter-war years, the status of the artist-chef has given way to technologist in the kitchen, and in many instances the replacement by women cooks or craftsmen has blurred the old distinction of rank and symbolic uniforms. However, variations in status still exist. When Whyte investigated the situation in the large kitchen of a Chicago restaurant,

---

* Since 1976, an unpublished thesis on chefs and cooks and a published text on restaurant organisation have, however, become available in this country. (7) and (8).

he discovered an official as well as an informal status scale. The
former was based on formally appointed grading, relating to prescribed
duties while, in the latter case, the social standing was rooted less
on function or dress as on background, skill, seniority, financial reward and, significantly, on the material handled. Those who worked on
the finished product enjoyed higher status than those working on the
earlier stages of production. No single variable exerted a major influence, but all factors mentioned operated to place the component
bodies of the kitchen brigade. Officially, the working supervisor of
the fish station ranked with other supervisors, but still his status
was depressed on account of the unpleasant smell of the material used.

Perceptive observation by Whyte and his assistants resulted in a
number of illuminating hypotheses. It was found that work stations had
a social ranking where the cooking function took top place. Skill and
pay were found to be most relevant and, as might be expected, everything revolved around this particular range. Next came the salad section, which had prestige because it dealt in finished products, and women
vegetable cooks spoke respectfully of the old salad station. Next in
line was the chicken preparation station, then chicken-cooking and vegetable preparation; located at the very bottom of the scale was the
fish station. Ranking could be observed by worker-behaviour towards
one another, but additionally, there were even finer status variations
than that to be discovered by the perceptive observer.

These distinctions are now worthy of more detailed consideration.
The larger stations had within them a ranking system of their own,
depending on the tasks performed, seating position at the work table,
division of time, male/female worker and work flow. Apart from the
cooking/non-cooking distinction, a status of the various vegetables
themselves was observed. Parsley at the very top, to be followed by
celery and other luxury and decorative items; green beans held top
position of the regular vegetables, followed by spinach and carrots;
then sweet and white potatoes and onions last, as the most undesirable
of all vegetables. Recorded comments by the researchers revealed the
characteristics of the materials which kitchen workers held in high or
low esteem:-

        Low - staining hands, sloppy to handle, smelly,
        dirty, greasy items;

        High - lack of odour, crispness, cleanness,
        freshness, aroma.

Status and prestige variations occurred as a direct extension on to
the workers who handled certain of these meats and vegetables, while
further distinctions in the work pattern were due to strength, seniority, full or part-time employment, age, work consistency and speed.
Workers with some of these characteristics were able to control or crit-
icise others who did not have them and thereby elevate their own status
position in the kitchen. Prestige differences occurred also when meat
was in short supply, at which time the fish station gained in importance. This research is most revealing because it shows how the prestige
value of, and tools used on, the materials can affect the status of
manual workers in kitchens and elsewhere. Old women and those who
cleaned vegetables part-time, spending the rest of the day on dish-

washing, had lower status, while the young and the strong were more favourably placed in the organisation of their work. Higher-status workers enjoyed the privilege of handling and working with higher-status vegetables.

If the prestige value of materials used enhances status, justifiable credence derives from this finding that status thus gained (or lost) must logically be very relevant to either intrinsic work attitudes or sources of friction. Further, if materials in certain occupations consist of grease, dirt and garbage and the tools used for the work are of the most primitive kind, not much imagination is needed to arrive at an idea of what this will do to the intrinsic meaning of work performed by those in what we may call deprived and stigmatised occupations. Our later, detailed study of kitchen porters will go some way towards exposing particular problems which possess people in such occupations, and endeavour to test some of our propositions put forward. How far extrinsic rewards in any particular occupation induce acceptance of work devoid of intrinsic satisfaction is a question deserving of consideration.

We have already indicated the importance of status where groups of people perform various tasks as is the case in restaurant kitchens. Intrinsic dissatisfaction results, however, also from the generation of tensions, particularly during the rush periods when cooked meals are served. Pressure tends to flow from the impatient customer to the entire staff. In most catering establishments, the quantity of food for consumption that cooks are allowed to prepare in advance is strictly limited by factors of cost and waste. When cooks fall behind, a chain reaction is set off from customer to service pantry to runners, since no one else can supply the food. For example, if any kitchen runner - whose status at the Chicago restaurant investigated was just above that of pot washer - orders the higher status cook to go beyond his maximum food limit, friction results.

Whyte gives examples of pressure at meal times also upon waitresses, and how they react to it. Routinely, customers are served in turn and delays tend to cause frustration. As she competes with other waitresses for her order, she needs to please guests and supervisors and has also to get on with pantry, bar staff and checkers. In turn, the pantry girls are constantly on the receiving end of the waitresses' temper. In times of such pressure, some girls break down and cry; others argue with one waitress, while the rest of that occupational group impatiently wait for their supply of cooked food, which builds up more pressure. The work flow requires the food to travel through various stages before it gets to the customer; but there is also a flow in reverse; a mass of dirty plates, dishes and pots. In rush periods, these rain upon the (usually) understaffed dish-washers and plongeurs. These people work long hours in hot and steamy sculleries and try to keep up with the demand. As we shall later see, members of these low-status kitchen occupations serve as outlets and scapegoats for the frustrations and bottlenecks in the organisation and as butts for the bad temper of the entire kitchen staff. Hall* in referring to dish-washers and hospital porters, suggests that their location at the bottom of the social structure generally precludes interaction with those of a higher status, while meaningful interaction with same-status members is not much better in the smaller establishments.

* Hall, Richard,1969,'Occupations and the Social Structure',Prentice Hall, London

Isolation is, therefore, more prevalent than any kind of viable colleague relationship.

The lower-grade kitchen worker is not often consulted on any matter
which thus severely limits any participating aspirations he may have.
His orientation is rarely substantive and he may view his choice inst-
rumentally as one of non-alignment with the organisation, owing to the
kind of position he holds and the treatment he receives. Thus, aspirations will, in most cases, be of low priority. Why this is likely will
later emerge from the investigation of additional cases. In his discussion of vertical mobility, Whyte found that the majority of waitresses
did not aim for the top, although some managed to achieve the more modest goal of hostess which involved, however, the sacrifice of tips. The
chances for upward social mobility of the Negro were also considered and
Whyte discovered here the severest constraints in most catering establishments on the opportunities to rise further than dishwasher in his
catering career.

THE HOSPITAL PORTER: A Behavioural Profile of an Occupation in the
World of the Care of the Sick. (9)

It is a popular conception that some of the less-skilled occupations
cannot be intrinsically satisfying and meaningful to an incumbent and
that extrinsic rewards (that is, mainly monetary) assume an importance
that transcends all else. This belief is certainly not substantiated
by our researches of the work of hospital porters in two of the largest
and most modern teaching hospitals in this country, a work group that
is currently very much in the news on account of the enormous impact
their protests for better recognition has made. It is highly significant that instead of finding their work activities alienating, the complete reverse appears to be the case and the emphasis of their work
orientation is on public service and 'care', as our subsequent findings
will show.

It is also held, with some justification, that we, the public, appreciate more the social contribution of some of the less pleasant and often
stigmatised occupations when such work is temporarily not done. We hope
to balance out the public image by a more precise and illuminating picture of what the work of the hospital porter really entails, how he himself sees the usefulness of his contribution to the general welfare of
our sick and how we might fairly reward those who do this work day-by-
day with the sort of commitment - in view of its peculiar ingredients -
that defies belief. Our findings are based almost entirely on observation and interviews with staff members of the two hospitals.

The Work Environment

To look at the structural picture and work routines first, one of the
hospitals (in a provincial town) has undergone vast expansion and provides for some 1,000 beds at this time. It was once known as the 'Work
House' to most locals and the attitude of the older patients was that
they have come there to die. Porters were used more functionally, initially as aides and later as nursing auxiliaries, but with the development
of occupational specialisation, the function of the hospital porter has
become a supportive one. The other hospital of equal size, only some
four years old, is situated in London, with an aerial view like a cross,

but as yet without a historical tradition. As is the modern trend, both are multi-purpose complexes with some 50 wards and staff that run into thousands in number and with more than 50 occupational varieties other than medical personnel. Both also are almost self-contained communities with shops, banks, post offices, newsagents, libraries and their own radio stations and request programmes.

Each of these hospitals employs about a hundred porters alone and that does not include catering or domestic ancillary staff. At the present time, duties of the hospital porters are spread over a number of departments: X-Ray, Pharmacy, Physiology, Orthopaedic, the Mortuary, Psychiatric, the Operating Theatre, Maternity and various general wards. The duties of some porters may include the general servicing of the whole hospital, such as Admission Lodges,Laundry, Bread and Milk distribution, Refuse Collection, Messenger Duties, and such. Rotating shifts are worked to cover needs round the clock. *

We gained the distinct impression that there operated certain key factors which tended to compensate for some of the more gruesome duties and give a taint of intrinsicality to the work, that reduces estrangement and abhorrence and provides an element of cohesion for the porter brigade, otherwise in danger of disintegrating. First, however, we shall look at the work routine which, but for this compensatory ingredient, would give rise to what some writers called 'the alien purpose' or the physically polluting and disgusting kind of work,+not so much in terms of dirt as perhaps of nausea. This may best be illustrated by describing some of the experiences of porters in the course of their duties.

The Hospital Porter's Work

The first job in the early morning is the collection from the various wards of the dead patients, who have to be transported to the mortuary and the bodies usually housed in metal boxes. The chargehand sends two porters for each body, but four people are normally involved in taking these to the morgue: the porters, the sister in charge and the morgue attendant. A porter then takes the death certificate to the office and the ward beds are prepared for new occupiers. Not all bodies are carried in boxes. There is the case of a 9-months-old child who died after many hours on the operating table. A porter carried it, wrapped in a blanket to preserve discretion. That man had children himself and this incident caused him a great deal of agitation. By the time this first job is done, the hospital is in the full throes of activity. Porters everywhere: attending to people at X-Ray, Accident and Emergency, seeing to urgent specimens, delivering gas cylinders, helping with laundry and kitchen rubbish disposal (which rates extra pay), directing entrants into the car park, delivering flowers and moving patients by chair or in

---

*Shift times: Day - 6-2 (or 7.30-4.30), 2-10 (or 1.30-10.30), sometimes compulsory overtime from 7.30-10.30; Night - 10-6 (or 10.30-7.30)

+C. Wright Mills' book 'The Sociological Imagination', Oxford University Press, 1959, and Penguin Books, 1970; and Everett Cherrington Hughes' book, 'Men and Their Work', Free Press of Glencoe, 1958.

bed to various departments. Some porters take perhaps better to some of the work than others. Porter A expresses it this way: '... some ward duties can make you sick. One has to touch patients with skin ailments all over their bodies, or lift old and frail people. We get used to it but some of us don't. The most unpleasant task is to put refuse from the wards into bags, like stained, smelly linen from bed wetting...' There are, in each of the hospitals, a dozen clinics which operate from 9 to 5 of the working day. That is really the busy period.

Porters work also in out-patient treatment rooms and they don't only move patients. Porter B's work on a particular day involved even a bit of auxiliary nursing and he told us: 'Whenever I have to remove plaster cast, my heart sinks. Blimey, I'm frightened I might hurt the patient. The other day, I was asked to take off a kid's plaster. This caused me no end of worry and tension... perspired all over while I was cutting it...' The variety of the work and its people-orientation holds, however, great attraction for many a porter. The Deputy Hospital Secretary explained that certain routine jobs are found rather dull and labour turnover tends to be higher. For example, delivering bread and milk is not liked because there is no contact with patients. Another dull routine consists of taking and collecting sheets and other linen from the laundry building. Here again, there is no contact with patients, the work extending over a 6-day week is not well paid and not part of the rotary arrangement. It can be seen that the intrinsic element for the porters is, therefore, contact with patients which they regard as an important part of their work.

The operating theatre is a central place in the hospital, but holds mixed attractions for porters, although it is more popular than moving furniture. It differs from work in the wards in a number of respects. When patients are under constant medical treatment or long-term, they really do get to know the porters; often even by name. One frail old lady insisted the porter take 10p every time he brought her a cup of tea. Patients strike up a rapport with the porters, although one might expect a great deal of anonymity in hospitals of that size. Some porters have been doing this work for years and we found also several father/son set teams on the job. Nor is the work completely male dominated, since the sex discrimination legislation of 1975, and those women who opted for hospital portering are doing as well as any man. Porters in the operating theatre may be permanently attached there and enjoy a higher status in the porter hierarchy. In this kind of setting, medical personnel have to work in teams with a fine division of labour and all members complementing one another. Clearly, in this situation, the porter gets to know the surgeons, sisters and others in the team. Such porters are seen as privileged in that they may not be part of the pool, rate special training and often higher pay. Even so, not everyone can take it, as Porter C indicated to us: '... it takes a strong stomach to work in the operating theatre. It isn't just the lifting of sick people (and the lifting of females by male porters can cause embarrassment) as the operations. Take a case of gangrene: the doctor would saw off a leg or an arm and hand the dripping limb to the porter to put in a bag. Some porters refuse to do it...' As a rule, the Hospital Secretary advised us, porters do not like moving bodies, nor do they get extra pay. Some porters have to assist with post mortems, which involves cutting bodies open or extracting parts; but this is mostly voluntary and the older porter who has been in the war takes better to the work.

At this point, it may be of interest to note that the porters who work in rotating shifts are regarded as part of the 'elite' of the porter brigade by their colleagues, because during their rotating 24 hours of duty they get to know most of what goes on in the hospital, that is the cycle of interaction. A hospital rule requires that some porters are always in the pool room, on call so to speak. There are telephones everywhere, even in the lifts; one of the hospitals has 1,400 of them. Once a job is done, the porter will normally return to the pool, but does check with the pool room by telephone whether any job can be done on his return journey. Thus, efficiency is preserved and waste avoided. The porters use their time with discretion. There are no deadlines, as in production work, but the flow of duties is such that there is little time for more than casual socialising. Even though a staff canteen is available there is comparatively little in the way of colleague relation-ship. The larger number of buildings and acreage over which the duties of individual porters are spread makes social contact among them diff-icult.

Career Prospects and Pay

We have discussed the work role of the hospital porter in some depth. There is a number of peripheral matters, some relating to informal code, some to dress, and some to occupational ideology, which we would like to briefly touch on, in addition to matters under the above heading.

With half a million patients in hospitals on any one day of the year, three quarters of a million waiting to get in and a load of about twenty million yearly out-patients, the 30,000 porters and ward orderlies should never be out of work. Job security is one of the factors that is liked, although labour turnover in some establishments has reached 40%. Some porters adopt an instrumental attitude and treat their work as a means to an end. But the majority gave us as a major reason for wanting to work in hospitals the positive value to society. (A Scottish hospital survey some years ago arrived at similar findings). They look upon the 'dependency' relationship with patients as highly important and intrins-ically satisfying. 'Care' is the significant term for them. Sick peop-le are appreciative of a few cheering words from the porter and, in his ideology, he regards himself as auxiliary nurse, social worker, allev-iator of pain and saviour of the medical staff's mistakes. Perhaps this somewhat illusory self-image is not quite consistent with the porter's general status in the hospital, for he is still on the lowest pay scale of annual workers and feels looked-down upon by management. Indeed, the porter is very conscious of the low esteem in which he is held by the medical staff, who tolerate him according to their prevailing mood or disposition. Some surgeons appreciate the porter who can set up an op-erating theatre; but older matrons consider it a social disgrace for him to fraternise with the female staff. Additionally to the intrinsic value of contact with patients, membership of a collectivity is now seen as giving the deprived porter more security in the event of disputes, better recognition and certain union benefits, as well as a group voice vis-a-vis the medical staff in the protection of his interest.

Career prospects for the porter are not good. He can, on occasion, work himself up to chargehand grade or deputy head porter, the latter only if staff exceed some 30 in number. Management policy is now to select younger people for work in the operating theatre. For them, a

scheme exists which involves training, certification on passing exams
and higher pay. The work requires more intelligence and also makes
greater physical demands, but carries higher status. All porters retire at 65, but can work on to 75 if they feel fit enough. The other
body of porters receives induction training lasting one morning, while
a new 14-day training scheme includes a series of lectures on infect-
ion, lifting patients, attitudes and communication. In some establishments, porters wear badges and special uniforms which symbolise their
function. A hospital porter has now the opportunity to increase his
earnings, but mostly at a cost of longer working hours. Additionally
to the basic rate, he can obtain increases for working weekends, for
shift and dirty work and there is also a London allowance for those
working in the metropolis.

Concluding Observations

By and large, there may be variations in the portering services depending on whether it is a General, Psychiatric, Geriatric, Children's,
Maternity, Infectious Diseases, Mentally Handicapped, Chronic Sick or
Teaching Hospital. But, in terms of how meaningful the work is to the
hospital porter himself, this can be gleaned from the sentiments expressed of the way in which he sees his diverse role performance as a
staff member with a vital contribution to make in the service of the
sick. We discovered a clear division in work orientation between those
porters who have regular contact with patients (and so, incidentally,
also with medical staff) and those others, regarded by all and sundry
as general 'dogsbodies' around the hospital. The former look upon
themselves as nurse-aids, comforters and morale boosters of patients
and relatives, monitors in patient-mobility, alleviators of pain,
stage managers of the operating theatre, providers of hygiene services
(like fumigation), caretakers of residual medical services (as for
example in the mortuary or post mortem room), communications link between the hospital and the outside world and guardians of the hospital's
security. This variety of roles assures porters of a definite occupational identity which clearly makes for greater job satisfaction and
stability at the work place. Such ideologies include a definite code
of ethics, one rule being for example that there be no stealing or pilfering from sick or dead patients, unless a culprit wishes to expose
himself to colleague sanctions.

The functional role definition of the non-medical, general category
of porter (who, day-in and day-out, carries, scrubs and cleans) that is
far removed from patient-care and contact, clearly explains his more
instrumental work attitude in the hospital and his morale is often reflected in informal dress (slacks, T-shirt and jacket) when a smart
uniform with badge would indicate a better status and recognition;
while also in evidence of lower responsibility are the instructions
from medical staff that certain areas are off-limits or out-of-bounds
to these porters. Some hospitals are, however, undergoing a process of
democratisation at this time, which shows itself in more consultation
on work routines and in the social setting of the more communal eating
arrangements (where doctor and porter may sit at the same table, although surgeons and consultants still enjoy separate 'hotel services'),
as well as generally according the lower-grade staff more respect.

THE IMAGE OF THE CAR PARKING ATTENDANT

An illuminating research in depth has quite recently been completed by
Graham Birch of Ruskin College in Oxford on the secret world of car
parking.(10) In addition, our pilot survey, looking into the public
image of this occupation gathered some opinions together which reflect
clearly the sentiment expressed by large sections of the community.(11)
Our question was addressed to a cross section of socio-economic groups
(including people in the professions and in various types of manual
work) as to what their impression was of the job of car park attendant
in terms of a general social evaluation and in regard to particular
members they have come into contact with. The answers obtained suggest
yet another category of worker, where a somewhat distorted image has
placed them in low esteem in society relative to other work in an occupational continuum of higher and lower social status and prestige.
The general tenor of the answers was along these lines:- (quoting
verbatim) ...

> It is just a sedentary sort of job, punching
> tickets and taking money; the work is not de-
> manding, there is no craft involved or spec-
> ial training and education needed; if a bloke
> can be replaced by a simple mechanical device,
> he cannot be up to much; car parks are handy
> places to hire cheap disabled labour and
> plonk them into boxes; a lot of these blokes
> are on temporary construction sites and hence
> a transient population; you won't find many
> young people doing this job as it is badly
> paid; some of these chaps are a bit physical
> and domineering with a take-it-or-leave-it
> attitude, chasing thieves is all they are
> good for; that occupation is a dying breed,
> it's all done by machine; mine acts like a
> king of his castle, treating non-regulars
> like dirt.

Hotel door-keepers and some of the private car park attendants carve
out a higher status for themselves by the exercise of discretionary
powers which enables the latter, for example, to mount a little car-
wash business on the side. Door-keepers of the larger luxury hotels
also have shown themselves to be entrepreneurially ingenious under conditions where a parking pitch is small. In the case of one of London's
West End hotels, there is room only for a mere ten cars. Thus, the
owner of a Rolls may pay the doorman a generous weekly retainer for re-
serving a space permanently. (12) This saves the owner of the car the
inconvenience of driving around the area to find a place to park. Not
surprisingly, the spaces of the park would be mostly full while short-
time parking and rapid turnover of cars would be a good business interest. By and large, the carless would rely on stylised media-perception
without perhaps ever having seen a car park attendant, and attempt to
construct their own mental image of what these people are like. Not
infrequently, this is how occupational stigmatisation originates.

Graham Birch, in his study, explains how the car parking industry in Britain started in London as a post-war maverick enterprise, when individual entrepreneurs took over bombed sites, often without the knowledge or consent of the landlords and allowed motorists to park for a definite charge. Operators staked claims to sites reminiscent of the American Gold Rush, and there were occasions when competition got so rough that rival operators would dump rubble on one another's sites to put the other out of business. If then tactics of this kind restricted parking space even further (already limited in the crowded streets), demand and supply laws would come into operation to drive up the price. Operators regarded the venture largely as a profitable short-term one while a small number of business-like entrepreneurs anticipated the possibilities of car parking as a viable growth-industry. Employment policies, however, differed little from their get-rich-quick rivals and the wages paid to staff tended to be very low.

The industry took off during the 1950's, when petrol rationing ceased and car ownership increased so rapidly as to exceed a million annually by 1963 and has not fallen below this figure since. The resulting congestion to town and city centres made the existing kerbside coin-operated parking meters, serving mostly short-term parkers, a limited success. Eventually, local authorities became aware of the impact of the car as an important element in the business and social life of the nation and began, alas very hesitantly, to make plans for the provision of regular parking space. A few boroughs built their own multi-storey car parks at charges just high enough to create a surplus on the rate account. Later, surface parks and the control of private parking development under the planning laws were additional measures taken.

In the private sector, a number of well-financed private companies had managed, during the following ten years, to obtain Council contracts with National Car Parks Limited, the most successful company eventually to dominate the market for parking services. A high proportion of the company's operations was under licensing and/or management agreements, which excluded it from the monopoly laws. The local authorities justified this by claiming that private companies had special expertise, ran the operations at lower cost and that such operators had tighter accounting procedures and a better security system to prevent fiddling.

Birch asks what sort of man becomes a car park attendant. He discovered a distinct division between those employed by private companies and those employed by local authorities. The work force in the public sector tended to be over forty-five years of age, with an earlier background of manual or unskilled clerical work. Council policy appeared to have been to use the car parks as a sort of safety net to find employment for some long-serving, unskilled staff who, owing to minor disability or ill-health, might otherwise be dismissed. Such staff tended to show gratitude by giving their best in return for modest but adequate wages, for which minimum nationally-agreed rates exist, but which are supplemented by extras for responsibility and shift work. Contrary to the practice in the private sector, information from council officials and the police suggests that fiddling is not common there.

The private sector reveals a totally different picture. Age groups and backgrounds are of wide variation. Some attendants might be men of eighteen to twenty, with a history of job drift, while others are quite close to retirement age, following a stable employment record.

Education, too, can vary from the semi-literate to the well-read and highly articulate. The example is given of one attendant who managed to use his hidden wage (fiddled cash customarily acceptable in the trade) for flying lessons, so eventually gaining his pilot's licence, while in another case a company chairman explained that some attendants prefer lower wages in exchange for a franchise to do such things as washing cars on the site. The industry has, in fact, a hidden wage policy where staff and management accept restrained fiddling as a normal part of the work environment (although a breach under criminal law), by way of manipulating the control machinery and/or falsifying accounting documents to facilitate the pocketing of cash paid as parking fees by motorists. Graham Birch found that car park operators see their park staff as merely human bodies to collect parking fees, where dishonesty is expected but no attempt is made to avail themselves of the contemporary industrial relations philosophy in use.

Clearly, hidden income serves as a mechanism to enhance the low (but now improved) earnings of this occupational group in the private sector of car parking, whilst at the same time, public esteem has continued to place this occupation among those at the bottom of the scale.

THE WORLD OF THE DUSTMAN (Manchester and Amsterdam compared)

According to a study of the life of dustmen by Guardian reporters who joined them for a short spell to observe their work routines, these men see their own position in a totally different light from the general image projected by the public. (13) Here, as in other occupations which involve the performance of heavy and dirty work, there is an increasing shortage of people who are prepared to do this, and labour turnover is high. Local authority associations, in evidence at an enquiry on refuse collection, mentioned the existence of labour difficulties, high rates of turnover and sickness, the competition of other industries and the social stigma attaching to refuse collection, all of which made recruitment difficult. To the irate ratepayer, binmen are all idle, shiftless do-for-nothings; they pour rubbish on his path if he does not bribe them at Christmas time and they knock off at lunchtime to squander their unearned wealth in pubs and betting shops.

The Manchester binmen are, however, conscious of their service to society and feel it is the public who are inconsiderate and careless with their rubbish in holed bins, which cause more often than not the smelly slime to run down their necks. Plastic bags are liked better, but people put broken glass in them so that every crewman has suffered cuts at some time or other. Crew strengths can be very uneven. There are over a thousand local authorities of which almost half have crews of three or less, frequently arbitrarily rather than scientifically decided, on the basis of work study or operational research. Most cleansing departments operate the "task and finish" system, which is said to have largely contributed to the impression that binmen skive off early. Under this routine, each crew follows a set daily or weekly route to be completed for a specified area, and the working day ends when that is done. Thus, it is not unusual for a team to start as early as 7 in the morning and be finished by lunchtime, or earlier. Whilst there are the benefits of getting the rubbish cleared away quickly and the vehicles to the depot for maintenance early, the

criticism has been that work targets are under-estimated or that the
job is not properly done, unless the binmen be superhuman. Arrangements
do, of course, exist for independent target assessment at a reasonable
pace, to include time allowances for walking, opening gates and replacing bin lids, so that bonus allocation may be justified. Early finishing does provide the incentive to work quickly - indeed, some crews do
the job at a running pace - although this could lead to the temptation
of a slovenly execution. As against this, supervision is effectively
provided by the public, who would soon complain if the work were not
properly done.

It was because of the answer of the binmen to the critics that they
should have a go that the Guardian reporters, with the agreement of the
City's Director of Cleaning, enlisted for a day. It was difficult to
get a depot to agree, owing to suspicion of the media and the natural
embarrassment of getting through the work at such speed, so that the
men were wary of 'showing up the job'. Early finishing is not always a
foregone conclusion: illness, bad weather, traffic or vehicle trouble
can seriously slow up the work. For example, a small lorry holding
only ten cubic yards is full within the hour and needs another hour for
tipping, while a bigger vehicle requires only two tipping trips per day.
In short weeks, say after Bank Holidays, there might be a backlog to
catch up on and, with some 5,000 bins per week to clear, it is not un-
common for a binman to walk between 8 and 15 miles a day. Wearing out
four pairs of commando boots per year is a fact and the lifting of even
the lighter plastic bags is hard work when one is coping with over 300
per man per day.

Looking further at work routines, we now come to the question of
'totting'. This means picking salvage out of refuse for sale to dealers and is practised by refuse collectors in some districts. Many
councils forbid this, either for reasons of hygiene or because they have
their own arrangements at the depots for recovery and there have been
prosecutions on the grounds that refuse is council property. Some authorities tolerate totting and others openly allow it. One council mentioned in the H.M.S.O. Report, in changing its vehicle fleet from barrier
loaders (where totting was easy) to enclosed rear-loading compression
vehicles, actually provided platforms at the back, so that men could go
on totting. (14) The practice persists, although it has been strongly
condemned as far back as 1930 by the public cleansing people. Not many
local authorities are happy about it, but binmen who find it lucrative
are not easily persuaded to give it up. The observers on the Manchester
round quote Brian finding a duffle coat on top of a bin and Pete, a
paperback thriller. The best pickings were said to be on special coll-
ections of bulk refuse, like washing machines or refrigerators and one
gets a tip, but there wasn't much to be found 'on the ash'. Public
health authorities find it quite unacceptable that salvage should be
picked out of bins or vehicles in the streets and say that such practices are dirty and aesthetically objectionable and should not be toler-
ated. Images such as this contribute to the perception on the part of
the public of the dustman as a polluted individual when, in general,
the norm in our culture is to deplore dirt, filth and pollution. However, such customs and practices as totting must be evaluated in a wider
context where they are closely bound up with a total reward structure
which in this and similar service industries tends to be low.

A possible extension of totting embraces the entrepreneurial activities of the binmen. The Guardian reporters found the faster lads to have second jobs like window cleaning or part-time work in a hospital mortuary, while others preferred to watch racing on television. But less formal enterprise occurs when early finishing of a tour enables a crew to collect rubbish from private business in a local authority vehicle and eventually to tip it in the usual space provided. All this makes the 'job-and-finish' system popular and many authorities turn a blind eye to the extra-work activities. When the day finally ends for them, some really hard menial work at fast pace has been done which (as will be shown) does affect the men's health and for which one can hardly begrudge them their reward. However, because of these opportunities, promotion to supervisor is often rejected in exchange for the freedom of unfixed hours and no deskwork.

A Social Analysis of Dirty Work

The latest reported research from a small exploratory survey of dirty and heavy work in the Amsterdam Sanitation Department has yielded some interesting information for those concerned with the social implications of the human shape of work. (15) Owing to better educational opportunities on the part of populations in Western societies, and a strong desire to elevate themselves socially, there has long been a trend to reject the performance of unattractive work, despite the increasing levels of unemployment. One researcher, not directly connected with the Netherland survey, refers in context to a 'secondary labour market', where low wages, unstable and uncertain terms of employment, an absence of social amenities and poor working conditions are the key characteristics in contrast to the regulated 'primary market', where a more favourable situation prevails. Among other reasons for this state, he suggests (and has evidence in support) that Governments too make use of such labour markets to get jobs done more cheaply. Dutch Government policy is to strive for wage differentials to compensate for unpleasant work, whilst in this country also the Department of the Environment has taken steps to improve the working conditions and welfare of those who work in refuse collection and disposal. The Dutch investigator complains that, in practice, little has come of these idealistic notions and he notes that in general labour is paid better the more agreeable the work and less well the greater the physical effort required.

Godschalk, the Dutch investigator who conducted the Amsterdam survey, in dealing with the inferior status of dustmen, observes that in the Western world at least, status no longer depends on 'style of life' as a whole, but that one's occupation is now the main determinant of prestige in the social hierarchy, where a man's work reflects the most important aspect of his social identity, so that occupational choice seems almost as irrevocable as that of a life partner. In consequence of his work, the dustman holds the lowest rung of the social ladder, and it is quite customary with schoolboys in Central Europe to be warned they will end up as sewage workers if they will not learn. With the advent of modern drainage systems, the refuse collector has, in this way, taken over the deterrent role to sloth. Studies in the Federal Republic of Germany, in the United States, as well as in India and Pakistan, have found his status to be economically low, true even of China where, officially, all status differences have been dispensed with.

31

Where then does this lowly evaluation derive from? A variety of complex issues bear on the matter. In an ascriptive society, people's ranks are given them by birth. A child in India, for example, born into a sweeper caste, holds the position for life. Some such occupations where, say, there is contact with dirt and human excrement, are clearly associated with ritual uncleanliness and stamp the incumbent an untouchable. The modern European dustman has the means to avoid this contact and his work may, indeed, be less messy than that of a slaughter-house worker or an operating surgeon. Thus, the answer to the question 'What constitutes dirty work?' is not immediately obvious. Our mode identifies such common characteristics as low prestige, low rewards, insecurity and the absence of training and career structure over and above the physical dirtiness of some of the work. Is any one or are all of these the key to explaining low evaluation and prestige? Ray Gold does not consider remuneration decisive, as some janitors earn more than their tenants. The low status (as we have seen) comes both from handling their garbage in full view of everyone and how tenants regard the janitor: namely, as an inferior lackey, concerned with everybody's refuse and dirt. Godschalk describes how this lack of respect shows up in the daily work routine. The public complain to his superior if he so much as lights a cigarette or eats a snack; and they will throw down rubbish deliberately and order him to clear it away. The dustman is a menial of whom no one is willing to take much account. Garbage bags containing broken glass are dumped by the kerb and people calmly allow dogs to relieve themselves against garbage bags left to be collected, to the exasperation of the dustman when he clutches this filth. In one extreme case, a sack was actually thrown down from the eleventh floor and burst open with a veritable bang beside the cleaner on the street.

This sort of treatment by the public keeps a dustman in a state of constant awareness of his low status and leads to feelings of shame, as is evident from interviews among employees in the Sanitation Department. Here is a small selection of replies: 'I know chaps who change their clothes because they do not want their neighbours to know what work they do.' 'If you happen to sweep near a tram stop, you see all the people staring.' 'Some of my mates hardly dare to sweep near a school, it embarrasses them.' 'I considered it a really inferior job, a job for morons.' 'They swear at you and say unpleasant things: he is just a numbskull.' (Dustman's wife): 'Sometimes, when people ask me what my husband does, I blush when I reply.'

As in the Manchester findings, the Amsterdam dustman's work is considered heavy work, with a loader picking up anything from 2,000 to 2,900 garbage bags and additional weighty articles per day. Staff shortages mean that the same amount of work has to be done by fewer people. Also, traffic hold-ups in the narrow streets involve a lot of speedy lifting and handling of the sacks to catch up on time, and long distances have to be walked each day. The departmental physician expressed the opinion that a dustman should not do such work beyond the age of 32, when training for lighter work might be given. Sickness absence among all grades of dustmen (loaders, drivers and sweepers) has been found to be three times the national average and a large part of this absence is accounted for by long illnesses. The majority had back complaints and those involving organs of movement. A study carried out by the Institute of Preventive Medicine discovered a high percentage of complaints

32

of heart and arterial conditions, of respiratory disturbances, digestive as well as psycho-social problems, in addition to the back and organ ailments. Since the burden of the constant staff shortages falls on those that are left to do the work, the incidence of sickness is evidently thereby increased. As a consequence of the heavy nature of the work and the constant tension, the majority of the dustmen are unable to attain the normal retirement age of 65 and are already declared unfit for work between the ages of 40 and 50.

Another question considered by Godschalk is what sort of people become dustmen. The vast majority derive from the class of unskilled labourers for whom, in many cases, schooling stopped at the primary stage. They have usually done various types of work before becoming dustmen and most were fairly young when starting on sanitation jobs. The proposition is advanced that unsuccessful parents beget unsuccessful offspring, where perhaps the dustman of today is the oldest son, who was prematurely taken from school to work as the greengrocer's errand boy because father was out of work, had deserted the family, or had been killed in a factory accident. That sort of situation would ensure fewer chances of satisfying work in later life. For such people, the sanitation department could offer a job that entailed no shift work, some job security, good social amenities and a relatively good wage, with basic pay augmented by a premium. Additionally, there are sickness benefits and a pension adjusted to a cost-of-living index. The general economic situation also bears on recruitment. Skilled workers out of a job often join (but there is an upper age limit of 45), as do self-employed who run into hard times. Resort is had to foreign labour when conditions are buoyant.

Finally, is there any intrinsic job satisfaction to be gained at all from this work? One of the attractions is the relative freedom for crews to organise the job themselves and perform it out-of-doors. The majority of the survey answers express no actual dissatisfaction with the work, although there is often an awareness of the lack of alternatives. Those that express satisfaction see the situation more in instrumental terms, that is, the need to make a living and help to maintain the family, enjoy job security and better pay in comparison with what they know about earnings of other unskilled workers. Promotion chances are exceedingly limited. Of 600 dustmen, only three have been promoted during the entire post-war period, management claiming that the rest of the candidates were not suited to higher positions. Making friends at the workplace counts for something, and there is an opportunity for a bit of totting for regular clients, consisting of the removal of empty bottles, packing cases, boxes and such, for shops, cafes and small businesses. This, together with the sale of useable articles found on the street, makes a welcome, tax-free addition to his wages. Respondents do not want to say too much about this in interviews, but there has been talk about bribes of section head or inspector with money or drink, so as to be able to hold on to their jobs.

COMMON CHARACTERISTICS OF THE OCCUPATIONS INVESTIGATED

Discussion

The present discussion aims to discover the extent to which common characteristics, so far as discoverable, offer us a basis upon which to

FIGURE 2.
MODEL DEPICTING COMMON CHARACTERISTICS IN SELECTED LOW-STATUS OCCUPATIONS

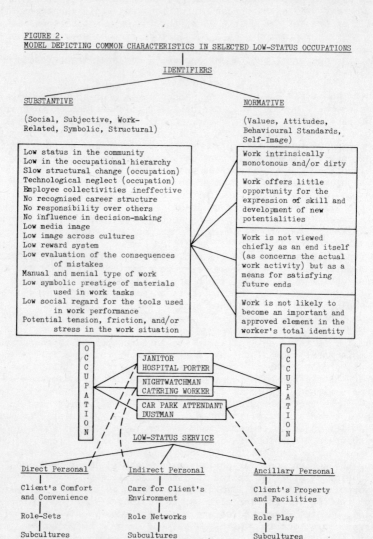

IDENTIFIERS

SUBSTANTIVE

(Social, Subjective, Work-
Related, Symbolic, Structural)

Low status in the community
Low in the occupational hierarchy
Slow structural change (occupation)
Technological neglect (occupation)
Employee collectivities ineffective
No recognised career structure
No responsibility over others
No influence in decision-making
Low media image
Low image across cultures
Low reward system
Low evaluation of the consequences
    of mistakes
Manual and menial type of work
Low symbolic prestige of materials
    used in work tasks
Low social regard for the tools used
    in work performance
Potential tension, friction, and/or
    stress in the work situation

NORMATIVE

(Values, Attitudes,
Behavioural Standards,
Self-Image)

Work intrinsically
monotonous and/or dirty

Work offers little
opportunity for the
expression of skill and
development of new
potentialities

Work is not viewed
chiefly as an end itself
(as concerns the actual
work activity) but as a
means for satisfying
future ends

Work is not likely to
become an important and
approved element in the
worker's total identity

OCCUPATION

JANITOR
HOSPITAL PORTER

NIGHTWATCHMAN
CATERING WORKER

CAR PARK ATTENDANT
DUSTMAN

OCCUPATION

LOW-STATUS SERVICE

Direct Personal

Client's Comfort
and Convenience

Role-Sets

Subcultures

Indirect Personal

Care for Client's
Environment

Role Networks

Subcultures

Ancillary Personal

Client's Property
and Facilities

Role Play

Subcultures

Note: Low-status occupations are likely to be identified if the common
      characteristics predominantly apply.

34

build a concept of occupational stigmatisation. In the first instance, we have drawn a socially-orientated perspective of the experiences in work of members of six low-status occupations. This has enabled us to lay bare the importance of intrinsic work needs and priorities. Gouldner has argued that work which inhibits intrinsic needs contributes to the unemployment of one's 'other self' (that is, that part of the self for which industrial society has no use) and we suggest that the absence of intrinsic work values forms an important variable in the determination of occupational stigma. (16) Our selected occupations can be found in the lower levels of most occupational prestige ratings and are taken to be fairly representative of stigma in work. The various important characteristics they have in common can be presented in the form of a theoretical model, which has been attempted here. Certain qualifications are necessary in the interpretation of this model. Not all the positive characteristics will apply to the same degree at all times in all six occupations; but they constitute a flexible indicator of stigmatisation symptoms which impose social penalties on members. In our later attempt to attach a definition to occupational stigma, we shall wish to introduce some additional variables. (See Chapters 3 and 6).

In the experiences described, we could not fail to note the effect in value terms of the meaninglessness of certain tasks performed, and we have also seen that the work environment involves not only the physical setting, but also the structure of roles played in particular undertakings, the inter-personal relationships and a formal authority-responsibility system in the organisation. These relationships will assume considerable relevance in subsequent discussion of work attitudes. A man's work is one of the things by which he is judged, and certainly, one of the more significant things by which he judges himself. The disagreeable chores Gold's janitor has to perform are an example in point. Much of the discussion about alienation concerns the extent to which modern industrial society reduces work to an unsatisfying chore, and thus destroys both the self-image of the worker and his image in other people's eyes. One instance is the vivid account describing the agony of a nightwatchman's work and how his own rating of the social importance of it transmits this image on to a wider public. The general feeling is that the nightwatchman produces nothing, sleeps on the job, that any moron can do it and that he is good for naught else, or why would he otherwise give up his regular sleep and social life? Tom Nairn speaks of the dream-like monotony of walking for hours in the night and found that all that really counted was the illusion of release and escape. Survey replies from a cross section of the public on the image of car parking attendants likewise yielded mostly derogatory opinions that label its members as a craftless, uneducated, cheaply-hired, transient, drifting or disabled breed of people, who fiddle the cash from customers. Berger discovered that members of all occupations develop occupational ideologies, illusory though they may often be. (17) The janitor has the notion that he is his own boss - a dubious proposition at best - but obviously self-enhancing and frustration-assuaging, while other hopes are of an early retirement or, if that is out of reach, a pre-occupation with possible property speculation.

The kind of work that Hughes describes as physically disgusting to most and hurting to one's dignity, and of the hidden 'dirty task syndrome' in any occupation, is undoubtedly that of the hospital porter.

35

In a recent interview with an ex-hospital porter, the type of work performed was briefly discussed and the former incumbent explained some of the more gruesome duties in this way:

> 'Some of the orderlies I have come into contact
> with impressed me as low, illiterate, anti-social,
> mentally retarded nits who did all the dirty, dis-
> tasteful jobs. Police, for example, often bring
> drowned people, fished out of the river. Such
> corpses are large and bloated and they have to be
> punctured before they can go into a standard-size
> coffin. The undertaker should do this, but for a
> small tip such work was left to the porters. Tall
> people are also a problem. To get them into the
> box, they have to be shortened and a porter would
> amputate the feet. Hunchbacks present the biggest
> difficulty because their backs have to be broken
> to fit them into the coffin.' (18)

It is not difficult to imagine why this action repertoire of the hospital porter remains normally hidden. Even so, significant others like John will have some conception of the nature of the duties in this occupation and thereby, our 'virtual' stigmatisation upon a porter's social identity. Incumbents become concerned with self-evaluation and how it can be preserved and may erect Freud's defence mechanism in an interview situation or other confrontation that offers image-creating facilities when favourable opinion of themselves is threatened. (19) Hence, the assurance by one particular porter at a Midlands hospital that the work is pleasant, satisfying and rewarding. We find in the hotel and restaurant industry a number of service occupations lowly evaluated in status and prestige terms. Caplow suggests that any occupation involving personal service is inherently degrading and there is a related notion that it is less honourable to work for an individual than to be employed in the same capacity by an organisation. (20) Among such occupations are various grades and types of porters, chambermaids and semi-skilled kitchen staff. In applying the idea of personal service to our selected occupations, including here also the guardians of property, we may find that, although the work is respected, the occupations themselves are not socially respectable. Thus, we are still left with the problem of relating the stigma discoverable in work tasks to the social identity of the performer and to the occupation itself. Our occupations, as we have pointed out, consist of service as well as of menial characteristics, but some service occupations in the lower status scale have tended to be consistently ill-paid, and reserved mostly for outcasts; and they have also tended to remain structurally static in an evolutionary sense and in terms of occupational mobility neglected by technology, in contrast to certain industrial routine work. One such occupation is that of the kitchen porter, at which we shall look more closely in a later chapter.

We have included tools and symbols among our characteristics in the model. Whether society stigmatises a group (the occupation and its members), or individuals who are part of it, tools and symbols - in many instances synonymous - so closely identified with work tasks are the means by which occupational stigma is pronounced and identified with that occupation. Primitive tools used to carry out primitive tasks tend to depress the status level of the user, while stigmatising symbols may

have an inhibiting effect on social interaction. The social performance of our occupational members entails little idealism in the moral
sense and we have also been able to observe among the ideologies in
the role-playing situations those which Merton called the 'self-fulfilling prophecy' (give a dog a bad name and he will live up to it). [21]
Thus, logically, the common characteristics we have indicated should
serve towards moving closer in our attempt to define stigmatised occupations, because they distinguish the particular role an individual has
to play to earn the label of stigmatisation. We have already noted
that members of each occupation serve in two directions: each serves
the superior in the hierarchy, as well as the recipient (present or
absent) as the beneficiary of the service. Warehouse staff find the
place in good order when they arrive; the janitor looks after tenants,
the hospital porter after patients, the catering staff after customers,
while the car parking attendant keeps custody of clients' property and
the dustman removes their nauseating refuse and waste. In the performance of these functions, the symbols or signs connote a focus or meaningful experience, capable of arousing feelings and ideas among people
sharing the same culture. Tools, for example, are concepts as well as
tangible objects. Thus, the use of these, it may be argued, corrobor-
ates the accepted purpose for which tasks they are required and identifies them with particular occupations. The brush, the shovel, the
torch or the trolley, the ticket or the bin. Human bodies, garbage,
the watchman's clock, the kitchen sink and such are the sort of symbols
that leave little doubt as to the connection with the particular type
of work discussed here. We have also noticed where task performances
require the handling of materials, such as fish or various vegetables,
that these carry symbolic ratings which reflect upon the people handling the materials, in that they transmit a degree of high or low status on to the users.

Our six occupations involve neither responsibility over other employees, nor any significant influence in the decision-making process. The
studies also indicate the absence of any formal career structure, while
the opportunity for vertical social mobility has been found only a rare
occurrence. Miller and Form's conceptualised work histories similarly
describe the pronounced immobility in the case of unskilled and domestic or personal service jobs. They also find that these occupational
groups experience many jobs in a lifetime and achieve only a fleeting
level of security. The 'heuristic' outlook, that is the curiosity to
find out, is usually absent while an individual's social origin and educational background may tie him to a particular occupational area. [22]
Whyte's action research of the American restaurant industry showed that
workers tend to perform according to the expectations of management.
Most managers entertain pre-conceived notions of the low-grade kitchen
worker stereotype and our research has endeavoured to test particular
hypotheses to discover the reasons for such stigmatisation.

So far, we have related our investigation of work values in particular
occupations to the subjective experiences of individuals without probing too deeply into the hierarchical relationships of the systems within which these actors function. It was not our plan, at this stage, to
establish more than that the stigmatised subordinates conform to (and
sometimes deviate from) norms over which they exercise only a modest -
if any - form of control in the power structure, because of the flouting
of rules, disobedience of instructions or refusal of an order may lead

to a variety of punitive sanctions. Discretionary decisions as part of
the work routine tend naturally to vary in our selected occupations, but
even in these lowly-esteemed categories of work, some psychological demands are made: in the case of the nightwatchman, for example, for habits of predictability of appearing for work and punctuality . We saw,
too, in this work that the consequences of a mistake (i.e. forgetting to
turn a key) may actually lead to head office investigation. The janitor
may neglect his boiler and cause it to blow up; the hospital porter may
wheel a sleeping patient to the mortuary and a cook may inflict discom-
fort on the customer. The consequences of mistakes in work have been
used as a variable in status evaluations and have attracted various interpretations. Hughes' low-status workers save their superiors from
making mistakes - an illusory though elevating ideology. Brown's 'time-
span' theory relates the importance of particular work to the time it
takes to discover a mistake, (23) while Jaques' ideas associate the prestige of work routines with the chances of making, and consequently arising out of, mistakes. (24). If all these propositions are to have any
sociological significance in status and prestige (and therefore in stigmatisation) terms, a correlation between type of work and such phenomena
would have to be proved in empirical research.

Tension and friction occur at times in all our occupational roles,
which may be due to a variance between formalised role definitions and
assigned duties in the organisation on the one hand and expectations of
an incumbent's performance on the other. Tensions may arise also out of
the subjective priorities, say, between an individual's normative aspirations for himself and the strength of his commitment to the values
underlying the organisational norms. The janitor may wish to retire
early in life or become a property tycoon; the kitchen worker may see
himself as a future entrepreneur; while dustmen and car parking men may
practise their private endeavours alongside their regular routines. The
effect of these aspirations or activities may go beyond evading the unpleasant formal restrictions of the job and, as we have seen, take the
form of a janitor's 'cut-throating' on the road to bossmanship, or in
the case of the kitchen worker legitimise his desires in the promotion
of a partnership venture and quitting the job as soon as he can. Tensions occurred also from the immediate demands at the work place by reason of the tasks to be performed (hospital porter cutting plaster or tenants spilling garbage), or in face-to-face encounters with others (supervisors and customers in catering). This shows the existence of cross-
pressures by members of a role-set upon an incumbent and the relevance
of the concepts of role and status of givers and receivers of services.

The inequality of status arises from the working conditions and the
servile nature of the work, which impose stigmatisation and operate to
remove parity, while causing the giver to define himself as rationally
and normatively inferior. Hence, tipping is sometimes regarded as a
mechanism for establishing social equivalence (using Simmel's 'gratitude'
concept) (25) and thereby restoring the balance of such an exchange.
Whether parity is attempted by means of an expressive or symbolic gratitude, its achievement is, in fact, rarely established; and one doubts
whether even socialisation into the economic ethos of our industrial
society succeeds in removing the stigmatising effect of such a transaction.

As to the meaning of the 'need' concept in work, we have shown in tracing historically how men regarded the value of work that the different

influences have come to survive in the form of particular cultural attitudes. When we looked at the intrinsic and extrinsic orientations of
incumbents, we saw that individuals in certain occupations formulated
priorities in the light of their stigmatised work routines. Caplow
tells us that the survival of any social institution like work implies
a reasonable degree of satisfaction from that activity. Yet, in the
occupational field of institutions, we find a survival of occupations
where the nature and toil of the work experience has hardly changed
over the years. The kitchen porter of today no longer feels the master
cook's wooden ladle on his back as in mediaeval times, but in many
other respects, the work has remained unchanged, while the incidental
frustrations have probably increased. We must, therefore, attempt not
only to find out what part the 'need' aspect of work plays in the performance of tasks in occupations subject to stigma, but also to venture
beyond the subjective-psychological, towards norms of the group in our
(control) occupation of kitchen porter, so as to discover what determines
the attitudes and reactions that cause stigmatised occupations not only
to remain, but also to remain static, social mobility-wise. Concepts
of need may, therefore, be found to originate not so much from personal
attitudes to the work environment as from a total societal conception
within a particular culture at a particular point of time. We may hypothesise that members of any occupation see the occupational universe
as a dichotomy and their personal, social position as members of an occupation in terms of the consciousness of being identified, and of identifying themselves with that particular collectivity. If that occupation happens to be a deprived and discriminated against one amongst
others in the structure, members will be acutely conscious of a lack of
achievement and recognition, and collectively identify themselves with
sub-cultural values that may generally be regarded as deviant. The
social consciousness of achievement, although related to work group
ideologies, is to be seen as an independent factor, represented by a
tangible, 'value-creating' effort for society; that is, a function constituting a fundamental pre-supposition in the minds of others in society. The proposition that certain occupational routines carry a higher social evaluation in our culture than those in some other occupations
has long been firmly established in the public image. What is, however,
a neglected area of investigation is why society places such poor value
upon the less tangible efforts of members in certain job categories and
thereby implicitly devalues their personal total social position as well
as that of their occupational group. If society chooses to define some
work in a stigmatising way, it need surprise us little if the individuals concerned exhibit the more instrumental pattern of commitment towards material possessions than that of the self-actualising kind of
need. This view, it will be noted, represents perhaps a slight modification of Gouldner's concept of an overriding need for the satisfaction
of one's 'other self' in the activity of work.

NOTES TO CHAPTER 2

1. Small, Mike. Catering Officer, Westfield College, Article in
    'Catering and Hotel Management', April 1971 entitled 'The
    Intelligence', Blandford Publications

2. Gold, Raymond L (1964) 'In the Basement - The Apartment-
    Building Janitor', Berger, P.(Ed.) 'The Human Shape of Work'
    McMillan, New York. The whole chapter relates.

3. Hughes, Everett, C. (1958) 'Men and Their Work', Free Press,
    Glencoe

4. Fox, Alan (1971) 'A Sociology of Work in Industry', Collier-
    Macmillan, London

5. Nairn, Tom (1968) 'The Nightwatchman' in Fraser, Ronald (Ed.)
    'Work' Vol.1, Pelican Books. The whole chapter relates.

6. Whyte, William F. (1948) 'Human Relations in the Restaurant
    Industry', McGraw-Hill Book Company, New York

7. Chivers, T.S. 'A Study of Chefs and Cooks', Survey for the
    Hotel and Catering Industry Training Board, 1971

8. Bowey, Angela M. (1976) 'The Sociology of Organisations',
    Hodder and Stoughton, London

9. Saunders, K.C. (1979), Article: 'The Hospital Porter' in
    'Employee Relations', Vol.1,No.4

10. Birch, Graham (1979) 'The Secret World of Car Parking',
    (Unpublished Dissertation) Ruskin College, Oxford

11. Saunders, K.C. (1979), Pilot Investigation of Car Parking

12. Saunders, K.C. (1980) Forthcoming article: 'Head Hall Porters:
    A Behavioural Study of Occupational Experience in the Hotel
    Industry', Employee Relations, Vol.1,No.5

13. Thoarnber, Robin, 'When the Dustmen Can Clock Off at 10 in the
    Morning', 'The Guardian', 6th September 1976, Page 10

14. 'Refuse, Storage and Collection', Report by Ministry of
    Housing and Local Government, 1967, HMSO, London

15. Godschalk, J.J. (1979), 'Foreign Labour and Dirty Work',
    'The Netherlands Journal of Sociology', Vol.15

16. Gouldner, Alvin (1970), 'The Unemployed Self', Fraser, Ronald
    (Ed.), 'Work', Vol.2, Pelican Books, Middlesex. The whole
    chapter relates.

17. Berger, Peter (Ed.) (1964) 'The Human Shape of Work', Collier-
    Macmillan, New York, Chapter 6

18.   McIntyre, John (1971) One-time Hospital Porter, now resident
      in Copenhagen, from interview by the author.

19.   Freud, S. (1922) in 'Complete Psychological Works', Vol.1
      (1886-1899), Hogarth Press, London

20.   Caplow, Theodore (1964) 'The Sociology of Work', McGraw-Hill,
      New York

21.   Merton, Robert (1957) 'Social Theory and Social Structure',
      Free Press of Glencoe. See also Miller and Form (Note 22)

22.   Miller, D.C. and Form, W.H. (1966) 'Industrial Sociology',
      Harper and Row, New York

23.   Brown, W. (1965) 'Exploration in Management', Penguin,
      Middlesex. See also 'Organisation' by Wilfred Brown,
      Heinemann, London (1971)

24.   Jaques, Elliot (1964) 'Time-Span Handbook', Heinemann
      Educational Books, London

25.   Wolff, H. Kurt (1964) 'The Sociology of George Simmel', Free
      Press, London.

3   An analysis of occupational stigma

Some General Considerations

In the previous chapter, we considered the actual and normative stigmatising propensities in six particular occupations which enabled us to
discover that large sections of people in our society are branded as
sub-citizens as a result of their membership of particular occupational
groups, as well as the mode of existence that their type of work has
forced upon them. In this section, we aim to advance this argument by
adding related propositions towards the formulation of a conceptual
framework and the construction of a substantive model, which we hope
will serve as an abstract, but simplified, representation of real phenomena and an aid to the understanding of occupation stigma.

In the past, sociological writers, whilst not entirely ignoring the
idea of stigma, have tended to favour in their choice of investigations
only definite areas, to the exclusion of vital others. Goffman (1),
Scott (2), Douglas (3), Jacobs (4), Polsky (5), Bendix and Lipset (6),
Titmuss (7) and Townsend (8), to mention but a few of the American and
English writers, have all, during the last few years, concerned themselves with problems such as mental disabilities, ethnic group relations
deviance, poverty, class differentiation and community care. Yet,
occupational stigma has remained a field comparatively untouched by
sociological research and the closest to which we have progressed here
is the consideration of types of work in terms of skill-categories,
status hierarchies and the effect of technology on occupational structure.

It appears to us that occupational stigmatisation is an active, socially harmful virus, affecting large sections of the work force in society, a virus which we have been prepared to accept for too long without
any degree of real concern. A fruitful attempt at finding a sensible
and comprehensive model incorporating some ordered ideas is what we
hope to achieve and, perhaps, thereby stimulate others to look further
into this area of analysis.

Can Occupational Stigma Be Defined ?

We do not know at this stage what ideas later, empirical investigations
will yield. We have, in our attempted definition, two end-points, representing an analytical continuum: on the one hand, the person (known
as the social actor), performing specified work as a member of an occupational group; and, on the other, the individual or collective orientations of organised (and at times unorganised) groups, exercising a
moral judgment, the reasons for which may be traceable to a variety of
influences as our inter-related propositions will show. Our definition
is intended neither to explain the origins nor the problems related to
the kind of social stigma of concern. We merely try here to identify
the subject matter as a base from which to proceed to more complex considerations bearing on stigma evidenced in occupations. With these directives in view, we may now attempt to identify our area of interest as
follows:

Occupational stigma is a discrediting attribute
accorded to individuals or groups who are performing certain occupationally identifiable roles
(in the service of their hirers), by other individuals or groups within a community, representing an active threat to full social acceptance for
the socially disgraced (by reason of their work
function) who are perceived as negatively departing from the work norm of those engaged in 'respectable' occupational activities.

The Socio-Structural Origins of Stigma

The term "stigma' is traceable to the Greeks, and refers to marks on the
human body that expose a blemished person as ritually polluted and to be
avoided in public places. In the later Christian period, 'stigma' referred to either skin eruptions as prima facie evidence of God's punishment or physical deformities. Secondly, most societies in the world
have traditionally regarded varying disabilities as stigmatising and the
deprived regarded as an economic burden. Their communities subjected
them to degrading treatment by placing them in asylums or otherwise withholding ordinary rights and benefits and, in this way, pronouncing these
disadvantaged as morally inferior.

In the twentieth century, however, industrial societies in the Western
world have accepted greater responsibility for rehabilitation of the
genetically and psychologically afflicted and for those whose abilities
the economic organisation rejects. Thirdly, social anthropologists have
contributed to studies of contemporary cultures, particularly of the
social behaviour of castes in India, which are of special interest here.
In the investigation of the Hindu, anthropologists found much concern
with the idea of 'pollution' in caste systems, when certain substances
are conceived as polluting, and attach low status to those whose occupations require them to handle such substances.

The Shudras (servants) are at the bottom of the scale of the 'untouchables'. Their very touch (or even shadow) is held to be polluting to
members of higher castes. Every caste is identifiable by an occupational
name and this division of society is said to hold good, theoretically,
throughout India. Rewards are mostly low and stigma derives not from
mere economic status alone, but from 'pollution'. The ritually 'unclean'
include outcasts who were at one time 'attached' to warriors as labourers
and sweepers employed not as sweepers, but as watchmen for government
bungalows and rest-houses. The next lowest in the hierarchy are the service occupations (Low Hindus): the washermen, barbers, distillers and
herdsmen, and all village servants. Stigmatisation operates, however,
less in the role of ranking of individuals than in the caste as an organised group, forming a distinct sub-culture in terms of religious distinctions, and also of production techniques and distribution. There were,
in 1931, fifty million people in 'unclean' castes and at the bottom of
the stratification system. Finally, we must now be alerted to the stigmatising conditions that disgrace individuals and groups engaged in specific occupational activities, where both, polluting job characteristics and
the personal disabilities of an incumbent act in tandem to demean the
self.

Occupational Stigma and the Individual

It has been shown that certain characteristics associated with the nature of work in an occupation act as contributory ingredients in bestow-
ing a debasing social identity. Some opinions deny the existence of
occupational stigma and say that the causes originate from self-imposed
economic deprivation or a related psychological make-up of the individual, whose immediate goal is subsistence, in return for which he is
prepared to carry out certain tasks demanded of him, so that the stigmatising characteristics of menial work are said to be of minor influence
upon the self. These same opinions attribute indifference to the type
of work performed, also to low intelligence which, it is alleged, prevent the incumbent from entertaining any consciousness as to the status
and prestige associated with his work. (9) If this argument stood on
its own, we would be driven to the conclusion that occupational stigma
either does not exist, or is not felt by the individual to be discrediting to him. This view has certainly found little credence in our six
occupational studies and reinforces the need for more empirical research.

Two problems pose themselves at once: firstly, can one trace any occupational identification attaching to stigmatised occupations? And a
second, more specific question, is the social stigma located in the
person himself - as is the long-held image of kitchen porters in the
catering industry - who, by reason of his membership (for the time being), discredits the occupation? In his discussion of stigma, Goffman
also suggests visual attributes and impressionistic characteristics
that may be displayed by a stranger coming into our presence, by which
we may place him and categorise him on this basis; that is, we label
him with a social identity within which Goffman includes personal attributes such as character blemishes, as well as structural ones like
occupation.

The additional question posed is, therefore, whether the stigmatised
seeks to conceal or display membership; that is to say, where he himself sees the location of the stigma. To Goffman, a stigma is really a
special kind of relationship between traits and the stereotype and he
is more concerned with those attributes which are incongruous with his
stereotype (in his discussion, the mental patient), whether such attributes are desirable or not. We shall be looking at particular occupational stereotypes more closely in the following two chapters, when the
hotel and catering industry comes under review. Goffman adds to the
idea of social identity two further concepts which will assist us in
our case studies theoretically to define relationships: one is ego identity, allowing us to consider how an individual feels about his occupational stigma; the other is personal identity, considering the individual in biographical terms. The identifying symbols inform socially
also: Smith, the kitchen porter, may at some time have to prove that
this is his occupation, but rarely to show he is a kitchen porter to
prove he is Smith. By the same token, exclusion from certain types of
employment may be on grounds of ethnicity, identified through a person's
name. Goffman's 'social' and 'personal' identity concepts are part of other
people's concerns and definitions regarding the individual whose identity is in
question, while ego identity refers to the stigmatised's subjective
sense of his own situation, continuity and character as a result of his
various social experiences.

An Individual's Occupational Identification

We have considered some aspects of the second question of the two we
have posed above. Before proceeding to discuss the subject under this
heading (the first point we raised), we return once more to Goffman, to
explain the criteria he employs to indicate the pattern of a stigmatised person's moral career. Four patterns are offered by Goffman,
which we intend to expand in the next chapters: (a) inborn stigma-
carriers adopt the ways of their disadvantageous situation and incorporate the standards where they fall short; (b) the capacity of a family
and neighbourhood to be able to form a protective capsule for the young;
(c) stigmatisation arriving late in life, or learning that one has
always been discreditable (that is, when the stigma was not yet known
or perceived); (d) those initially placed in an alien community and
having to learn to re-adapt. Persons who are subject to a particular
stigma have, therefore, certain learning experiences regarding their
plight and there are certain changes in the conception of self. Such
a moral career, says Goffman, is both cause and effect of commitment
to a sequence of personal adjustments.

We shall now move from the discussion of the relationship of stigma
located with the individual which marks him out as morally inferior and,
thus, also his occupational membership, to the effect that occupational
affinity (and stigma, if a stigmatised occupation) has upon the individual, returning to the question we first posed. The process of identification is of consequence in one's conduct, but the self and its mechanism is also related to continuing occupational structure, the bones
of the work-a-day society, figuratively speaking. And our cultural
expectations direct members of our society to have an occupation, that
is, to join a group, acquire a label and behave in a particular way.
Members incorporate an identity and perspectives that shape their conduct.

Carper (10), an American writer, discusses some of the threads from
which the fabric of occupational identification is woven and divides
this work identity into four major elements. Firstly, occupational
title. A name carries a symbolic meaning, which tends to be absorbed
into the identity. Names also specify an area of endeavour tied to
those that bear the name and place of this area, in relation to similar
activity in a broader field. Further, they imply many characteristics
of their bearers, as we have noted, and the meanings become converted
into ideologies which itemise the type of person in question. All these
things implied by the occupational title are evaluated and society reacts to such evaluations. The title may be an object of attachment or
avoidance with all that this implies. A kitchen porter may feel proud
of his occupation so long as he is in the kitchen, and his ideology
pronounces that the chefs cannot work unless he provides them with clean
pots in which to cook. No sooner has he left the kitchen for the outside world than he will try his damnedest to present a more acceptable
image to society, by passing himself off with an adopted identity.

Secondly, Carper names commitment to task. There are two kinds of
attitude: either, some sharply delimited work tasks only and performed
in a particular way are proper, and that one is the kind of person who
does this kind of work; or, the opposite attitude, that there is no kind
of task which is not possible. There may be shades of grey, of course,

but the element of attachment or the lack of it, to a specific set of tasks and the way in which one does them, is said to play also an important part in the identification with one's work. This was verified in our case studies. Thirdly, a person may see his occupational life tied to a particular organisation or, if not that, to a restricted range of work places. Allied to this, identification may embrace the hope for a variety of statuses, seen in terms of upward social improvement. There is a continuum about these along which various kinds of work identification may be found. Identifications may vary in the degree to which they reflect dependence on informal systems of sponsorship control. This category is really bound up with role relationships, to be more closely investigated in the following chapter.

The fourth dimension refers to an incumbent's social position. Here, Carper holds that occupational identity contains an implicit reference to a person's position in the larger society, tending to specify the positions appropriate for him to enjoy by virtue of the work he does. Class position or opportunity for class mobility may be favourably correlated to entrance into or membership of a particular occupation. Stigmatised occupations have not been shown as conducive to social mobility in community esteem. Possibly, these four identification factors may all be causally or functionally related and mutually reinforce each other. Again, later empirical investigation may clarify the position further, when our eleven-city survey will bring important information to light.

Society's Reaction Towards the Occupationally Stigmatised

We have been concerned with theoretical concepts as relating to the influence an alienated or deviant person may have on the social esteem in which an occupation is held and the influence identification (the reverse or a variation of it) which an occupation may have on an individual, and how he may rationalise in the social situation in which he finds himself. No discussion of stigma can be meaningful without careful regard to societal reaction towards those members who, through this double exposure, are condemned to social apartheid. We have seen that stigmatised occupations may have inbuilt characteristics that result in certain social consequences. An occupation may, for this reason, permit the employment of deviants in need of subsistence. In the hospitality industry (hotels and catering), for example, seasonal requirements and the practice of 'living-in' attract transients to certain kinds of work, where some of the more formal institutional controls are dispensed with (e.g. few recruitment formalities, leaving formalities or taxation requirements for casual labour).

Stigmatisation may revolve around person and occupation and move from his own stereotyped expectations to the public, whose perception he helps to structure. In turn, society tends to single out for attention those attributes that meet its expectations, as for example, the sort of jests directed against the kitchen porter we mention in Chapter 3. There are, therefore, a priori reasons to suppose that there is an occupational personality attached to an incumbent, as well as a societal view of an occupation that is stereotyping, stigmatising as the latter often is. In the following chapter, the sub-cultural implications of a stigmatised occupational personality will be more closely examined. For the moment, we may accept that the stigmatisation process affects the individual in a predictable way. In his contact with others in

society, their reaction may take the form of fear, pity, hostility, revulsion, tension and disgust. More than that: he will also have to
cope with inter-personal sanctions such as laughter, gossip, rejection,
shunning, ridicule, isolation and the withholding of affection. Additionally, society will bring to bear its various institutional means for
dealing with those whose abilities and usefulness it rejects. Whether
this takes the form of economic leverage, rehabilitation or punishment
will depend on the social definition of the degree of responsibility
that society accords to the individual or he may be burdened within the
situation in which he finds himself.

Interpreting Occupational Stigma

We have yet to determine the relationship between the transient population of an occupation and occupational stigma. We may well hypothesise
that these sections of the community who do not believe in the social
necessity of regulated work, or regard leisure as merely a tool of
rhetoric, adhere to cultural ideas of leisure far in advance of our
time. Lower status occupations may well appear as unworthy of lengthy
occupancy. High labour turnover in such occupations may be seen as one
of a number of social indicators signifying the stigma effect. Or,
there may be large numbers of persons who, by their mode of life, can be
taken to protest against the domination of work in the way we spend our
time. The hobo, the tramp and those whom we call 'vagrant', may regard
leisure as a source of self-identity, distinguishing it from the concept of 'free time', which is simply the antonym of work. Dumazedier
(11) has suggested that a man's leisure is the major determinant
of his self-consciousness and that his style of life during leisure is
the basis for adopting attitudes and values that influence his behaviour
in all other spheres of his life.

David Riesman (12), discussing the social role of leisure, also talks
of a society where it is held to occupy a central place for the 'other-
directed' man, that is one who seeks his source of direction in those
groups of people among whom he is thrown at any given moment in his
career. In this new, affluent employee or leisure society, the social
character of the worker loses individuality and independence and becomes increasingly group-centred. Riesman contrasts this behaviour
trend with what he calls the 'inner-directed' person, who sticks to his
opinions and follows his own conscience and is the product of an earlier
society, when values and norms changed only slowly and mobility was
limited. The modern, much maligned type in American society - the
other-directed - has no opinions of his own, and waits for a sign from
others, so that he can adapt to them. In 'our' society, they are the
work-shy or unemployable who will work in stigmatised occupations, only
for the purpose of survival. The notion of menial tasks as obvious
antecedents to kitchen portering lends itself to a hypothesis which explains the stigma attached to occupations by regarding it as vestigial
or the ritualistic, simple, or pre-industrial cultures that persist in
contemporary society. We have seen how the Hindu culture differentiated
the Shudras as ritually 'unclean' or impure in relation to their performance of polluted tasks as members of certain occupations, usually
menial or dirty.

Some sociologists reject the view of a leisure-centred, not too distant future,in which all work would be relegated from the prominent role

it now holds in society. Wilensky (13), another American sociologist, argues that the nature of some work is so stultifying that it effectively prevents the development of satisfying forms of recreation; and that work-based relationships and the values and attitudes generated within them, shape the style of life. Blumberg (14), a Boston lawyer, writing on corporate social responsibility, equally maintains that work still occupies such a large part of man's time that it must have a pervasive effect upon the entire pattern of life and, for this reason, should be made more satisfying (and, by implication, less stigmatising) and that this goal be treated as the main task of our civilisation. Blumberg strongly rejects the view that work need no longer be treated as a social problem on account of the greater importance that people attach to leisure, to which we may be permitted to add that not only is work itself a social problem, but stigmatised work is a social cancer.

The Grading of Stigma

We have suggested that our culture has, in some respects, not matured because it still carries residual values from simpler cultures, which is evidenced from the social condemnation of dirty and servile jobs. We have also advanced the idea that some sections of the transient population, or those who work only when they must, might conceivably adhere to an advanced leisure philosophy or sub-culture. We proceed now to advance a further proposition, that of a possible continuum of stigma, still looking at the problem as a two-way relationship between the individual and his occupation. It must, however, be clear from our discussion so far, that we regard occupational stigmatisation as a cultural phenomenon in Western society; it should also be stated that some countries have become more active than others in the encouragement of cultural directives through all kinds of publicity, educational, administrative, legal and political, in modifying such cultural attitudes as are not regarded desirable for progress and welfare in the broadest sense. We refer, of course, mainly to the stigmatisation of certain types of work.

Certain social differentiation will tend to remain in all societies. In the Israeli kibbutz, job rotation has been tried in order to reduce such differentiation. Its success is largely symbolic, however, having run into competition with the economic necessity for effective co-ordination. (15) Francis Hsu (16), a Chinese-Western anthropologist who studied social mobility in China, found occupational status to be elevated by imperial degrees and honours, by bureaucratic positions, distinction in literature or arts or exemplary conduct, according to Confucian principles. Prior to the immediate present, reports indicated a change from the traditional contempt of manual labour towards Mao's vision for all Chinese to be willing to work with hands as well as head. (17) Considerable research on the measure of success between a country's ideology and the social reality of occupational stigmatisation would be essential before we can claim some knowledge to yield benefits for sociology and possibly other social sciences. If we now attempt to abstract the occupational sub-system from the general social system and suggest a continuum of polar occupational types, we may, according to Raymond Mack's typology, postulate occupational determinateness in terms of statuses (i.e. definition of rights and duties) and rigidity of role expectations. (18)

Put more simply, Mack identified two ideal types and coined them the
'determinate' and the 'indeterminate'. The determinate has rights and
duties in work well defined; entry requirements into the occupation
(say, lawyer) are elaborate; expectations of role behaviour will be
narrow in range and definite. The indeterminate will be the opposite
type. Entry (say, to kitchen portering) is not defined by any specific
amount or type of training or educational requirement; there is no licensing or code of ethics; role expectations are vague; rights and duties
are not formalised by specific rules and the range of role behaviour is
wide. Mack also attaches some subjective evaluations to the statuses
of these two types in his high-to-low rating of the continuum of occupations, holding the income variable constant - excluding the influence
of income, that is. By this interpretation, determinate occupations
would then enjoy higher prestige than indeterminate ones. Indeterminate
occupations (e.g., unskilled labour) are held to be more strongly orientated towards monetary rewards; to rely upon a larger number of specific groups in society on which to model themselves (known as reference
groups) in their occupational history than the determinate role players;
downward generational mobility (like son filling a job of lower status
as compared with father) may be a more frequent pattern of entry; further indications of indeterminate occupational roles are evidenced in
less realistic aspirations, a wider range of income mobility and means
rather than ends to hold a place of prominence.

These propositions will be tested later in this study, but it is
quite clear by Mack's typology that stigmatised occupations would display the kind of characteristics which he identifies under the label of
indeterminateness. It will also be clear that these ideas by no means
conflict the association of occupational stigmatisation with cultural
phenomena, since in any given commmunity or society, the whole pattern
of thinking, striving and behaving of its members derives from a prescription of various roles in life which exert a powerful influence on
the personality formation of individuals and groups of people who are
all enmeshed in various networks of relationships in systems and sub-
systems of the many institutions in society, be this in family life,
work environment, some role in a voluntary activity, central or local
government field.

Goffman's Stigma Continuum

Goffman's concepts relate to physical and mental disabilities and their
management. He sees the continuum between the 'occasionally precarious'
and the 'constantly precarious'. Again, reconciliation with Mack's
ideas is possible if we concede to Goffman that Mack's determinate occupational role incumbents are not at all times and in all situations
absolved from precariousness. The relationship moves even closer in
the case of the occupationally stigmatised, who, as we have already
seen, finds himself constantly in a precarious social situation. His
chosen self, merely a 'resident alien', a voice of his occupational
group that speaks for and through him. He is in a special situation,
though different, yet still a normal human being in terms of a wider
group in society; and, since difference must be conceptualised collectively by whole society for it to matter, the stigmatised's difference,
which, says Goffman, it would be foolish to deny, derives from society
itself. Thus, we are in harmony with cultural phenomena also. The existence of a distortion of the structure and of the value system must

be recognised as present in society, reflecting as it does the social victimisation of actors (the stigmatised role players), who play the part of survival in a particular way; and so moulding, shaping, rein- forcing and elaborating the occupational status hierarchy in the sort of graduation or continuum we have been talking about.

Brief Comments on Figure 3, showing the Anatomy of Occupational Stigma

We shall conclude this part of our theoretical discussion of stigma in occupations with a short reference to Figure 3 below. The presentation is intended to illustrate a broadly-based set of dimensions of the con- cept of stigma, as related to place and time in terms of worker and occupation. It traces the derivation of stigma to a multiplicity of variables in the work place and outside, further to be considered later in this study. It was our endeavour also to draw into the idea of occ- upational stigma various relevant middle-range theories and show how these may be used to refine our framework designed to aid understand- ing and make a small contribution to new knowledge in this field. The earlier case studies are designed to give our theoret- ical propositions empirical reality, make them operationally more mean- ingful, help in the testing out of some of our hypotheses and isolate the factors of major influence in the attraction and contamination of occupational stigma.

A Preliminary Hypothesis of Centrality

Having regard to the visual presentation, and its inter-related prop- ositions, it is already feasible to advance a provisional hypothesis which emphasises the central area of interest in this study:

> CERTAIN SPECIFIED, STIGMATISED OCCUPATIONS ARE
> CHARACTERISED AND IDENTIFIED BY THE FACT THAT
> SUCH WORK IS INTRINSICALLY MONOTONOUS OR DIRTY,
> GIVES LITTLE OPPORTUNITY FOR THE EXPRESSION OF
> SKILL AND THE DEVELOPMENT OF NEW POTENTIALITIES,
> IS NOT VIEWED CHIEFLY AS AN END IN ITSELF, AS
> CONCERNS THE ACTUAL WORK ACTIVITY, BUT RATHER
> AS A MEANS FOR SATISFYING SHORT-TERM NEEDS
> (WANTS) AND WILL NOT BECOME AN IMPORTANT AND
> APPROVED ELEMENT IN AN INCUMBENT'S TOTAL IDENTITY.
> NON-WORK ACTIVITIES FOR THE PRACTITIONERS OF
> SUCH OCCUPATIONS ARE LIKELY TO BE MORE CENTRAL
> TO THEIR LIFE STYLE THAN WORK ACTIVITIES.

FIGURE 3.
ANATOMY OF OCCUPATIONAL STIGMA (inter-related propositions)

The location of occupational stigma may be attached to the actor, found in
the social system where he is employed, in the community and society, or in
all of these.

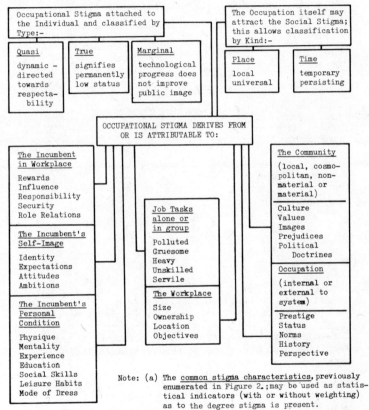

Note: (a) The common stigma characteristics, previously
enumerated in Figure 2.; may be used as statistical indicators (with or without weighting)
as to the degree stigma is present.

(b) Measure of stigma type (see Figure 3. above)
indicates the direction of movement -
whether static or dynamic.

51

1.   Goffman, Erving (1968)'Stigma', Pelican Books

2.   Scott, Robert A. (1970) 'The Construction of Conceptions of
     Stigma by Professional Experts' in Douglas, Jack D. (Ed.)
     'Deviance and Respectability', Basic Books, New York

3.   Douglas, Jack D. (Ed.) (1970) 'Deviance and Respectability:
     The Social Construction of Moral Meanings', Basic Books,
     New York

4.   Jacobs, Jerry (1970) 'The Use of Religion in Constructing the
     Moral Justification of Suicide', Douglas, Jack D. (Ed.) in
     'Deviance and Respectability', Basic Books, New York

5.   Polsky, Ned (1971) 'Hustlers, Beats and Others', Pelican
     Books, London

6.   Bendix, Reinhard and Lipset, Seymour M. (1963) 'Class, Status
     and Power', The Free Press of Glencoe, III, New York

7.   Titmuss, Richard M. (1960) 'The Irresponsible Society', Fabian
     Society, London

8.   Townsend, Peter (1962) 'The Meaning of Poverty', The
     British Journal of Sociology, Vol.13

9.   Hegarty, J., Clewett, T., Bates, M.(October 1971), Lecturers,
     Department of Catering, The Polytechnic, Wolverhampton,
     Interviews

10. Carper, James (1970) 'The Elements of Identification with an
     Occupation', Becker, Howard S. (Ed.) in 'Sociological Work,
     Method and Substance', Allen Lane, The Penguin Press

11. Dumazedier, J. (1967) 'Towards A Society of Leisure', Collier-
     Macmillan, New York. See also Roberts, K. 'Leisure' (1970)
     Longmans.

12. Riesman, D. (1967) 'The Lonely Crowd', Yale University Press

13. Wilensky, H.L. (1969) 'Work as a Social Problem', in Becker,
     H.S. (Ed.) 'Social Problems: A Modern Approach', John Wiley,
     New York

14. Blumberg, P. (1968) 'Industrial Democracy: The Sociology of
     Participation', Constable, London

15. Schwarz, Richard D. (1955) 'Functional Alternatives to
     Inequality', American Sociological Review, Vol.20

16.   Hsu, Francis L.K. (1949), 'Social Mobility in China',
        American Sociological Reniew, Vol. 14

17.   MacDougall, Colina, 'A Little Dirt on Every White Collar',
        Observer Magazine, 7th November 1971

18.   Mack, Raymond W. (1956), 'Occupational Determinateness:
        A Problem and Hypothesis in Role Theory', Social Forces,
        Vol. 35

4 Two service industries and their workers: a social profile of occupational evolution

Introductory

No previous research could be traced that singles out the kitchen porter for treatment on a social, historical basis. Isolated data can, however, be found which describes the origins of associated life among social actors and their work in kitchens and we were able to glean snippets of social activities as part of an environment of the provisionof hospitality and lavish entertaining out front and slavery in kitchens behind the scenes. Our prime objective in producing this outline is to a lesser extent to highlight conditions in kitchens, important as this undoubtedly is, as perhaps the discovery of a pattern or configuration of historical occurrences that will enable us to adduce that the role and status of the kitchen porter has changed but little; and, perhaps also provide a perspective on the problems of occupational stigma in our age, as well as to make the point that cultures may remain virtually unchanged over time, despite some drastic alterations in an underlying pattern of social order; and that ideas of culture (stigma) frequently survive long after societies that generated them ceased to exist.

The Ancient and the Mediaeval World

The ancient and mediaeval world accepted poverty, pain and servitude as a way of life from which one could not escape. Cicero saw nothing unusual in the ownership of one man by another. Plato (1) once suggested only half jokingly, when a poor and humble worker succumbed to the miseries of life to an early grave, that it was the better for him to be out of it and freed from all his troubles. Many slaves were taken to work in factories and mines, as well as into rich households as private servants. Kitchens in ancient times were closely related to the diets of the people and this affected the type of apparatus used for the preparation and cooking of food. The upper classes in Greece enjoyed elaborate diets and slaves used and cleaned such equipment as charcoal braziers, cauldrons, troughs and beehive ovens. Much of the Greek-type kitchen equipment is still used today and kitchen workers then, as now, of low status, consisted mostly of male slaves, but unlike today were able to advance to high rank if they showed any ability at cooking. (2)

Porter-Slaves in Roman Times

Roman cooking, at first Greek-influenced, surpassed this phase, the recipes in the book by Apicius covering a wide range of foods and requiring an extensive amount of equipment, as substantiated by written evidence and found in excavations, particularly at Pompeii. Sumptuous banquets, served in Roman Emperor times, needed the employment of many slaves for the performance of various kitchen duties. These 'porter-slaves' were branded on chest, back or face, or their ears pierced, in order that their masters could trace and reclaim them if they absconded. Such marks of slavery remained an imprint for ever, even if they later rose to a rank of cook. Some slaves, regarded as the lowest possible form of human life, were the washers-up, the stokers (Focarii), the sweepers (Scoparii) and the Lecticarii, whose portering job it was to

carry their lazy or high-ranking masters to and from the dining table.
Another unhappy duty of a slave-porter consisted of blowing constantly
at the kitchen fire to keep up the flame which fired the large cauldrons for boiling, eventually to be cleaned out by slaves. Saucepans of
all shapes and sizes were used and cleaned by porter-slaves in a corner
of the kitchen. The head chef (Archimagirus) was subject to flogging
in front of the guests if one complained of a badly cooked dish. He
would then return to the kitchen and subject the porters to a bigger
ration of the same.

Casual Labour in Mediaeval Times

During mediaeval times, the kitchen was the social centre of the large
household. It was a place where anyone wanting a snack, rest or gossip
went. As a result, the kitchen was described as a noisy, crowded place
with people working or lounging about; a place where cats, dogs, birds
and other creatures could be found: hot, smoky, stinking with body
smells and cooking, filthy and harbouring germs of every description.
Noblemen's kitchens had to be huge (Hampton Court, Gloucester Abbey),
for they were catering for some 700-800 and needed to accommodate the
practice of whole-ox roasting. Kitchen sections compare with larger
hotels today, consisting of the Great Kitchen, the Privi Kitchen, Cellar, Larder, Buttery, Scullery, Ewery, Saucery, Chaundry, Spicery and
Poultery. Casual labour was used in most of the large kitchens, especially for working the spit and cleaning the mass of varied equipment in
use. These tasks were given to wandering tramps, loafers and vagabonds
for a pittance in coin and food. It was only when neither down-trodden
spit-jacks nor tramps could be found that donkeys and dogs were used
for some of the jobs. (3)

The Kitchen Porter in Fifteenth Century England

In Fifteenth Century England, eating and drinking formed one of the
chief pleasures of life for people of means. In many of the socially-
elevated households, the cook enjoyed a respected ranking, symbolised
by a wooden spoon which he carried to mark his status and which he used
for tasting dishes or for beating offending kitchen porters. We may
gain a good impression of the working environment in kitchens from
Ellacott's description of the atmosphere there when Archbishop Neville
held a great feast for 6,000 guests upon his installation at York in
1467:-

> As the preparations and serving of the meal progressed,
> the air of the kitchen, big as it is, became stifling
> with fire-heat and the greasy steam... the air of the
> great lord's kitchen was so heavy with grease that to
> 'breathe was to feed'. The master cook stalked here
> and there, smelling, tasting and occasionally advising;
> the servers scurrying to and fro, kitchen porters cross
> and re-cross with fuel, buckets of water, waste tubs
> and greasy pots. Now and then, the master's ladle
> (made of cast iron in those days) was heard to swack
> upon some worker who stole to a corner with a tempting
> left-over from the dinner table. (4)

The Archbishop's banquet compares with the biggest organised today.
Few cities even today can accommodate such a larger number. At a period when unemployment, sickness and destitution mirrored the unsettled
nature of the times, Neville's great feast required 104 oxen, 500 deer,
1,000 sheep, 304 calves, 200 pigs, 400 swans, 2,000 geese, 1,000 capons,
104 peacocks, 13,500 other birds, 608 pike and bream, 300 qrs. of
wheat, 1,500 hot venison pasties, 13,000 jellies, custard tarts and
other delicacies, 300 tuns of ale, and 100 tuns of wine. And this is
probably not all. Our intention here is not to discuss the philosophy
of the social injustices of the age, of which students of our social
history are aware, but to illuminate a situation within the context of
time when a large brigade of kitchen workers of the lowest of statuses
used and cleaned a vast quantity of primitive equipment that was to be
found in the kitchens during this period. Not all those huge quantities of food could be consumed by the guests. The left-overs were
passed out to kitchen porters and other servants, while the remainder
went to the poor.

The Renaissance and the Obligation to Serve

We now come to the Renaissance, when a man worked not just to be able
to live, but because it was the right or moral thing to do. This work
ethic or gospel of work spread all over England, Germany, Scandinavia
and elsewhere in Europe. Aubert, when discussing the positions of Nor-
wegian servants during this time, explains how the role of serf was
eventually replaced by that of the free servant; how a general prescription was issued by the legislative authorities which made it a legal
duty for all able-bodied men and women, under threat of penalties, to
seek employment in the service of others. (5) This and other enactments
show that this occupational role was based on ascribed status. The
housemaid worked long hours and, in addition, was forced to invest some
of her 'private' emotions in the family for which she worked.

Joan Walley illustrates the situation in France as follows:-

> (quoting a conversation between the mistress and her
> maid). 'Come down and bring towels and linen and coal
> and take the bellows and blow up the fire, take the
> tongs and mend it so that it burns, boil the pots,
> fry some fat, lay the table and bring a long cloth,
> put water in the hand basin.'

> 'Ma'am, where are the copper, cauldron and pans?'
> 'Art thou blind? Dost thou not see them...? Thou
> has still to wash and scour the pewter bottles and
> the quart and pint pots, platters, bowls and saucers,
> and put all this iron gear in its proper place, the
> roasting iron, the flesh hook, the trivet, the covers
> of the pots and the spits...'

The Sixteenth Century - Life for Domestic and Kitchen Workers

Our short digression from the toils of the kitchen porter to the servility of the housemaid is less intended to highlight social or occupational differentiation than to show that domestics, as well as kitchen workers, belonged to a common servant hierarchy existing within the largest

households at particular social levels of the times. Also, Orwell's observations three centuries later, that the plongeur's intensely exhausting work is the sort of job that would always be done by women were they
but strong enough, could well explain the absence of female porters for
the heaviest tasks in the earlier historical period. (6)

The Sixteenth Century kitchen of the wealthy, where most of the larger scale catering took place, was headed by a male cook. The heavy
and exacting work in those kitchens was too much for women who, as was
noted, played a more prominent part in a service capacity for their
'masters' than supporting the onerous tasks behind the scenes. A mass
of dishes and plates had to be dealt with after meals, with little in
the way of amenities for washing them. For centuries, the luckless
dishwasher seems to have relied on hot water and an occasional scouring
with sand. There is no record of soap being used for washing dishes,
although it was first made in England early in this century. At the
time, kitchen sinks were usually made of stone or hard wood and waste
pipes discharged outside the kitchen without, however, the benefit of
drains. It was the task of the porters to carry the waste water in
buckets in the absence of a piped sink.

The Seventeenth Century Work Ethic

Where Protestantism in the last century gave respectability and sanction
to the profit motive when it removed the stigma from personal enrich-
ment, exerting as it did a leading impulse for thrift, frugality and the
virtue of hard manual work, the Seventeenth Century was a time of conflicting views and values of religious heterodoxy. It was also the
time of Cromwell and his Puritan followers and a time in which the common man spoke his mind. Religious sentiments of the period, often 'acted
out' (through supplication, prayer, confession and other rites) some of
the psychological products of strain. The Protestant ethic conceptualised that a life of action counted for more than insular reflection.
Indeed, to Luther (leader of the German Reformation), it meant that the
scullery maid who did her chores well was as near to God as any priest
in the pulpit. The Puritan morality went a step further. To be poor
was not merely a misfortune, it was to fail in one's mission and mock
God. It might be hypothesised that this kind of morality encouraged
the gospel that 'thou shalt love thy master' and encouraged servility
as an appropriate ethic, but we wish to avoid speculation here for the
evolution of the servant class is a vast subject of research in its own
right.

This century was also marked by great contrasts between the heights of
individual wealth and the depths of poverty. It was a time of relief
for the impotent poor; for the masterless poor to be set to work; for
apprentices to be bound out for the removal from parish rates; and for
the vagrants to be shown the error of their ways, by locking them away
from the concern of society. 'Bridewells' were prominent and servants
had to produce testimonials from their masters to prove gainful employment or they were liable to be whipped as vagrants and thrust out of
the parishes. Such vagrants were glad of casual work in the kitchens
at a time when labour (particularly domestics) was cheap. (7)

The Eighteenth Century - Position of Servants

As we move into the Eighteenth Century, comments on the contemporary
scene show that the occupations of 'service' were considered somewhat
demeaning. Stigma attached to much of the servant class. There was,
however, a certain readiness for both men and women to become domestics:
and, seemingly, an absence of gloomy discontent and acute sense of degradation, or personal indignity, so often found among servants in more
recent times. However mild it may have been, the stigma did exist;
deriving in part from the nature of the servant's social role. The
climate of Eighteenth Century England stamped the servant as valueless
to the community; as a group who contributed little or nothing to the
common well-being. (8) Contemporary writers time and again supported
this view in their incidental remarks. Such as one Nathaniel Forster
who called attention to the 'numbers of servants in gentlemen's families, who consume without mercy the product of the state, with very
little return of advantageous labour'. (9)

This century mirrored the poverty of the labourer more as a sign of
idleness and sin, at a time when his employers prospered rather than as
a burden he had to bear. Industrialisation with institutional and ideological changes engendered an awareness in the worker that his status
was that of a second-class citizen and that he was personally responsible
for the poverty from which he was afflicted. This disruption of the
traditional way of life coincided with the denial that the ordinary employed man had a legitimate place in society; and, if poverty there be,
it resulted from defects in character rather than from the inscrutable
forces that tended to stigmatise and undermine his self-respect. (10)
The aristocracy asserted that the 'higher classes' were obliged to
think for, and protect, the 'poor', while the latter had to be submiss-
ive and depending on their 'betters'. When this view was put into practice, it caused considerable social isolation among groups of work
people in catering and industrial enterprises. (11)

Hecht admirably analyses the status hierarchy of the Eighteenth Century servant class. We shall present the structure in our own graphical
form. The valet was his master's servile companion, accompanying him
everywhere, whether this be shopping, travelling or visiting. The valet
did not always play the role of a male domestic; but when he did, his
status was high and he performed the duties of house steward. Below
him in rank came the butler and the gardener. The butler's domain was
the pantry and wines. The status of the cook (male) depended on whether
there was a kitchen clerk; if not, his control over the culinary department was complete and the rest of the kitchen staff worked under his direction. We then have the bailiff, who may be regarded as a kind of
land steward, managing the master's farm. The bailiff ranked just above
the valet. The groom ranked lowest among the male upper strata of servants and his task was mostly the maintenance of furniture. The lower
(inferior) strata of manservants was topped by those who wore livery and
of whom the coachman ranked highest. Below him came several domestics.
The mainstay of the household was the footman, whose duties consisted
mostly of waiting when indoors and acting as messenger or escort when
outdoors. Other members ranked in this hierarchical order: horse
groom (to be distinguished from the groom of chambers above), underbutler, undercoachman, park-keeper and the gate porter, who at times
acted also as underbutler. It is not difficult to imagine where

un-uniformed, low-grade kitchen staff ranked. It has been surmised that this body of the kitchen brigade ranked even below the main body of livery servant, including the domestics and after such species as youths who bore such titles as postilion, yardboy, provision boy, footboy and page.

Hecht finds that Eighteenth Century maidservants often represented prestige value in a household, although they were not always considered an essential part of the 'display equipment'; indirectly, they contributed their support to the style in which their employers lived. Maidservants ranked under the chambermaid and their role was mostly utilitarian in character. Included in this group are the housemaid - the maid of all work - followed by the laundry maid and the dairy maid. The slight variations that are said to exist in the ranking order were difficult to determine and remain unclear. Immediately below the lady's maid came the housekeeper (sometimes coupled with cook), otherwise the lowest upper servant on the female side was the cook. Below the chambermaid ranked the housemaid, whose work was hard and arduous. (12)

Within the context of English society in the Eighteenth Century, the domestic servant class had a special significance, as it was an important agent in the process of social change. The general cultural tone was set by an elite, composed of the highest nobility, the wealthiest gentry and their satellites, from which no level of societal structure escaped the impact on its mode of behaviour and its scheme of life. We considered the servant class of this century at some length, not only because it embraced within its hierarchy all manner of low-grade domestic and kitchen workers, but also because it was the single largest occupational group of the time.

The Nineteenth Century

In this, the Nineteenth Century, we shall continue to give the servant class further, detailed attention, not only for the reasons already indicated and because it constituted still the largest occupational group in the country, but also because extensive banqueting and activity in large households under the prevailing social conditions were functionally similar to the newly-developing hotel and catering industry. Nor will the location at the bottom of the servant hierarchy of the kitchen staff have escaped notice. Strongly in evidence is a pattern where status relationships are based less on contract than on the label of one's place or station. (13) Job involvement tended to be closely bound up with the fortunes of the employer and the mode in which role expectations were met in the master-servant relationships, for neither party could disentangle private life from the work-a-day existence.

Domestic Service

Domestic service in this century thrived for two main reasons: first, because economic necessity forced poor, larger families to place their children - mostly daughters - into service, as one of the few means of maintenance; and second, because servants 'knew their place' and accepted it as their lot in life to 'serve their betters'. The new age brought into being a large, leisured class, not related to the professions, industry or trade. Territorial aristocracy still ruled the rural parts and led society in London and in its country house gatherings.

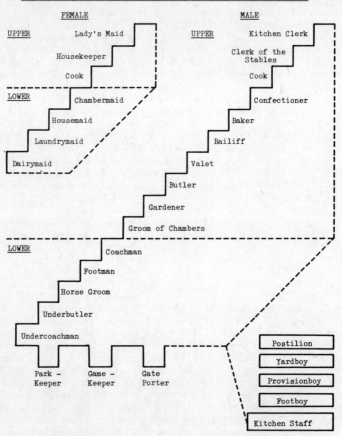

FIGURE 4.
STRUCTURE OF THE SERVANT HIERARCHY IN EIGHTEENTH CENTURY ENGLAND

FEMALE

MALE

UPPER — Lady's Maid

Housekeeper

Cook

LOWER — Chambermaid

Housemaid

Laundrymaid

Dairymaid

UPPER — Kitchen Clerk

Clerk of the
Stables

Cook

Confectioner

Baker

Bailiff

Valet

Butler

Gardener

Groom of Chambers

LOWER — Coachman

Footman

Horse Groom

Underbutler

Undercoachman

Park –
Keeper

Game –
Keeper

Gate
Porter

Postilion

Yardboy

Provisionboy

Footboy

Kitchen Staff

Note: Among the large numbers of servants in many households at
that time, maids, keepers and porters, rated low in the
hierarchy. Placed lowest of all is kitchen staff.

Expression was given to rampant individualism and enjoyment of its own pleasant life. These gatherings and large-scale banqueting required the operation of large kitchens, whilst at the same time, open roasting and cooking ranges were not yet technically efficient.

Quennell (14) discusses the conditions of work at the time. Open ranges, devouring coals and pouring smoke are said to have been the cause of the Nineteenth Century London fogs. The distinguished doctor, Sir Frederick Treves, estimated that fog in a London square mile contained six tons of soot and killed people by the thousands. Blackened implements, kettles and burnt-out boilers, plus the temperature of the fat from the joint splattering over, resulting in unpleasant smells. The elaborate meals created masses of washing up. The soot that coated saucepans, collected from being over the fire, had to be scrubbed off before they could be washed. Puddings were eaten much more than they are today, and the suet clung to the cloths they were boiled in. They were the most horrible, greasy objects to wash and, as hot water did not come from the tap, it would usually get cold before the scullery maid had finished the washing up in the big, wooden sink. The soda put into the water to disperse the grease roughened and reddened the maid's hands still more. (15) Incidentally, the duties of porters included the cutting off of ice from the ponds and lakes, which was required for the ice-houses used for cooling drinks. It has been suggested that many a porter did not survive the change of temperature from hot kitchen to ice-house.

Although conditions of Elizabethan times, when servants slept on prickling straw, had now passed, it was still customary in most great houses to sleep men in the cellars and women in the attics, often in a long, single dormitory. This practice of 'living-in' has later been adopted by hotels, in order to maintain staff requirements in times of acute shortage. Only towards the end of the Nineteenth Century has the idea that 'anything is good enough for servants' given way to the need of meeting the new scarcity; nor was it usual until that time to give days off or annual holidays, it being considered quite enough for servants to get the occasional afternoon to themselves and to have the opportunity to attend church on Sunday. By the middle of the century, a London maid of all work got between £6 to £10 per year, with allowances for tea and sugar and beer; at the end of the century, an ordinary middle-class household was paying a 'rough girl' something like £6 per year. From the Eighteenth Century, another development occurred which had profound social implications; servants began to demand tips, which so outraged employing classes that they combined to try to put an end to it.

Marshall (16) talks also of another complaint against the servants. Instead of being content with their subordinate position in society, they were rankly extravagant in the matter of clothes, respectably dressing above their station, instead of saving towards a respectable and frugal old age. By this time, a further charge brought against men servants was - with the days of elaborate livery over - that hair was worn unpowdered. Thus, the demand for the perfect servant never varied, but the dependence which most people had upon their servants did give a bargaining power which enabled them to redress the balance somewhat, as for instance by demanding tips for extra jobs for visitors.

Victorian prosperity allowed even middle-class families to have an abundance of servants. An upper middle-class family might have the whole range of butler, footman, lady's maid, cook, kitchen maid, scullery maid and laundry maid. Even the poorest clergyman's wife had a cook and servant girl, while the husband employed an all-round man for odd jobs, to look after the garden and horse. A nobleman employed between twenty and 100 servants in his great house. One in nine females over the age of ten was a domestic servant. (17) The career structure took the following direction: a young girl would start as a kitchen maid (making tea, coffee, biscuits, jam, cordials and preserves) or as parlour maid (looking after china and serving the table). If she started as chambermaid, making beds and repairing linen was her task. A step up was to become a cook, but the best post she could hope for was to become a housekeeper in a large establishment.

By 1870, servants were still plentiful and their demands for wages and nights out still moderate. Some became attached members of a household, while others came and went, dimly recollected. The services were arduous, for the tall, narrow town-houses of the middle-class were not fitted with labour-saving appliances. (18) An architect by the name of James Laver, who wrote widely on the character of England in pre-war days, correlated architectural with social stratification when comparing the physical location of rooms in the Eighteenth Century country house with the Victorian London house. (19) Whereas, earlier social divisions were at least, in the physical sense, on the same level, in the Victorian house, rooms were arranged on top of one another, so as to confront society with a perpetual symbol of its hierarchical structure, the servants becoming quite literally the 'lower classes'. The Quennells point to the implications of house construction upon the work of servants. (20) Quite apart from carrying coal and food upstairs, stone-paved halls with long passages, kitchens, sculleries and front door steps needed continual scrubbing; heavy furniture constant polishing; and two to three substantial meals prepared each day. Work began at six o'clock in the morning and went on until the last dishes and pots were washed and put away at night. Although the laws of the 1891 Factory Act limited women's hours to twelve per day, it did not apply to domestic servants who continued to work longer hours well into the Twentieth Century.

It will not have escaped attention that some of the practices that have grown up in this century, such as living-in and tipping, were carried over into some of the service industries, particularly hotel and catering. Servants suffered also the disadvantage of the scattered nature of their employment, which made it difficult for them to form associations, even at a time when the Nineteenth Century trade union movements showed how effective combination could become accepted and recognised as part of the social structure. The scattered nature of catering establishments today has been one of the principal reasons why organisation for the protection of common interest has proved so difficult to attain.

Paupers, Floaters and Wanderers

This discussion would be incomplete without mentioning another large class equally far removed from domestic service or factory. We are referring to the destitute. The agrarian and industrial changes of this period, together with the high prices and miseries of the war years, led to much destitution. The population grew and unemployment with it.

Affluent industrial England was also the age of paupers and workhouses, of navvies and vagrancy, of the factory toiler and trucking; and of street criers and scavengers, many of whom were living squalid lives, nosing around the 'dustbins' of the more fortunate for scraps of food. (21) The humiliation of failure was institutionalised in the forms and ceremonies of the workhouse and the stigma of pauperism.

In mid-Victorian times, there was a surplus of unskilled labour, particularly in London. Today, London has a desperate need for many thousands of workers in the hotel and catering industry and there is a chronic shortage of kitchen porters. But, kitchen porters are said to be recruited from the strata of social groups that formerly made up the Victorian poor, hence diagramatic analysis of this population will serve us to compare and contrast later with our findings of the present day.

Our Visual Categorisation of Itinerant Social Groups among the Victorian Poor

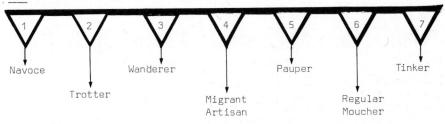

These groups of individuals were the least charted sections of the then contemporary society. The Victorian age was also one of financial ups and downs, which made the life of servants frequently insecure, since it was the practice of the employer class to set up temporary home by taking over a house for a short stay, or seasonal splash, and filling it with all manner of servants, only to dismiss them a few months later and so causing them to swell the floating army of the unemployed. Let us briefly see how this floating, heterogeneous population was made up. Group 1 were a caste of rough, nomad labourers with their own habits and traditions: Group 2, also referred to as the costermongers, consisted of street sellers, drinking lots of beer and always at loggerheads with authority, as well as in competition with the 'shopocracy'. Group 3, the wanderers, were a variety of the poor, constantly shifting in and out of the main centres of population, remaining a mysterious class of nomads to the settled inhabitants. Group 4 were unsuccessful tramping workmen, so ragged and wretched that they could not avoid begging; Group 5, the paupers, are the most familiar to students of social history. Although seeking work, they suffered the aura of disgrace attaching to any form of indoor relief, strongly discouraging bona fide seekers of work, and leaving the casual wards largely to delinquents who had no sense of dignity to lose. Group 6 have been described as ragged and filthy, padding along the dusty verges of the summer roads, a universally unwelcome sight without necessarily presenting the physically collapsed appearance later associated with tramps. The mouchers were fond of scrounging and pilfering. Finally, Group 7, the tinkers, represented a different kind of nomad, well known for mending pots and pans; they were gipsy-like in appearance and habits, although their way of life was more squalid and dirty; but they were well known for their aptitude for rough metal work.

Booth (22) has provided us with some empirical data which is relevant for comparative purposes. He writes that 3 per cent of the London pauper population consisted of inmates of hotels and lodging houses and other institutions that existed in the late Nineteenth Century. Potmen working in London in inns, hotels or clubs, earned £1 per week from work as kitchen porters, hall porters, luggage porters and scullery men. Booth identified the principal causes of pauperism from an analysis of case investigation. It is convenient to categorise them by means of a diagram.

<u>Reasons for Pauperism and Transience</u>

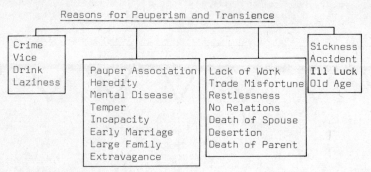

| Crime
Vice
Drink
Laziness | Pauper Association
Heredity
Mental Disease
Temper
Incapacity
Early Marriage
Large Family
Extravagance | Lack of Work
Trade Misfortune
Restlessness
No Relations
Death of Spouse
Desertion
Death of Parent | Sickness
Accident
Ill Luck
Old Age |

Booth found in the 1880's that one third of the London population lived in poverty, and that over half of this poverty was the result of poor working conditions and irregular employment. About one quarter lived in circumstances which they could not control, such as infirmity, illness or some of the causes listed above, other than drink or thrift-lessness, of which the poor were often accused. Categorisation of the poor was somewhat crude and mainly served bureaucratic purposes without regard to the social elements of administration, although the founding fathers of sociology can by no means be said to have been indifferent to social problems. It was not until the inter-war years that policies based on stigma and deterrence were increasingly considered inadequate to meet the needs of accelerated industrialisation. Before turning to the Twentieth Century, there are further dimensions to be looked at briefly: one of which is that of recruitment. We have already seen how the itinerant social groups among the Victorian poor obtained work. As for the paupers, the inspectors believed that the able-bodied paupers were the central problem. Their attitude hardened and they introduced still sterner tests towards the end of the century. The idea was a test of work in workhouse stone-yards. It failed to deter. In times of unemployment, men queued at the workhouse gates for the right to any kind of work for payment. One Board of Guardians in London (at Poplar) created a test house of a new kind. Children, the sick, the aged and infirm were removed to another workhouse (Bromley) and the main work-house converted into a 'House of Industry', organised into 'such a sys-tem of labour, discipline and restraint as shall outweigh the advantages of subsistence'. Men had to pick 5 lb. of unbeaten oakum per day and women 3 lb. Failure to complete the task meant either bread and water diet or a charge and appearance before a magistrate the next morning. The test house became the terror of the London poor. Pinker, more

recently, and Mayhew, writing earlier in the century, note the vast difference in social status between skilled operatives and unskilled workers. Equally, he observed among the unskilled workers neither union
organisation nor, like the artisans, political consciousness - they were
as unpolitical as footmen. (23/24)

The Vagrant Hypothesis

We now come to consider the 'Vagrant' hypothesis, as seen during the
Nineteenth Century. How such social groups are regarded by society depends largely on the structural and cultural factors of the times,
which influenced people's propensity for social distance, condemnation
of the dependent, compassion for greed or humiliation, and for social
consciousness or humanitarianism. Such outsiders as paupers and vagrants experienced either institutional sanctions or conceptual liquidation, by being accorded inferior status in the social hierarchy, if
indeed they counted as a part of it. Caplow (25) associates skill with
the regularity of employment, implying that irregularity of employment
is an acceptable way of defining the unskilled. Charles Booth,(26) in
his investigations, directly relates poverty to the peripherality of
the labour force. One of his categories, the casual worker, (one tenth
in East London) is very poor, a kind of anomaly in industrial society,
constituting a test generally of the state of trade - a sort of 'dist-
ress meter' - the ideal of such persons being to work when they like
and play when they like; a leisure class, bounded very closely by the
pressure of want, but habitual to the extent of second nature.

It will be convenient to look at the views of an earlier writer, Henry
Mayhew (op.cit), who was particularly interested in the unskilled worker
and vagrancy. He defines a vagrant as:-

> ' ... an individual applying himself continuously
> to no one thing, nor pursuing any one aim for any
> length of time, but wandering from this subject to
> that, as well as from one place to another, because
> in him no industrial habits have been formed, nor
> any principle or purpose impressed upon his nature'.

In the Government Reports of 1839, Mayhew explains, the Constabulary
Commissioners found in almost all the cases, the prevalent cause to be
an 'impatience of steady labour'. Mayhew agrees, but stresses that, in
order to understand the question of vagrancy thoroughly, one must go
further and find out what, in its turn, is the cause of this impatience
of steady labour, or as he re-stated the problem -'whence comes the desire to obtain property with a less degree of labour than by regular
industry?' Today's pragmatic interpreters of this social group in the
hotel industry might take a leaf out of his book from Mayhew's penetrating reply to the question he posed:-

> ' ... the evils upon the uncertainty of labour ...
> and the mischief attendant upon it is that remaining
> to be exposed... many classes of labour are necessar-
> ily uncertain or fitful in their character. Some
> work can be pursued only at certain seasons; some
> depends upon the winds - as dock labour; some on
> fashion; and nearly all on the general prosperity of

the country. Now the labourer who is deprived
of his usual employment by any of the above
causes, must, unless he has laid by a portion of
his earnings become a burden to his parish, or
the State, or else must seek work, either of
another kind or in another place. The mere fact
of a man seeking work in different parts of the
country, may be taken as evidence that he is in-
disposed to live on the charity or labour of others...

Mayhew, continuing his brilliant analysis, a little later hands out a
prescription hardly out of place for today's managers, thus:-

' ... labour and effort are more or less irksome
to us all. There are however two means by which
this irksomeness may not only be removed, but
transformed into a positive pleasure. One is by
excitement of some impulse or purpose in the mind
of the workman; and the other, by the inculcation
of a habit of working. Purpose and habit are the
only two modes by which labour can be rendered easy
to us; and it is precisely because the vagrant is
deficient in both that he has an aversion to work
for his living, and wanders through the country
without an object, or indeed, a destination...'

This proposition, we feel, has a good deal to commend it, but does not
today contain the whole answer to the problem, as our theoretical chapter on stigmatisation has already shown. There is a multiplicity of
variables contributing to explain the generations of protestants and
itinerants; or, as Mayhew referred to this group - 'those impatient of
steady labour'. It is hoped that our survey-in-depth analysis will have
identified some of the variables and thereby increased our understanding
of this phenomenon.

This concludes our Nineteenth Century profile of the social changes as
these affected the life and labour of people engaged in catering and
service occupations, and the hotel industry itself. The Twentieth Century brought once more important changes, not only in the foundations,
however fragile, which had been laid for the further development of the
social services generally, together with the stages of legislative response in the structure and organisation of the hotel industry and manpower within it, but also in the form of a bloodless social revolution
below stairs.

It is found, as we advance with our survey into the Twentieth Century,
that scant documentation of the conditions in hotel kitchens can be
traced and that only within the scattered writings of historians and
travellers, who have commented in passing on the social scene of hospitality. Accounts rarely reach into the rear world normally hidden from
the resident of a hotel, where there may be observed a strict division
between service and production, between the splendour of uniforms and
the functional dress of those performing menial tasks. Orwell, one of
the outstanding writers, who has himself experienced the life of a
'plongeur', helps us to understand the feelings of those who performed
this work by his vivid social documentation, which we shall be looking
at. As for servants, the last generation of employers complained about

the difficulty in obtaining 'satisfactory' servants; the present generation (early Twentieth Century) has a problem of finding them at all.
The position was so acute and pressing that a Government enquiry became
necessary to investigate the causes and cure of the servant shortage.
In this final section of our historical analysis, the aim of which has
also been the co-ordination of social facts within the ambit of our interest, we shall briefly describe the wider social scene, in terms of
growth of the hotel industry and the conditions - including the legislative adjustments - under which activities within the social system of
the kitchen take place.

Recruitment of Servants

As for recruitment of servants, writes Molly Harrison (27), the Mop Fair
was a popular way of hiring servants in the country. It was a kind of
servants' carnival, where the market place would be filled with stalls,
public houses with customers and servants standing in rows, by the side
of the market place, displaying a traditional sign to indicate their
particular abilities - brushes, brooms or mops were carried by them.
There was a universal reluctance of working-class girls to enter domestic service, especially so if it included 'living-in' in private houses,
for domestic service had an evil reputation among those who were in the
best position to know its conditions, i.e. the servant class themselves.
There was less disinclination for service in hotels and boarding-houses
and still less for daily work. In the towns around 1873, writes Royston
Pike (28) the hardest-worked class of women were domestic servants, especially in schools, hotels and lodging houses. Particularly unpopular
was also the work in slaughter houses and bakehouses. Slaughter houses
loaded the air with effluvia of decomposing animal matter in drainage
systems. Concomitant activities were gut-spinning, tripe-dressing,
bone-boiling and paunch-cooking. Bread-making in bakehouses took place
in the coalhole, in front of the kitchen, with currents of cold air
upon the men at work in high temperatures. Dirt, cobwebs, flour dust,
growling animals in the troughs where bread was made and the air over-
loaded with foul gases from the drains, ovens and the fermentation of
the bread, plus the emanation of the workers' bodies; such work and the
increased employment in domestic service, was often a reflection of poverty and the lack of more remunerative employment. We shall refer to
legislation passed concerning conditions in the hotel and catering industry at a later stage in our discussion.

   Side by side with our historical analysis of occupational groups in
household service and in kitchens, there has occurred in this century
another important and (as far as this study is concerned) parallel development; that of hotels, catering for large numbers of residents
temporarily away from their homes. Whilst in the latter half of the
Nineteenth Century, meals served in many homes were more elaborate than
they had ever been in the country's history, hotel kitchens also assumed
a central position in terms of luxurious cooking and the mix of kitchen
workers employed behind the scenes. We shall be looking at the hotel
as a social system presently, but the briefest of outlines of hotel development here will provide the background knowledge for the understanding of social relationships later.

Nineteenth Century Hotel Development

The rapid growth of hotels in this country is closely associated with
the transport revolution and the invention of the steam engine. The
name 'hotel', first used in London after the mid-Eighteenth Century,
was common in Paris and signified large houses in which apartments were
let by the day, week or month. (29) The hotel differed from previous
methods of accommodating guests in that it provided something more luxurious, backed by a whole complement of staff, including manager, liv-
eried porters, page boys, receptionists, plus chefs and kitchen brigade
behind the scenes. No literature exists to indicate conditions in hotel
kitchens and about life for the lower occupational grades, although
Dickens, Shakespeare, Chaucer and such travellers as Cobbett and Defoe
make ample reference in their writings to establishments supplying food,
drink and shelter to pilgrims, travellers and residents. No one is
certain of the location of the first hotel in the United Kingdom.
London, although acknowledged as the capital city of the world, lagged
behind America and the rest of Europe in standards until the opening of
the Savoy in 1889 by D'Oyly Carte, with Gilbert and Sullivan as principal shareholders. Innovations such as bathrooms, artificial light and
the invention of the hydraulic lift, strengthened the claim of the Savoy
as a leading hotel in the world, but the lift also altered hotel design
in that it made it an economically viable proposition to build higher
than three floors without causing the food-loving clients undue exert-
ion. As the great network of railways spread across the country, many
of the coaching inns disappeared, whilst others became ale-houses or
farmhouses. The great Victorian railway hotels which replaced them at
termini such as Birmingham, Manchester, Leeds, London, Sheffield, York
and Newcastle, were not just the product of the railway age, but also
reflected a rise of national prestige and vast increase in wealth in
the country at that time. The large hotels in London, writes Medlik,
were the Great Eastern at Liverpool Street, the Grand, adjoining St.
Pancras, the Euston and others at Paddington and Charing Cross. Other
luxury hotels sprang up to swell the Ritz era in hotel-keeping. As the
railway network spread and social conditions (including holidays with
pay) improved, the hotel industry began to respond to the increased demand for its service. Such spas and seaside resorts as Bath, Brighton,
Cheltenham, Harrogate and Tunbridge Wells increased the number of their
hotels. Sir George Young (30) describes the erosion of the traditional
monopoly of the South coast by the increasing affluence, as a result of
the industrial revolution and points to the efficient municipal activity
in those holiday areas, compensating for the inactivity of the hotel industry. Examples are the enlargement of piers, building of parks, par-
ades, municipal gardens, roadworks and reinforcing sea defences, as well
as the provision of such amenities as baths, bandstands, aquaria and
similar, to meet the needs in the area of the nearby industrial complex.
The second half of the Nineteenth Century showed also a revival of the
spas, on account of the healing waters, and towns such as Bath, Harrogate, Buxton, Droitwich and Matlock, regained their previous popularity.
Other means of transport gave a further boost to the emergence of hotels
during the Twentieth Century, when we shall return to the subject to indicate the impact of this change.

The Origin of Tipping

Tipping is said to have started in Tudor England (31), when footmen were rewarded for bringing gifts such as salmon or cherries. It was also the custom to give tips at the end of a visit. By the Eighteenth Century, these demands had become a real barrier to social intercourse, as many a parson complained. Defoe called it a ruinous business to dine out with nobility. According to a magazine published in Aberdeen around 1760, employers attempted to combine to stop the giving and receiving of 'vails'. (32) In some great houses, a fixed schedule of service charges existed, which so outraged a visiting German baron to one of the stately England homes in 1740 that he accused the footman of pocketing as much as would keep the baron supplied for a week at a local tavern. The system of vails was largely stamped out by the end of the Eighteenth Century, only to return in another form a hundred years later. (33)

The discussion has so far provided us with background knowledge to the Nineteenth Century practice of tipping. Authors and historians do not share one view about the origins of tipping. According to Eichler (34), tipping appears to have originated with barbers. People applied to the barber to be bled, as bleeding was regarded as a cure for most ills. It was, in any case, customary for the barber to perform minor operations in surgery. The barber received no definite payment for bleeding operations and patients tipped him whatever they were able to afford. This custom, having spread in England, was regarded as an excellent means of securing quick and efficient service. Presently, small boxes appeared hung conspicuously in inns and road houses, with signs above, bearing the slogan 'To Insure Promptness'. It will be noted that the initial letters of these three words read 'tip'. Wildblood (35) explains in her book that is has been the custom from mediaeval times for guests to bring their own servants on visits. As late as the Nineteenth Century, it was not unusual for the valet or lady's maid to accompany master or mistress, but this fashion became less popular by the middle of the century (except with royalty or aristocracy), as it was considered in bad taste to bring servants, unless leave to do so was asked first. The poorer invites on country visits suffered the most in satisfying servants with gratuities, although hospitality was lavish enough. Gold was expected by manservants of the great houses, but the poorer visitor did not need to be ashamed to tip in silver.

We shall pick up the thread of this theme again at a later stage and appraise it in terms of the effect upon the lower grades in the hospitality industry, particularly those working behind the scenes and not in direct contact with the recipient of the services to the provision of which they make a direct contribution.

The Twentieth Century

The Edwardian Era

The Edwardian era is frequently defined as beginning with the death of Queen Victoria in 1901 and ending close to the outbreak of war. There had been a transformation from Victorian self-satisfaction to Twentieth Century self-questioning. Social conscience grew, the under-privileged were enfranchised and became politically more vocal; a seemingly inevitable pattern of social planning emerged, which was reflected in the innovations of the old age pensions, unemployment benefits, health insurance and the labour exchanges. Some of these measures encountered

bitter political opposition but, frequently, the working classes themselves were not totally enthusiastic about them all. Perhaps the then
limited knowledge of sociological research on which effective social
planning depends, and more so an understanding of society itself and,
therefore, industrial relations, may be attributable to this state.
Disillusionment about the inequalities contributed to the unrest. Booth
and Rowntree revealed the deep suffering of the poor, extending still
to about a third of the population, while the wealthy displayed what
Veblen+called 'conspicuous consumption'. Below the three basic social
classes - working, middle and upper - at the very bottom of society,
were to be found the unemployables, the misfits, the tramps and the des-
titutes. Social groups from which some years earlier the radical polit-
ician, John Bright, (36) wanted to withhold franchise on the grounds
that they lacked the independence necessary to resist corrupting influences. To Bright, they constituted the 'residium', persons of almost
helpless poverty and dependence. Later, Booth found also a term to
label these groups as the 'Submerged Tenth', whilst Winston Churchill
in 1908 referred to them as if hospital patients, but in need of 'De-
casualisation'.

The Supply of Casual Labour

The heterogeneity of the hotel and catering industry, and its consequential peculiarities - to meet the services demanded by patrons, to adjust
to a pattern of activity that is continuous, to adapt to seasonal fluc-
tuations in demand, and its neglect to establish a formal negotiating
machinery - have long presented problems. Thus, there has been (and
still is) a propensity to attract ancillary grades of kitchen employees
from the transient social groups who are currently available and seeking work that can be commenced at once. Recruitment was in accord with
the fluctuating needs that the high labour turnover and the varying
provision of services of a hotel engendered. Members of the 'residium',
often desperately seeking subsistence, even survival, competed for the
opportunity to exchange some periods of disagreeable work for a few hot
meals and irregular pay.*

  Casual enquiries, work houses, the Salvation Army and, eventually,
the special employment exchange (set up in 1930), for the hotel and
catering trades, formed an unsystematic intermediary for the supply.

Working Conditions in Kitchens

The use of gas and electricity for domestic cooking belongs almost entirely to the Twentieth Century, but until well after the turn of the
century, the main fuel used in hotel kitchens was coal, coke and charcoal. Page and Kingsford (37) describe effectively the work experience
of those predominantly rooted there:-

---

* This statement embraces several elements: irregular opportunities
for work; lapses in work habit; casual and intermittent work; low wages;
absence of tips, the inapplicability of the Truck Acts, resulting often
in deductions for board or other payment in kind; payment in tokens, to
be exchanged in special shops or stores; and fines for breakages or
trifling misdemeanours. Some opinions hold that chefs and porters may
have been covered by the Acts.

+ Veblen, Thorstein (1912) 'The Theory of the Leisure Class',Macmillan,
New York

'The cook worked sometimes for fourteen hours
or more. The heat from the stoves was immense,
and the fumes and smoke drifted round the kitchen,
creeping into lungs and eyes of everyone there.
The life of those who worked in such kitchens
was a hard one. Because of the great heat, the
cooks perspired freely and to counteract the
thirst this produced, they drank heavily. Beer
was always ready at hand, and the more work the
cook did, the more he drank, and the more he
drank, the less capable he was of doing good
work, the more cruel and vulgar he became.
Heat and sweat, drunkenness and vulgarity, ill
temper through lack of sleep, and constant noise,
these were the conditions which caused the young
cooks sometimes to be brutally treated by their
superiors. The general atmosphere was one of
chaos and disorder. The cook had the well-earned
reputation of being no better than a vulgar
drunkard, who stank most of the time of food,
burning fuel, beer and sweat'.

These writers then go on to describe the efforts of the then famous
chef, Escoffier, to improve these conditions by imparting social skills
and replacing beer with barley water.

In addition to suffering from the environmental conditions and the
temper of the cooks, the kitchen porter performed the disagreeable work
to which reference has been made on the previous page. A brief description is here given from Fuller (38) which still applies today to some
of the older hotels in our sample:-

'Work in the plonge was hardly an attractive task
and labour not easy to obtain, and there is usually
a substantial turnover of operatives working in the
plonge... The 'plongeur' (literally one who plunges)
is the kitchen porter who has the important task of
cleaning the pots and pans. For copper pots, traditional procedure was to have two deep sinks, one
fitted with a steam jet to heat water in which the
pans were placed, adding soda. The plongeur had a
long fish hook to fish out the pans from the hot
water and clean them with a pickle made from one
third salt, one third silver sand and one third
flour, mixed with vinegar to paste. Traditionally,
he did this either with bare hands or with the
skins of used lemons, rubbing all over the pan inside and out to bring a shine and effectively removing particles of food. Pans are then rinsed,
wiped dry and placed on racks in order of size,
each group together and handles pointing all one
way. (This operation is still carried out in many
plonges today)'.

The burning question that is always asked is why there prevails this
continuing association of the vagrant, the tramp, the drunkard and the

71

pauper with intermittent or casual low-grade work in general, and kitchen portering in particular. Seen in the historical context of the
period we are considering, there was much speculation, but less understanding of 'depression economics' and the causes of unemployment and
poverty. There had been a relative neglect of sociological theory which
might have brought to light earlier sophisticated models which help to
explain more adequately the problem of social need than the contemporary
empirical sociologists have helped to provide in aiding the reformist
lobbies.* (We refer to value-orientation among social administration
specialists such as the 'institutional' and 'residual' models, the former requiring a comprehensive organisation to aid the deprived, and the
latter focusing on the residual (declining) minority of the needy, in
the wake of economic growth and affluence). Although Booth has been
criticised on the grounds that his description of poverty and unemployment was largely static, and failed to take account of the vicissitudes
of the trade cycle, he, more than anyone writing at that time, offered a
rational answer to the burning question of this association. He does
this firstly by attempting to show the numerical relation which poverty
and deprivation bear to regular earnings of a floating population in
parts of London. Whilst categorising under eight headings, precise information is given of groups that are of particular interest to our
analysis. We present these by way of a diagram:-

Our Presentation of Charles Booth's Categorisation of Work Groups in
London, 1902 (39)

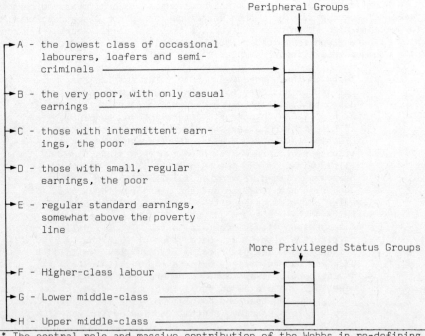

Peripheral Groups

A - the lowest class of occasional
    labourers, loafers and semi-
    criminals

B - the very poor, with only casual
    earnings

C - those with intermittent earn-
    ings, the poor

D - those with small, regular
    earnings, the poor

E - regular standard earnings,
    somewhat above the poverty
    line

More Privileged Status Groups

F - Higher-class labour

G - Lower middle-class

H - Upper middle-class

* The central role and massive contribution of the Webbs in re-defining
the aims of social welfare by their academic study of welfare instit-
ions - with a historical rather than sociological perspective however -
is given wide recognition by historians.

Group A ......   1.25% of the population, as estimated by Booth, are
                  the class of 'occasional labourers, loafers and semi-
                  criminals', whose life is one of 'savages, with vic-
                  issitudes of extreme hardship and occasional excess'.

Group B ......   10% of the population, depending on casual earnings,
                  seeking work from day to day, mostly as porters
                  around the markets or at canals or wharves. These
                  are the 'very poor'.

Group C ......   8% of the population, characterised by Booth as a
                  category performing the economic function of provid-
                  ing for variations of labour input to accommodate the
Total approx.   business cycle and random ups and downs in trade; the
    20%   central core of sweated labour.

Health and Poverty Diet

From our historical analysis, the position which emerges becomes already very clear in one major respect: namely, that for the vast majority, not an 'impatience of steady labour', but a multiplicity of
conditions over which they seem to have little control, account for the
symptom of peripherality. There is one, additional factor that has
tended to be insufficiently stressed by many of the contemporary writers, which dealt with the conditions of the urban labour force: that of
health. Medical care in the Twentieth Century derived from the need
for efficiency in industry and warfare. Rowntree (40) had collected
alarming figures of a rejection of nearly one half of the would-be
army recruits in York, Leeds and Sheffield on medical grounds between
1897 and 1901, while General Maurice (41), veteran of a number of
African campaigns, asserted in 1902 that sixty per cent of recruits
were physically unfit for military service. He also talked of 'the
certainty of the street-bred people of Britain approaching exhaustion
in their new urban environment'. Alfred Marshall (42) comments upon
the conditions of the people in London thus:-

> ' ... residence for many generations amid smoke, with
> scarcely any of the pure gladness of bright sunshine
> and green fields, gradually lowers the physical con-
> stitution ... as a result, London has a labour force
> containing large numbers of people with poor physique,
> and a feeble will, with no enterprise, no courage, no
> hope and scarcely any self-respect, whom misery drives
> to work for low wages... '

   Health, therefore, constituted an additional, important variable that
helps us to explain the diminished capacity for work of large numbers
of people. Equally, poverty diet is a concomitant that creates the
very effects which Marshall emphasises above. While the popular press
of the times gave the possessions and activities of the rich continuous
publicity, the poorer sections, reading of costly menus, became aware
of their own outlay on bread and dripping. Arthur Ponsonby (43), a
radical Member of Parliament in 1909, scathingly contrasted the problem
of poverty and the problem of riches by comparing a rich man of 'no
occupation' with a poor man also of 'no occupation' (through illness).
We quote:-

' ... the former, married, two children, four houses,
London house, 62 rooms, 36 indoor servants. Each year,
on the day after the Lord Mayor's sumptuous banquet,
the remains of the feast were condescendingly distributed
to the 'deserving' London poor'.

Small Sample of Selected Occupations for the Purpose of Comparing Long-
est and Shortest Working Hours. Source: Charles Booth (44)

48 hours per week or less	72 hours or more
Plumbers	Bakers
Woodcarvers	Market Porters
Shipwrights	Barmen
Bookbinders	Potmen
Mat-makers	Railway Porters
Feather-curlers	Waiters
Saver-flushers	Barmaids
Scene Painters	Servants

Note:-

(a)   It will be noted that long working hours were predominant in the
      service and catering occupations and those occupations needing
      less skill and training.

(b)   Potmen and Potwashers defined: Had to be good pewter cleaner at
      first, but later used as a general servant and porter in public
      houses, earning 10-14 shillings if living in. His social and
      occupational status was inferior to that of barman, itself a low-
      status occupation.

Small Sample of Selected Low-Grade Occupations (in terms of dirt and
servility), showing Working Hours and Pay. Source: Charles Booth (45)

Occupation	Pay	Working Hours	Remarks
Sweepers	20s p.w. mostly	48-56	-
Dustmen	24-30	48-69	-
Lavatory Attd.	18-26	50-60	-
Drainage Wks.	25-30	50	-
Urinal Flushers	21-30	48-60	-
Waiters	10-20 plus board	12 hrs. per day	-
Waitresses	15 with board	10 hrs. per day	-
Charwomen	2/6d per day part-time		-
Grave Diggers	1s per ft. dug	10 hrs. per day	Day may also be 6d per hr.
Washers	8-10s p.w.	21-28 part time	-
Bath Attendants	21-25 plus tips	hrs. not fixed	Long hrs. welcome
Caretakers	24-25	not fixed	-

Occupation	Pay	Working Hours	Remarks
Domestics	£6-9 per yr.	around 80 hrs.	younger and lower grade
Domestics	£26-36	not specified	older servants
Footmen (tall)	£32-40	when required	livery in use
Footmen (short)	£30	when required	livery in use
Second Footman (tall)	£28-30	when required	livery in use
Second Footman (short)	£20-22	when required	livery in use
Kitchen Porter	£1 per wk.	unspecified	-

Ponsonby (op.cit.) also quotes one observer of the social scene as saying: 'the less poor of the capital regularly helped the more poor.' It is peculiar to London, this custom of placing leavings where the first comer who is hungry can see them, and it materially helps to keep the man in the street from starving'.

Responsive to such alarms, the Balfour Government established an Inter-Departmental Committee on Physical Deterioration early in the century, collecting much useful evidence (including the need for meals to underfed school children), which gave rise up to 1914 to further social legislation embracing also unemployment relief, later consider- ed ineffective by the Edwardian social and economic planners. (Notably Sidney Webb and William Beveridge).

Orwell's Impressionistic Documentaries

Moving forward from Edwardian times into the post-war period (1918 and after), Orwell's previously mentioned more personal, impressionistic documentaries, embodying some grains of social analysis, aid our under- standing of the prevailing social climate and conditions in hotel kit- chens among the lower-grade porters and assistants. When Orwell wrote of his experience in Paris and London in 1929, at a time of the dole, depressed areas, malnutrition and slum, he came very near to starving before eventually finding work as dishwasher in the subterranean world of dirt, sweat and curses which supported the carpeted elegance of an expensive hotel restaurant. The point he makes is that poverty is not merely an inconvenient absence of material comforts, but a real degrad- ation of character; and he asks what it is that makes a nation ready to tolerate the misery of large numbers of workless, roaming the count- ry in search of work. Orwell exercises a kind of intellectual control over his experiences by his illuminating interpretations. He has this to say of the life as a plongeur comprehends it:-

> 'When one comes to think of it, it is strange that
> thousands of people in a great, modern city should
> spend their waking hours swabbing dishes in hot dens
> underground. The question I am raising is why this
> life goes on - what purpose it serves, and who wants
> it to continue, and why I am not taking a more rebellious
> attitude. I am trying to consider the social sign-
> ificance of a plongeur's life. I think I should start
> by saying that the plongeur is one of the slaves of
> the modern world... he is no freer than if he were
> bought and sold. His work is servile and without art;

he is paid just enough to keep him alive; his only
holiday is the sack. He is cut off from marriage,
or, if he marries his wife must work too. Except
by a lucky chance, he has no escape from his life,
save into prison... if plongeurs thought at all, they
would long ago have formed a union and gone on strike
for better treatment. But they do not think, because
they have no leisure for it; their life has made
slaves of them... people have a way of taking for
granted that all work is done for a sound purpose...
some people must feed in restaurants, and so other
people must swab dishes for 80 hours a week. It is
the work of civilisation and therefore unquestionable.
This point is worth considering'.

Orwell goes on to question whether the plongeur's labours are really
necessary to civilisation. Society feels this must be 'honest' work,
because it is hard and disagreeable and makes a sort of fetish of manual work. The plongeur earns his bread by the sweat of his brow, but
it does not follow that he is doing anything useful, as he is only
supplying a luxury which, very often, is not a luxury... where, after
all, is the real need for smart restaurants and big hotels? They are
supposed to provide luxury, but in reality provide only a cheap,
shoddy imitation. Smartness means, in effect, merely that the staff
work more and the customers pay more... essentially, a smart hotel is
a place where a hundred people toil like devils in order that two hundred may pay through the nose for things they don't really want.

 Back in England, Orwell is not just describing poverty, but writes
from within it. This personal contact enables him to alternate detail
with social comment and he develops theories about tramps, stripped of
literary flesh, which perceive some association between vagrants and
their willingness to work:-

    'It is queer that a tribe of men, tens of thousands in
    number, should be marching up and down England... but
    one cannot even start to consider the case until one
    has got rid of certain prejudices. These are rooted in
    the idea that every tramp is ipso facto a blackguard.
    In childhood, we have been taught that tramps are black-
    guards, and consequently there exists in our minds a sort
    of ideal or typical tramp - a repulsive, rather dangerous
    creature, who would rather die than work or wash, and
    wants nothing but to beg, drink and rob hen-houses. The
    tramp-monster is no truer to life than the sinister
    Chinaman from the magazine stories, but he is hard to
    get rid of. The word 'tramp' evokes his image and the
    belief in him obscures the real question of vagrancy'.

Somewhat condensed, Orwell's hypotheses run as follows:-

1. People suggest the most fantastic reasons for what makes a tramp
    take to the road. A criminology book refers to the tramp as an
    atavism, a throw-back to the nomadic stage of humanity. But the
    obvious cause of vagrancy is staring one in the face. A tramp
    tramps, not because he likes it... but because there happens to

be a law compelling him to do so. A destitute man, if he is
not supported by the parish, can only get relief in the casual
wards, and as each casual ward will only admit him for one
night, he is automatically kept moving. He is a vagrant because
in the state of the law, it is that or starve.

2.   Very little of the tramp-monster will in fact survive inquiry.
      Take the generally accepted idea that tramps are dangerous char-
      acters. Apart from experience, one can say a priori that very
      few tramps are dangerous, or they would be treated accordingly.
      A casual ward will often admit a hundred tramps in one night,
      and these are handled by a staff of three porters at the most.
      A hundred ruffians could not be controlled by three unarmed men.
      These often bully tramps because the latter are docile, broken-
      spirited creatures.

3.   Or take the idea that all tramps are drunkards - an idea ridic-
      ulous on the face of it. No doubt, many tramps would drink if
      they got the chance, but in the nature of things, they cannot
      get the chance. At this moment, a pale watering stuff called
      beer is 7d a pint in England. To be drunk on it would cost at
      least half a crown, and a man who can command that much at all
      is not often a tramp.

4.   The idea that tramps are impudent social parasites ('sturdy
      beggars') is not absolutely unfounded, but it is only true in a
      few per cent of the cases. Deliberate, cynical parasitism, such
      as one reads of in Jack London's books on American tramping
      (Hoboism) is not in the English character for the English are a
      conscience-ridden race, with a strong sense of the sinfulness of
      poverty. The Englishman's character does not necessarily change
      because he is thrown out of work; one cannot imagine the average
      man to turn deliberately parasite. If one remembers that the
      law forces him to live as a vagabond, the tramp-monster vanishes.
      Tramps are not ideal characters, but they are human beings and
      if they are worse than other people, it is the result and not the
      cause of their way of life.

5.   The 'serve them damned well right' attitude is no fairer than it
      would be towards cripples or invalids. The futile, acutely un-
      pleasant life of the casual ward and the tramp's daily routine
      has already been described; but there are three special evils
      that need insisting upon. The first is HUNGER, almost the gen-
      eral fate of tramps. Since the casual ward's rations are in-
      sufficient (probably meant to be), anything beyond must be got
      from begging, that is, breaking the law. The result is that
      nearly every tramp is rotted by malnutrition. The second great
      evil (a good second) is that the tramp is entirely cut off from
      contact with women. To elaborate, there are firstly very few
      women at a tramp's level of society. The sexes are not equally
      balanced for, in fact, below a certain level, society is entire-
      ly male. (L.C.C. night census, 1931, of destitute men and women
      found the latter to constitute only some 10 per cent of the men).
      So, if the tramp finds no women at his own level or above - as
      far out of reach as the moon - he is condemned to perpetual cel-
      ibacy from the moment he takes to the road. There are the

effects of homosexuality and occasional rape; but, deeper than
this is the degradation of a man who knows he is considered unfit for marriage, while starvation of the sexual impulse can be
almost as demoralising as physical hunger. Cut off from the
whole race of women, the tramp feels degraded to the rank of
cripple or lunatic. The other great evil of a tramp's life is
enforced idleness. The vagrancy laws are so arranged that when
he is not walking the road, he is sitting in a cell; or, in the
intervals, lying on the ground, waiting for the casual ward to
open. It is obvious that this is a dismal, demoralising way of
life, especially for an uneducated man.

6.   Besides these, one could enumerate scores of minor evils - dis-
       comfort (no clothes, ill-fitting boots, hardly ever sits in a
       chair). Purposeless existence. (Walking the road and from pris-
       on to prison). Wasted energy. (Innumerable wasted foot-pound
       of energy could be used to plough thousands of acres, build
       miles of road, build dozens of houses). What is needed is to
       de-pauperise him, and this can only be done by finding him work -
       not work for the sake of working, but work of which he can en-
       joy the benefit.

We feel that Orwell's words are well worth the space given to them. He
adds an idea which, to this day, has not been taken up: that the idle
and underfed should grow their own food. Thousands, however, are being
diverted or divert themselves to the plonge, so that they may eat, as a
next best solution and thus hoping to avoid, temporarily at least, the
scores of evils Orwell is talking about.

Conditions of Work for the Lower-Grade Catering Worker

Before switching our discussion to the - in the later part of this century - declining problem of servants, authentic information has come to
hand which describes conditions in hotel and institutional kitchens during the inter-war period. This will complete the historical picture of
the lower-grade worker in the catering working environment and his association with poverty through the ages.

This personal information about the conditions for the lower-grade catering worker in hotel and institutional kitchens relates to the inter-
war period to 1938. We quote Mr. H.O. King (46) from Bromley Area Health
Authority, who was then employed as a Catering Manager of a Surrey hospital and has himself experienced life in kitchens in the 1930s, before
achieving higher occupational status, following many years in the industry:-

       'The kitchens during this period were not well equipped,
       badly ventilated, with poor lighting, tables or work tops
       mainly of coarse wood. Although mechanical aids were al-
       ready on the market, many kitchens were without such
       luxury. In these kitchens, porters, domestics and appren-
       tice cooks would be expected to carry out the bulk of the
       manual work. I have often had to carry up several flights
       of stairs sacks weighing 100 lbs. to 140 lbs during my
       earlier apprentice days. Crockery and cutlery were hand
       washed and potatoes peeled by hand, the latter in a very

dirty condition on delivery. Floors were scrubbed on
hands and knees, and solid fuel still used because of
its cheapness. This required the usual lighting, heat-
maintaining and cleaning processes throughout the day.
I would start each morning at 6 a.m. and seldom finished before 7 in the evening, working a full six days
and going into work for approximately two hours every
Sunday, to prepare various doughs, for Monday start.
Working hours were well in excess of 48 and my weekly
pay was five shillings, equal to 25p; at the end of my
apprenticeship, the wage was increased to £1.5.0. or
125p. In my time, you were expected to supply your own
uniform and small equipment, knives, etc. required for
the job. Discipline was strict - one was expected to
do as one was told at the discretion of the employer.
Work was generally scarce and one was extremely cautious,
and worked that much harder. To the best of my knowledge, these conditions applied to small and large
hotels all over the country'.

Recent investigations conducted in London confirm the association between
casual kitchen workers of a lower grade and the desperate endeavours of
the unemployed poor to obtain work in the kitchens of the (then) newly-
built hotels in the early Twentieth Century. The Piccadilly Hotel opened in 1908, some three years after the Ritz. These are part of a string
of hotels springing up before or at the beginning of the century: the
Savoy in 1897, the Carlton in 1899 and the new Claridges. This was a
time of the great luxury hotel; a time when the upper class was untroub-
led by taxation; a time when labour supply was literally unlimited. The
development of the combustion engine and the use of petrol saw the petr-
ol-driven motor cars on the roads. In London, the motor taxi appeared
and electric trams, together with the new motor bus, gave large numbers
of people new mobility. A topographical separation of the classes with
the working classes in the slums, the lower middle classes in the inner
and the middle classes in the outer suburbs, took place, this whole sub-
urban revolution having been made possible by the transport revolution.
Thus, these new forms of transport, together with the extension of the
railway network over the country, the invention of motor cycles, coaches
and new road surfaces, gave renewed impetus to hotel building. In London, further large hotels appeared. Among others, the 1,000-room Regent
Palace, completed in 1915; the re-built Grosvenor House in 1927; the extended Strand Palace in 1930; and the Cumberland in 1933. The Trust
Houses had over a hundred hotels by this time, managing to recover in the
late 1920s when economic conditions in the south-east and in London improved.

Mode of Recruitment

We said above that there was an abundant labour supply. There was hardship for families in the depressed industrial areas and the country had
nearly three million out of work. How did the hotels recruit their
kitchen porters in those days? Some of the large, luxury hotels, built
early in the century, were reluctant to meet our request for such historical detail as would throw light on the mode of recruitment of unskilled kitchen employees before and during the inter-war period. Hotels
that co-operated readily referred us to some likely employees without

undue formality. The summary view of their experiences confirmed what
was to be expected in times of economic depression: that on every day
of the week, large numbers of casual applicants congregated outside the
hiring locations at the rear of the large hotels, in the hope of being
favoured by discriminating head chefs, who themselves picked the staff.
Demand for casual labour in the luxury hotels was considerable, because
services not only operated on several floors, but the ratio of staff to
guest was more likely to be 3:1. (The Savoy still has a staff of some
1,550 to look after a maximum of 500 guests).(47) Wages consisted of a
nominal amount, or no pay at all, although meals were included. (48)

   Living-in accommodation was not often provided for kitchen workers of
a lower grade. Hoteliers saw no need for that, partly because there was
an abundance of applicants and partly, such workers performed outside
the environs of the guests. Quarters were usually provided for controll-
ing chefs, intermediate grades of managerial staffs and chambermaids, on
the principle that the hotel could not function without them. Plongeurs
and other manual kitchen workers lived mostly in the type of hostel that
Orwell describes, and which did not cater for a permanent abode. Zweig,
(49) describing the social layers of working class at the time, gives an
unbiased indication of the social strata from which these hotel workers
in kitchens might have been recruited:-

          'Many labourers fall into the category of casuals and
          vagrants ... the status of a man is, in fact, conditioned
          by the whole pattern of his way of life ... at the bottom
          layer can be found the chronically unemployed men, the
          hard core of unemployment; the disabled or physically
          handicapped, subnormal or maladjusted men, or emotionally
          unstable or broken in health and spirit. Next come the
          labourers in whom five categories can be distinguished -
          light, general, heavy, craftsmen and the handyman, a
          'Jack of all trades'.'

Lack of Data on the Social Conditions of Catering Workers

Three more layers are then identified by Zweig, advancing in status towards the upper stratum of the working class. These, however, concern
us less in this discussion. Various universities (Liverpool, Bristol,
Birmingham, Southampton) conducted surveys on the incidence of poverty;
and Prof. Bowley from the L.S.E. surveyed in Reading, Warrington, North-
ampton, Bolton and Stanley during the inter-war period also, as well as
conducting a later study of 'London Life and Labour' (1928-1935). All
these studies were characterised by their identification of a correlation
between poverty and employment. (50)

   Much of the detail we produced to make our points was hard to find,
for so far as it exists at all, it is buried in specialist periodicals,
scattered around a large number of books and to be obtained only from an
account of the personal experiences of - ferreted out - particular people. The lack of information concerning the recruitment and conditions
of work of lower-grade hotel and catering workers since the establishment of hotels constitutes a serious gap in the social history which,
apart from our modest attempts, constrained by resources and time, no
one has yet endeavoured to fill. Regrettably, the industry's failure to
collect data acts as a significant limitation on both research and the

shaping of policy.

The Situation of Servants in the First Half of This Century

A very brief survey of the servants' situation in the first half of this
century, followed by a consideration of the state of hotel development
and the greater participation of Government in social welfare matters,
is to concern us next.

In pre-1914 times, the more affluent families led still leisured lives
with an army of servants to wait upon them. Lavish eating, frequent entertaining and extravagant dressing was the rule. Servants' duties had
altered little and, although other parts of houses (drawing, dining and
bedrooms, studies and libraries) changed decor, in line with fashion,
the kitchen quarters remained virtually the same. The kitchen range
still dominated (but gas cookers could be found in some kitchens) and
meals were large and complicated, in line with grand-scale entertaining.
By 1911, the preparation and sale of food and drink and the provision of
lodging gave work to about $1\frac{1}{2}$ million people, while the largest of all
Edwardian occupations - domestic service - employed some $2\frac{1}{2}$ million, of
whom over two million were women in service. The growth of the service
industries and of transport concentrated these activities in the urban
areas then undergoing rapid expansion. Middle-class ladies found it im-
possible to recruit cook-generals, a sign of the impending domestic revolution. Other job opportunities for the more enterprising (such as
shop assistants and office workers) led to a gradual reduction in servant supply, which by 1914 became so acute as to force the Government to
set up a body to look into it. As the munition factories opened their
gates to women, so the kitchen doors began to close. The pre-war servant now driving tram, working on land or in the factory, was reluctant
to return to her post in the kitchen, a situation regarded as an ominous
sign of the collapse of the forces of law and order. The ill-paid,
overworked servant became so scarce that resort had to be taken to ex-
traordinary gadgets and innovations. By this time, only about five per
cent of households had resident servants and their treatment and status
vastly improved. In 1919, the Women's Advisory Committee reported to
the Ministry of Reconstruction on the 'Domestic Servant Problem'. For
the first time, this problem had been elevated to warrant Government
attention. But, wide dissension among members produced a host of probable and improbable solutions and a refusal on the part of some to sign
the report. Floods of letters to newspapers from the middle-classes
considered it the duty of the Government to restore supply of domestic
labour for private households, by way of refusing unemployment benefit
where vacancies in domestic service existed. Government did not support this notion; nevertheless, local exchanges withheld 'dole' money to
girls whose employers reported that they had been in service before the
war.

In the year 1923, another Government inquiry was set up to investigate
the continuing shortage of female domestic labour, and how far the effect of the then Unemployment Scheme contributed to this situation. A
great deal of evidence was taken, among other witnesses, one from Councillor Jessie Stephen, representing the Domestic Servants' and Hotel Workers' Union. Dawes writes as follows:-

'A social stigma now surrounded the job of servant:
'skivvy' and 'slavey' were commonly used by other
members of the working class to describe the occupation. Girls who had taken jobs in domestic service
and felt themselves objects of ridicule and derision
in the newspapers as a result, gave evidence to the
committee, saying that they did not mind the work,
but objected to being ridiculed; and to suffer un-
told misery by reference to their being servants
with whom other people did not want to mix'. (51)

Indeed, the report itself is dominated by reference to the status of
servant. It mentions the constant caricaturing of maidservants as dirty,
harassed, impertinent and somewhat grotesque creatures, and the use of
contemptuous terms as 'skivvy' and slavey'. Also, reference was made
to offensive and unjust articles and letters about domestic workers,
attacks and witticisms felt keenly and resented by the girls... and the
domestic workers lack of opportunity for cultivating a talent for music
aroused only ridicule and sarcasm in the daily press. Although the report suggested that domestic service had failed to keep pace with the
changes of English industrial life, it came up with little that was new
and like the 1919 report was consigned to the archives of State papers,
to be quickly forgotten.

By the 1930s, the number of women in domestic service had shrunk to
just over 700,000, although nearly five per cent of all households in
England still employed a 'resident' domestic - frequently living in
basement quarters. Looking back to Rowntree's first survey in York, he
believed that by 1899, some thirty years earlier, close to thirty per
cent of the population kept a resident domestic servant, but this finding may not have been typical of all England. Looking forward twenty
years, only about one per cent of all households had resident servants
in 1951 and by 1961, barely 0.6 per cent of all households in the country had domestic servants. This indicates the extent of the change in
domestic service by the mid-Twentieth Century.(52)

The 1930s was also a time when the 'Hudson Syndrome' began to give
way.* The Great War had temporarily breached the rigid class divisions,
only for employers to hanker again after the status quo when it ended.
Subserviance and 'manners' were still demanded and servants remained
near the bottom of the social ladder. Dawes writes that only the unemployed or criminals, down-and-outs or prostitutes were lower. The mass
of women servants under the age of thirty finally obtained franchise in
1928 and rigorous attempts some ten years later by Londoner, Mrs.
Savilla Connolly, to form a Domestic Workers Union dissipated when the
Second World War broke out. +

* We have coined this term from a quotation by Hudson, the butler, to
Rose, the kitchen maid, in the last episode of 'Upstairs, Downstairs'
(A.T.V., September 1974), when he said: 'There is a natural social order
that we question at our peril.'
+ Dawes (op.cit.) gives other, additional reasons why this union failed,
following an inaugural meeting in 1938 at Transport House and official
recognition - the scatter of location of work places, the difficulty in
attending meetings of branches and the sensitivity of servants to pressures from 'upstairs'.

During the inter-war period, the 'servant' problem persisted. The war had improved job opportunities and given working class women a measure of independence, much preferred to household service. The spread of education and the influence of the popular media helped further to deteriorate the image of work 'in service', but this transformation in social attitudes was eventually halted (and for a time even reversed) by unemployment and the economic depression. Long hours, unspecified and indefinite disposal to meet the whims of the employer, restricted opportunities for social life and leisure, lack of home life of her own and rigid class distinction were the rule. Nor was state education attuned to producing servants, and teachers in elementary schools contributed to shaping the image by recommending it only to the dullest of girls.

In 1931, the (then) Minister of Labour set up a Domestic Service Commission as a result of the introduction of a Parliamentary Bill to improve the working conditions and create a 'Servants' Charter'. Employers' resistance, Government lethargy and the lack of an organised pressure group among the service people, however, delayed significant change in social attitude until 1945, a time which most of us remember.

The inter-war period was also one of invention, of motor car, cycle, taxi and coach, while road surfaces experienced improvement and innovation by way of tarmacadam and concrete. Motoring for business and pleasure increased, side by side with public pressure upon Parliament for statutory holidays-with-pay, which together with gradual social changes of the removal of class barriers and the improved living standards of poorer sections of the community further increased the number of hotels in the country. Nonetheless, as pointed out by Medlik, the close dependence of the hotel and catering industry on general economic prosperity resulted in some serious difficulties during the early 'thirties by way of unemployment in the industry, curtailment of holiday and tourist traffic and a decline of the profitable seaside hotel.

By the early 1930s, the domestic servant was still not insured against unemployment, there was still no minimum wage or limit on the number of working hours. Neither was there any kind of inspection to ensure minimum standards of servants' living quarters and sufficient diet. The Wood Report of 1923, although referring mainly to female domestic staff, made many valuable suggestions, following a close study, such as the need for training, the need to regard domestic service as a skilled occupation and the need for obliterating distinctions between domestic service and other workers. The Wood Committee made good points also on the question of status, the uncertainty of conditions and restrictions of domestic work; and, finally, on the social stigma attached to this work and the damage done by cheap jokes and ridicule in the Press.

The Drift of Servants into the Expanding Hotel Industry

Conditions at the time made it seem logical that substantial numbers of male and female domestic staff drift into the expanding hotel and catering industry. A 1945 Ministry Report (53) on the 'Post-War Organisation of Private Domestic Employment', dealing with men and boys, puts the situation this way:-

'Private domestic work in the future is unlikely to offer
much scope for boys, but there will be many openings for
cooks, waiters, valets, porters, etc. in hotels and restaurants after the war. Some lads do not find the prospect
of industrial work attractive and to them the more personal
life of a hotel may appeal. A boy who has learnt to be
handy in his home and has some elementary instruction at
school to that end, will find any period of training necessary for indoor duties thereby shortened and his position as to wages improved.'

Households, in general, were also experiencing change which employers'
resistance could not stop. Frank Dawes explains:-

'In the previous generation, every cook had to undertake
the heavy work of kneading dough for bread-making and
every household had to endure the steam and tempers of
wash day. In the 1920s and the 1930s, bread and cakes
came from the bakery and the washing went to an outside
laundry. Jams and ale were bought ready-made instead
of being made at home by the servants. Little restaurants
sprang up all over London, relieving domestic staff of
the work of preparing late dinner. More and more household tasks were being handed over to outside specialists'.

Many employers of domestic staff were now also finding it expedient to
treat them well and encourage involvement in family matters. The introduction of labour-saving devices served the double purpose of making the
work more bearable, as well as replacing servants, when there was difficulty in obtaining them as a result of other opportunities in the labour market. One striking innovation in the 1930s was hire purchase.
It enabled people without capital to buy household goods and gadgets
for 'labour saving', a new concept much in vogue with the respectable,
middle-class woman, now having to perform menial domestic tasks.

Competing employment opportunities occurred also in the hotels and
catering industry. There had been an enormous growth, not only in hotels and restaurants. Other residential and catering establishments such
as milk bars, hostels, holiday camps, homes, caravans and boarding
houses (and some years later motels) appeared, together with a transformation of Army and industrial catering from a pioneering stage into
efficient and sophisticated services. Whilst the hotel industry suffered some adverse effects from the slump, a number of well-known hotels
were built during it: the Mayfair, Grosvenor House, Park Lane Hotel,
Strand Palace and the Dorchester are some of the projects that had become operational between the years 1927 to 1932. Medlik attributes
early post-war prosperity of the hotel industry in the 'twenties to
widespread reaction to the restrictions and privations of the war, which
resulted in a desire for travel and enjoyment and to the rapid development of transport, which furnished hotels with the new custom of the
increasingly restless body of holiday makers. The same tendencies helped the industry to mount a prompt recovery after the depression. An additional factor for the emergence of new hotels during the economic difficulties could be the lavish spending of visitors from overseas, although the hotels concerned were somewhat reticent in giving information.

White gives one instance of the Maharajah of Patila who, in 1925 hired the entire fifth floor of the Savoy Hotel of thirty seven suites,
had a silver bath installed and a special kitchen built for his chef
and fifty staff to prepare curries and other native delicacies.

For the hundreds of hotels throughout the countryside during the
1920s and 1930s, most of which were adapted from old-established inns,
fortunes defied prediction. In the more remote areas, custom was made
possible only by the motor car on a casual basis, or through the reputation for food and comfort. John Fothergill (54), an innkeeper, received also patronage from farmers on market days, dealers and corn merchants, commercial travellers and the local freemasons. The local
Grammar School held its biennial dinner there, also. By the 1930s, as
more and more people owned cars, an increasing number of hotels began
to concentrate on the provision of good and well-cooked food, interesting wines and rooms with bath. The wider use of refrigeration then
also helped considerably to combat losses due to fluctuating custom,
during a time of unseasonable weather. (55)

Hotel Development - The Impact of the Seaside

The profile of hotel development to the Second World War would not be
complete without a brief look at its impact on the seaside scene. We
have already seen the disappearance of the general servant from the attics and basements of boarding houses, on account of their decline and
the quiet departure of her somewhat superior sister from private service. The grand hotels had gravitated to the coasts by way of the Continental spas and the big cities. They were de luxe affairs for the
carriage trade from the start. The whole range of services would be
available as in the 1890s, with the addition of a palm court, to provide for social rendezvous of the genteelest kind. Such hotels had been
planned also to accommodate the servants that the holiday-making families brought with them. But, the profitable peak did not last. The
upper bourgeoisie that constituted the main clientele during the golden
pre-war years were not replaced by the nouveau riche of the immediate
post-war period. Metal traders, rag-trade merchants and food whole-
salers, together with some preening themselves with Lloyd George's
knighthoods, took over the seaview suites. Some of the hotels that had
been requisitioned for officers' convalescent homes were, by 1920,
handed back in good shape, with a bonus on top. But, times began to
change, as already shown. The wages of hotel staff had risen, industrial unrest limited dividends and profits fell, forcing the grand hotel
to advertise for casual customers once frowned upon. Indeed, some of
these hotels were obsolescent before the first guest signed the regist-
er. Inadequate plumbing, carrying of hot water into rooms by an army of
chambermaids and mounting overheads, even the better-planned, with
lifts, running water and continental menus, suffered a decline of patronage when the rich migrated to the Continent or rented houses for the
season. The inevitable fate of some of the grand hotels was conversion
into apartment buildings while a number have managed to survive to the
present day only by catering for those categories of patrons able to
pay substantial rates. (For example, the Grenville Hotel at Bude, open
from May to September, charged 21 guineas per week in 1966). It was
precisely because of a lack of sufficient customer orientation of the
commercial accommodation sector, in response to the potential demand for
seaside holidays that Butlin embarked upon the flourishing venture of
holiday camps.

APPRAISING THE HISTORICAL EVENTS

The Perseverance of Stigma

Tracing one occupation and its historical vicissitudes over a period of
some 800 years cannot be done in isolation. We soon found in the aggre-
gation of social forces that gave rise to the preservation and perpetuation of social stigma, that we had to proceed at a number of levels
to discover the multifarious strands that correlate with this problem.
Not only did this necessitate historical excursions into the early social scene of the ancient and mediaeval world of catering, right through
the Middle Ages, Rennaissance and subsequent centuries, but entailed a
consideration of the hierarchy and conditions of household servants as
the forerunner of inns, restaurants and hotels. The Feudal System,
with its key features of extreme status, functional and structural differentiation and the protection the system offered to serfs in terms of
security of a kind in contrast to the insecurity and hardship for many
that the next, following, more complex society, brought. The sweeping
changes in material culture and equipment, the new social forces of
production, the economic re-organisation known as the Industrial Revolution, all reacted upon the mass of the British people as no political or religious event had ever done before. The effect this had within
the areas of vagrancy, unemployment, poverty and progressive social legislation in terms of stigma upon our strata of low-grade service occupations justifies once more an inter-disciplinary transgression we
have thought appropriate to permit at this stage.

NOTES TO CHAPTER 4

1. Plato,'Republic III', Loen Classical Library. Translated from the Greek by P. Shoney, Part 3, Heinemann, London, 1930

2. Walley, Joan E. (1960) 'The Kitchen', Constable, London

3. Page and Kingsford (1971) 'The Master Chefs: A History of Haute Cuisine', Edward Arnold, London

4. Ellacott, S.E. (1960) 'The Story of the Kitchen', Methuen, London

5. Aubert, Vilheim (1955-56) 'The Housemaid: An Occupational Role in Crisis', Acta Sociologica, Vol.1

6. Orwell, George (1963) 'Down and Out in Paris and London', Penguin Books

7. Ashley, Maurice (1965) 'Life in Stuart England', Batsford, London

8. Firth, Violet M. (1925) 'The Psychology of the Servant Problem' The C.W. Daniel Company, London

9. Forster, Nathaniel (1767) 'An Enquiry into the Cuases of the Present High Price Provision', British Museum Catalogue, London Two Parts. See also Hecht (note 12), p. 178

10. Matza, David (1963) 'The Disreputable Poor', in Bendix, R. and Lipset, S. (Eds.),'Class, Status and Power', Routledge and Kegan Paul, London

11. Ashley, Maurice. See also 12. See also Lawrence Stone (1965) 'The Crisis of the Aristocracy', Oxford University Press, Oxford

12. Hecht, J. Jean (1956) 'The Domestic Servant Class in Eighteenth Century England', Routledge and Kegan Paul, London

13. Toennies, Ferdinand (1949) in Wilson, L and Colb, W.L. (Eds.) 'Sociological Analysis', Harcourt, Brace and World, New York

14. Quennell, M. and C. (1950) 'Everyday Life Series' (1733-1851) Vol.III, Batsford, London

15. Dawes, Frank (1973) 'Not in Front of the Servants' (Domestic Service in England 1850-1939), Wayland Publishers, London

16. Marshall, Dorothy (1949) 'The English Domestic Servant in History', Historical Association, London

17. Cowie, L.W. (1973) 'A Dictionary of Social History', G. Bell and Sons, London

18.   Trevelyan, G.M. (1952) 'Illustrated English Social History',
       Vol.4, 19th Century, Longmans, Green and Co, London

19.   Barker, E. (Ed.) (1947) 'The Character of England', Oxford
       University Press, esp. Chapter 23, Sir James Laver 'Homes and
       Habits'.

20.   Quennell, M. and C. (1965) 'History of Everyday Things in
       England (1851-1914)', Vol.IV, Batsford, London

21.   Megson, Barbara (1968) 'English Homes and Housekeeping (1700-
       1960)', Routledge and Keegan Paul, London

22.   Booth, Charles (1902) Series I (Poverty), Part II, Chapter III
       and IV, 105-238 and Series II (Industry), Part IV, Chapter IV
       p. 350-380. 'Life and Labour of the People of London',
       Macmillan, London

23.   Pinker, Robert (1971) 'Social Theory and Social Policy',
       Heinemann, London

24.   Mayhew, Henry (1969) 'London Labour and the London Poor, 1861'
       (III), See. Vol. III, Dover Publications, New York

25.   Caplow, Theodore (1954) 'The Sociology of Work', McGraw Hill,
       New York

26.   Booth, Charles, as quoted in Morse, D. (1969), 'The Peripheral
       Worker', Columbia University Press, New York

27.   Harrison, Molly (1972) 'The Kitchen in History', Ospry Publish-
       ing Ltd., London

28.   Pike, Royston (1967) 'Human Documents of the Victorian Age
       (1850-1875)', Allen and Unwin, London

29.   Medlik, S. (1972) 'Profile of the Hotel and Catering Industry'
       Heinemann, London

30.   Young, Sir George (1970) 'Accommodation Services in Britain
       1970-1980', London University Educational Books, London

31.   Rutland Account Books (1539) (see Eichler below).

32.   Marshall, D. (1949) See Note 16 above

33.   Dawes, F. (1973) See Note 15 above

34.   Eichler, William (1924) 'The Customs of Mankind', Heinemman,
       London

35.   Wildblood, Joan (1963) 'The Polite World', (guide to English
       Manners and Deportment from the 13th to the 19th Century),
       Oxford University Press, Oxford

36.   Bright, John (1850s) An active Parliamentarian during the
       Victorian years, Quaker, orator, cotton manufacturer, believer
       in Laissez-Faire economics, the moral and intellectual strength
       of the middle class, whom the labouring poor regarded as a
       benevolent monitor.

37.   Page and Kingsford (1-71), see Note 3 above

38.   Fuller, John (1971) 'Chef's Manual of Kitchen Management',
       Batsford, London

39.   Booth, Charles (1902) 'Life and Labour in London', 1st Series,
       Chapter II, Macmillan, London

40.   Seebohm Rowntree, B. (Quaker cocoa manufacturer) surveyed
       conditions in York and in 1901, under the titles of 'Poverty:
       A Study of Town Life', 'Poverty and Progress'. He dealt with
       the poor physical standards of the recruits for the South
       African War.

41.   Maurice, Gen. Sir John Frederick (1841-1912) 'Dictionary of
       Universal Biography'. Note: Sir Frederick participated in
       numerous military campaigns; later published books mostly on
       the subject of defence and military power. Also worked in
       the Intelligence Department of the War Office

42.   Marshall, Alfred (1925) 'Memoires' by A.C. Pigour, Macmillan,
       London

43.   Ponsonby, Arthur (1871-1946) Diplomat (background Eton and
       Balliol), headed a number of Ministries from 1924, became
       Leader of the Opposition in the Lords in 1931; published works
       on 'The Decline of the Aristocracy', Diplomacy, Reform,
       Religion and Politics, Years 1912-1921.

44.   Booth, Charles (1902) 'Life and Labour of the People in
       London (1891-1903)', Vol.5, Macmillan, London

45.   Booth, Charles (1902) op.cit. Vols 3 and 4

46.   King, H.O. (personal letter to author, 1974) Then Catering
       Manager, Cane Hill Hospital, Bromley Area Health Authority,
       Surrey. Information on conditions in kitchens in the '30s.

47.   Information obtained from the following sources:-
       The Press Office, Savoy Hotel, London
       A Director of Strand Hotels Ltd.
       A Deputy Head Chef, Ritz Hotel, London
       An Assistant Manager, Piccadilly Hotel, London
       Telephone conversations and personal interviews with executives
       concerning the conditions in kitchens during the early Twent-
       ieth Century (August 1974)

48.   White, Arthur (1968) 'Palaces of the People' (A Social History
       of Commercial Hospitality), Rapp and Whiting, London

49.   Zweig, Ferdynand (1952) 'The British Worker', Pelican Books,
       London

50.   Bowley, Prof. Marian, conducted surveys of life and labour in
       London 'Livelihood and Poverty 1915' (covering some provincial
       towns) 'New Survey of London Life and Labour, 1930-1935',
       'Social Survey of Merseyside 1934' and other publications in
       L.S.E. Library and researches under the auspices of L.S.E.

51.   Dawes, F. (1973). See Note 15 above

52.   Marsh, David C. (1965) 'The Changing Structure of England and
       Wales, 1871-1961', Routledge and Kegan Paul, London

53.   'Men and Boys' (1945), official report dealing with post-war
       organisation of private domestic employment, Cmd. 6650,
       H.M.S.O., London

54.   Fothergill, John (1922) 'An Innkeeper's Diary'.

55.   Cathcart Borer, Mary (1972) 'The British Hotel Through the
       Ages', Lutterworth Press, London

5   The hotel organisation and its institutional elements

In the following section, we wish to concern ourselves with the institutional parts of a hotel unit. Similar to other business enterprises,
every hotel, wherever located and whatever its size, has a history and
some element of tradition (unless just established, when such tradition
may derive from other hotels in a group or from newly-employed experienced staff, wearing it or bringing it with them). The hotel will also
have goals, objectives and purposes, which may be explicitly incorporat-
ed in printed communication, or implicit in the behaviour of its representatives by their attitude and applied skills. The utilitarian
characteristics of a hotel will be represented by the amenities it has
to offer, whilst its image will be projected in a tangible sense by various kinds of symbols that are meaningful to actual and potential patrons. We shall deal with each of these aspects in turn.

History and Tradition

Hotels are established over a historical time scale and their tradition
closely linked with the founders' ethics, the clientele catered for,
the quality of the staff, the amenities it can offer and the particular
geographical location. As is the case with all organisations, hotels
reveal a close relationship with the social and physical environments
within which they function, and have arisen because of certain needs
generated by people, which are not adequately served by organisations
already existing. Tradition is sometimes known as editorialised history,
often expressed in a specific way, or by specific customs. Particular
institutional agencies, such as hotels are, will often develop peculiar
traditions of their own. Some examples will make this clear. The theory of service without familiarity goes back to the time when hoteliers
bowed to clients who, by a slight nod of the head, would give a faint
sign of recognition; or the reverence and glamorisation of the French
conquest of culinary England, perpetuated by the chefs, and symbolically
transmitted to their apprentices. (This will be elaborated upon later).
Well-known examples of surviving customs and traditions are the 'charm-
ing-up' of newly-weds by flowers, the placing of bibles in hotel bedrooms or for the manager of the smaller hotel to display his carving
skills to the guests. Publicising official codes of ethics and association with Royalty adds to the weight an establishment will attach to
the value of tradition. The feature of food itself and the traditional
concept of hospitality has always had an important place in history.

The Hotel Business as a Legal Creation

The smallest hotels may still be owned by a sole entrepreneur or run together with family. Partnerships also exist, but by far the most popular legal creation is the limited liability company, which has a separate entity from the people who compose it. Such hotel companies will
display their oral or written tradition in a particular manner. Indeed,
such companies are social groups within the State that gives them a democratic right to form a corporate body if they are prepared to comply
with the formalities the legal model prescribes. Contracts, franchises,

articles of association and such are part and parcel of the traditional
institutional elements which endow these corporate bodies with the legitimacy to exercise their stated objectives. With current trends towards amalgamation, mergers, absorptions and takeovers, this kind of
dynamism is reflected in various legal species, including holding companies and their subsidiary flock, as well as those transcending national boundaries. Whilst we may observe an intimate relationship between
the country's laws and its society, as shown by these legal structures,
severe difficulties are seen in adjusting to the contemporary business
structure on account of the divorce between ownership and control, the
tension between profit maximisation and public interest and the struggle
for employee's rights.

Symbolic Characteristics

We may divide these into extra-mural and intra-mural characteristics or
traits. Every hotel will endeavour to emphasise status-elevating symbols and
attempt to veil those that may not project the desired image to outsiders.
Whyte offers a definition which will serve us excellently here:-

> 'A symbol can be an object, a word, a place, a
> condition (such as cleanliness), a natural phen-
> omenon (such as the sun, wind, etc.) or a person...
> this sounds vague until we add the qualification
> that symbols refer to relations between people,
> between people and objects, or a combination of
> the two. In addition, we should mention symbolic
> acts such as shaking hands for example, as a
> gesture of friendly relations... seemingly mean-
> ingless on most occasions, but significant when A
> refuses to shake hands with B... symbols can only be
> understood in terms of concrete examples and can be
> classified in several different categories: total
> community symbols, organisation symbols, and status
> symbols.' (1)

We are more concerned with the latter two in the category, specifically applicable to hotels. As indicated under the heading of history
and tradition, the status of a hotel will be associated with an imposing building, possibly showing a flag, a distinctive hotel front, neon
lighting, its name and how it is displayed and the location of the hotel. All these are external projections which, together with star classification of the Automobile Association and other associations, symbolise a kind of arbitrary hierarchy not unlike that sometimes accorded to
(but never in print) particular categories of educational institutions,
or to associations of the same profession where several of these exist.
These classifications are far from popular with hoteliers, because they
imply a particular level in a status hierarchy, while the expressed
reason is merely to advise a client of the services and charges available. The older hotel will trade on history and tradition and the new-
er one on style. Design-wise, some of the more recently-built hotels
have brutalised architecture that alienates even the vandals and produces debilitating psychological effects in the environment where they
are located and people that are withdrawn, callous and indifferent. (2)
But, we also see aesthetic designs that are a joy to look at. Clients
may, and do, judge comfort and functional efficiency by the shape of a

FIGURE 5.
ELEMENTS SHAPING THE HOTEL'S PERSONALITY AND CHARACTER

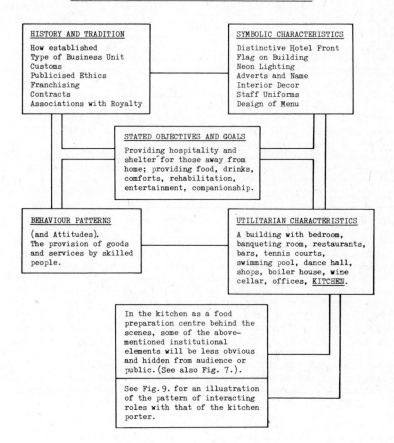

HISTORY AND TRADITION

How established
Type of Business Unit
Customs
Publicised Ethics
Franchising
Contracts
Associations with Royalty

SYMBOLIC CHARACTERISTICS

Distinctive Hotel Front
Flag on Building
Neon Lighting
Adverts and Name
Interior Decor
Staff Uniforms
Design of Menu

STATED OBJECTIVES AND GOALS

Providing hospitality and
shelter for those away from
home; providing food, drinks,
comforts, rehabilitation,
entertainment, companionship.

BEHAVIOUR PATTERNS

(and Attitudes).
The provision of goods
and services by skilled
people.

UTILITARIAN CHARACTERISTICS

A building with bedroom,
banqueting room, restaurants,
bars, tennis courts,
swimming pool, dance hall,
shops, boiler house, wine
cellar, offices, KITCHEN.

In the kitchen as a food
preparation centre behind the
scenes, some of the above-
mentioned institutional
elements will be less obvious
and hidden from audience or
public.(See also Fig. 7.).

See Fig. 9. for an illustration
of the pattern of interacting
roles with that of the kitchen
porter.

Note: The hotel guest is rarely conscious of the multiplicity of
influences that shape the hotel's personality and character.
A further influence, not to be overlooked, is that of the
guest as an outsider bringing values and attitudes to bear
upon the establishment and its staff.

building from which they hope for some degree of institutional care.

Intra-murally, decor, adverts, letterheads, staff uniforms, design of menus, linen, crockery, china, silver, floral arrangements, television in rooms, ice machines, even a stand-by hairdresser, are the obvious symbols most of the observant guests will expect to see. There are, however, more subtle mechanisms of interaction and style of doing things which are meaningful, not so much to unsuspecting clients, but to the initiated, for whom they have a special significance. Some ill-ustrations will make this clear.

Until very recently, when a customer died on the premises in one of the class hotels, the staff was sworn to secrecy on penalty of dismiss-al, so that newspapers would not get hold of the story. Every effort is still made to keep death on the premises within the confines of my-stery, but reporters may hear about it in course of police and coroner inquiries and, by a small bribe to waiter or room-maid at the staff en-trance obtain at least a few, garbled details. Disposal of bodies is a studied technique, such as workmen carrying, usually in the late even-ing, a receptacle very like a settee, to the back entrance to transfer the load to a waiting van. This procedure is symbolic for staff, as is the re-conditioning of every room in which death has occurred. (3) Many hotels, too, dispense with room numbers that end with 13, and as the story goes, one rich, middle-aged widow at the Metropole refused room number 292 because these add up to 13.

The more experienced hotel guest knows the meaning of the Golden Keys symbol worn by members of the renowned organisation of concierges, who perform magic for guests with problems. This occupational category of Head Hall Porters is one which is discussed more fully in a separate research study. *   Uniformed hotel staff wear their apparel only part-ly for the recognition of their assigned function: in the cultural sense, uniforms worn by hotel people constitute symbolic crutches. We saw in our earlier chapter how the hospital porter's self-image offers intrinsic rewards in a patient's care, or how a nurse's uniform, comp-lete with pins and keys, conveys the physical signs of a therapeutic relationship with the patient. So, also, uniformed hotel staff, whose vocational skills serve the patron's convenience and comfort, personally rather than institutionally, for which it is symbolic to reciprocate by way of gratuity. It is seen, therefore, that symbols operate in pers-onal inter-action, although they may represent a collective meaning.

This subject of symbolic traits is far from exhausted, but we must now limit ourselves to the theoretical perspective that underlies it. In order to be able to draw useful, socially valid conclusions, or make realistic predictions, the following qualities in symbols must be util-ised: referends must be accurate and validly represented to convey meaning. To illustrate, Green and Johns (4) explain in context that sneezing as an indicator of a cold is a case where the former is caus-ally linked with the latter. Secondly, there must be organisation. The process of combining symbols helps us to think and link them together into meaningful patterns - words that may evoke associations. These authors call this quality 'connotation'. Thus, a 'hotel' may denote a class of objects, but for a given person connote comfort and hospital-ity; and, finally, the aspect of sharing is a useful, but not essential, attribute, for it is possible for a symbol to be private, say, the

* Saunders,K.C.(1980)'Head Hall Porters: A Behavioural Study of Occupation-al Experience in the Hotel Industry'. Employee Relations Vol.2, Number 2 .

sound of an alpine-horn, symbolic of the mountains in Austria. Shared
symbols are most useful if they are well known and varied, so as to
obtain mutuality of interest. We are reminded of an incident observed
in a London restaurant where the waiter of Austrian origin served an
Austrian tourist of similar age. Strangers, when the order was taken,
by the end of the first course, they had established such rapport as to
give the impression of intimate friendship. Evidently, a shared interest in the meal experience and cultural background, where words evoked
an exchange of mutually experienced associations, helped to create, in
a short space of time, a social encounter typified by the utilisation
of such symbolic traits as we are here discussing.

Behaviour Patterns

Some of the symbols we have identified are merely an expression of customs and traditions. Certain customs may, themselves, be rooted in
specific traditions. Such structural elements are, therefore, inter-
related. To Russell Gordon Smith (5), nine-tenths of all we do or say
or think or feel, from the time we get up to the time we go to bed, is
not independent of self-expression, but in uncritical, unconscious conformity with rules, regulations, group habits, standards, codes, styles,
and sanctions that were in existence long before we were born. The behavioural scientist makes fine distinctions when referring to personal-
social conditioning and uses the terms, conventions, practices, habits,
folkways, morals and mores. We shall confine ourselves here to that
part of culture known as 'custom', as a multi-embracing behaviour pattern and referred to by Ruth Benedict (6) as the 'lens without which one
cannot see'.

The hotel industry recognises customs which are centrally observed or
which may be peculiar to certain occupational grades within the industry only (as we shall later see when we focus our attention on symbols,
customs and superstitions of the chef); and customs or practices exemplified in specific hotels as institutional agencies and evolved there
alone. These might well be an outgrowth of the manner in which time,
environment, faithful patrons and old-established staff have mutually
shaped the character of the establishment. A good understanding might
be gained of such customary behaviour patterns if we offer examples
based on what has been widely observed and relayed to us in general
conversation with a variety of people in the trade - chefs, porters,
catering supervisors and waiters. Some of the customs are also client-
orientated, whilst others may be only of occupational significance.
When waiters lay tables, two forks of the same size laid-up equals bad
luck; crossed knives means conflict between waiters which could result
in physical violence; spilt pepper is good luck; glasses upside down
equal a fight, that is, customer wants a fight with anyone after drinking; two teaspoons in a cup equal a wedding or a death; if a knife is
dropped and another picks it up, the dropper is not to say thanks if
ill-luck is not to ensue. Some of these symbols indicate to individuals how they should respond in certain situations, not unlike smoke
signals, beating drums, or carving signs on trees, practised by other
cultures. Customs expressed in this way should be seen in the spirit
of Radcliffe-Brown's and Malinowski's anthropological teachings, in
that these contribute to the cohesion of organisational life through
their meaningfulness in role-playing situations, although the origin
and persistence of a custom itself is not always rationally determinable.

We do not hold with the 'cookbook' approach used by some psychologists that any response to oral function, like eating or drinking, is to be seen as a universal symbol of mother-fixation. Freud has warned against interpreting symbols in this way.

Indications by means of gestures between individuals in the process of particular social action, although stimuli, do develop into symbols of significance because these are addressed to self and other simultaneously. In the examples we are about to give here, they express a subcultural pattern peculiar to service-giving in that trade, or a historical origin and continuing to transcend the life of particular social groups. Guests arriving at night without luggage at a luxury hotel may expect to be shown the door, or at best be regarded with suspicion; expensive baggage conveying a certain image of status; customer to be regarded as marvellous or otherwise by hall porter, depending entirely on the size of tip; all these are well enough known by staff and clients in the hotel world as is the 'customer being (mostly) always right'. Gestures or signs may occur when a hotel is full and the guest knows the purpose of a top pocket in the manager's waistcoat, or when all tables are fully booked and restaurant manager's finger rests in his waistcoat pocket. Customer putting a note in the appropriate place or taking out wallet is a meaningful enough sign to expect privileges to be rewarded or good service to be reciprocated, if one wants to put it that way. We shall see later that superstition also plays a role in which there is an overlap of custom and tradition symbolically expressed in the symbiotic situation of hotel kitchens.

Utilitarian Characteristics

Similar to other institutions, the hotel requires a multitude of physical paraphernalia for the performance of its function. It is not merely a question of building, furnishings, wine cellar, engine and boiler rooms, costly machines (such as dishwashing machines) and other resources. In all establishments where large-scale food preparation and cooking take place, one may speak of centres of food and science and frequently, art, where stores contain a vast inventory of ingredients and a turnover in perishable commodities frequently the size of a supermarket. We have noted already how early hospitality in history was geared to travel and provided by monasteries and pilgrim hostels and, later, of the significant grandeur of the luxurious railways hotels and regency hotel architecture in London, side-by-side with the provincial grand hotels. But, functional architecture was not always a major concern and we may find instances of obsolete plant handicapping many an older hotel which can, at best, afford only remodelling of parts, an added new wing or two and good deal of patchwork.

During the last few years, hotel architecture has had to respond to the social and technical forces bearing on the current scene. Sophisticated central kitchens with stainless steel equipment and cook-freeze apparatus or DEBBIE (Duplex,Electronic,Bookkeeping,Billing,Information, Equipment) from the Cumberland Hotel, dealing with 7,000 bill charges daily and occupancy details of nearly 1,000 rooms, are examples of technical progress here. Bedrooms have become smaller, ceilings lower and furnishings simpler. (Imposing chandeliers mounted on high ceilings made cleaning a costly, major operation of the older hotel, notwithstanding the availability of cheaper staff). Technical innovation and

functional influence on physical plant has also meant a more economical
use of labour and a number of personal services is now left to the care
of the clients themselves.

Looking deeper than utility pure and simple, as social scientists
must, we note in this part of our discussion also the mutual inter-
action of both the normative and the utilitarian aspects of hotels as
social institutions. Utilitarian traits, like resources and equipment,
change standards and norms which react on the social composition of the
client population, demanding in turn new concepts of physical plant.
As Sommer points out, the emphasis on the individual's phenomenal world
of earlier times delayed the study of the physical environment, because
of its pre-occupation with laboratory studies and a reinforcement model
of human behaviour. The effects of environment are generally too diff-
use and subtle to be explained by an animal pressing a lever to receive
a food pellet... nor have many behaviourists studied the effects of con-
finement per se on animals, or are knowledgeable about cage dimensions.
Although we wish to avoid an equation of Sommer's examples with hotel
patrons, we feel he has made his point. (7) Package travel has re-
emphasised movement in herds and, hence, greater simplicity where
people sleep, with service that is more silent and less visible, alongside the elaborate common rooms, lounges, banqueting rooms, dining and
drinking areas, where they mix for maximum inter-action and mutual observation, all demonstrating how social changes in one institutional
sphere, through the functions of actors, can activate reactions in
others.

The Hotel's Objectives, its Institutional Personality, Ethos and Character

Goals
We state at once that it is not our own aim to review the mass of management literature that has been written on organisational goals. Some
writers would maintain that it is hardly legitimate to conceive of an
organisation as having a goal unless it be that there is a continuing
consensus between the members of the enterprise about the purposes of
their inter-action.(8) Hotel people would claim that their organisation has been set up for a definite purpose with explicit, publicised
and usually legally registered, objectives, filed in the form of a
Memorandum with the Registrar of Companies. As our diagram shows, this
document will no doubt reveal a stated purpose upon the company's in-
corporation (or comply with another form of legitimation if not a limited liability company) that it intends to provide hospitality and shelter for those temporarily away from home. But, any social frame of reference recognises that stated objectives derive their meaning through
the actions of people whereby one might see the organisational goals as
symbols for the legitimation of action by those who represent, say, the
hotel, vis-a-vis the world outside it. Silverman (9) argues along
these lines and suggests that goals might be placed in the category of
cultural objectives which members use to make their actions accountable.

We accept that a hotel has a relationship with the wider society but
regard it as a misconception to look upon it as a replica or microcosm of
the community at large. A hotel may or may not have features similar
to the community in which it is situated, but may be quite antithetical
to the social structure and culture of the particular environment in
which it was built. Hotel people perceive it as a special community
with its own, unique social organisation, cultural norms and practices.

Indeed, the hotel as an institution may, and has a tendency to, develop its own normative and interpersonal style of operation, which may be quite foreign to the locals. Most hotels, large or small, are perhaps quasi-closed communities in some respects (particularly so when most of the staff live in), with a special pattern of staff-client inter-action and cultural norms that reflect the 'personality' of the undertaking. Each hotel might be seen as a sub-culture of its own, whose norms and cultural character one can only discover by perceptive observation over a period of time. Hotel cultures, therefore, differ not only from that of the local community but also as between different hotels.

Given all these propositions, that objectives originate initially from the founders, receive formal legitimation, are acted out symbolically towards the wider world of which the hotel is not necessarily a replica, managerial people at the helm see goals as basically particular end-states towards which human behaviour and physical resources must be directed; and which enables them to judge - as the organisation travels along its life of fulfilling endeavours - whether in the light of the success of other, similar hotels, there is an attainment of goals, assuming that the organisational structure is right for it. It has to be borne in mind, and the formulation of objectives seen in this light, that this industry differs from most other business undertakings in a number of respects. Medlik (10) explains this on the following lines: the hotel bed/night, its most important product, cannot be adjusted to demand, because it is fixed by the size of the building and, once idle, can never be recouped or put into storage for future use. Like some foods, this also is a perishable product. Secondly, the hotel's location is fixed and cannot follow the customer, so that the product has to be consumed at the place where it is produced. The key factors of the right location, correct capacity and high level utilisation are, therefore, crucial to the viability of a hotel. Catering shares these problems to some extent, with the difference that foods would need to be neither purchased nor cooked if not required, were it but possible always to foresee the casual or chance requirements that might arise. Thus, by the nature of its declared purposes, the organisation's behaviour mirrors the character of its intentions.

At this point, it is as well to obviate semantic confusion by attaching our meaning to some of the terms we have used. 'Planned future results' have been variously referred to as goals, targets or objectives and 'overall results' as steps on the way. Both refer to 'desirable future results' and we therefore propose, for our purposes only, to drop any distinction between these terms as we proceed with our analysis. Objectives will always mean temporary estimates of desirable future results that require a willing expenditure of resources. This meaning does not preclude a sub-division of particular types, in any case essential through the heterogeneity of the hotel services provided. What we need to avoid is to confuse with objectives certain matters which are related to them, i.e. mission or purpose, the reason for which the hotel exists; policies, which are broad statements of general intent that specify what is permitted and expected; procedures, which are the more specific instructions of how it is to be done; strategy, which is the compatible combination of policies, objectives and programmes; and, by assumption, is meant a probable development of some importance which cannot be predicted with accuracy.

Personality

We must now attempt to explain why we think a hotel has a 'personality'
of its own, and why goals provide the key to its character. To begin
with, every hotel system has a life cycle in which, according to Hertzler, four stages can be identified. Firstly, the incipient organisation
period which is one when,as a result of a social movement or crisis,
the need for this institution to exist at all appears and groups begin
to organise. Next, some form, leaders, role definitions and functions
emerge. The period of efficiency then follows. The institution is now
accepted and functions are performed (hopefully) with enthusiasm and
efficiency. Thirdly, a period of formalism is then experienced, when
the various codes and ideologies become more or less fixed in the institutional structure. The last period referred to is the period of
disorganisation, which trails formalism. Here, some flexibility is
lost and the institution suffers diminished vitality in meeting its
needs. When that stage is reached, re-organisation or replacement of
the system may be the only solution. (11)

 It will now be obvious that the speed at which the organisation contracts institutional arteriosclerosis during the four-stage journey of
its existence will be closely associated with its personality and character. We shall look briefly into the anatomy of these criteria in an
ideal-typical sense, so to speak. Our propositions will be largely
based on the ideas of Gellerman and Perrow. (12/13)

 Human influences like hunches, intuition and instinct still compete
with, or supplement, the cold analysis and logic in managerial decision-
making. The forces that mould these guesses will frequently reflect a
common core of the subjective attitudes among the principal executives
towards key problems which give the hotel (or any other system) a distinct atmosphere and philosophy of its own, and thereby making it different from any other hotel. Such influences may collectively be seen
as the hotel's personality. The composition of these collective dispositions will be the hotel's unique working atmosphere, its emotions,
hopes, attitudes and biases. The problem of identifying personality
may never crop up in meetings or be the subject of self-appraisal; but
it will enter into the social action process via the specific goals,
policy and attitudes of the hotel, the prevailing guidelines for doing
things and the norms for evaluating the performances of staff, so as to
acquire an outlook on service-giving that is its very own.

 Personality, therefore, consists of a body of unwritten traditions
and assumptions that are rarely ever questioned. If tastes and preferences there are, which may or may not be realistic or logical, the hotel will also have its blind spots or unsuspected assets. It is, therefore, hard to obtain a thorough understanding of the hotel's personality
without a deliberate analysis of it. If this were done, the main shap-
ing-forces that emerged would be the dynamism in reaction and adjustment to economic and market conditions, its dynamism in revolution
(whether, for example, tradition assumes the power of authority or
whether new blood energises the old hotel, or merely puts it at cross
purposes) and the pace-setters, whose traits the hotel takes on, if a
charismatic individual's personality does not clash with that of the
undertaking. Of the (approx.) 36,000 hotels of varying size, neat categorisation into personalities such as 'paternal', 'impersonal',

'aggressive' or 'passive', is not possible and that practically rules
out reliable comparisons or predictions, not least because some of the
characteristics may exist in contrast or combination. An example of a
high-class London hotel comes to mind. It literally thrives on tradition, but has an aggressive marketing team; spends huge sums on room re-
novation, but the dining room floorboards are left creaking and mice
have been seen there; it offers high-standard cuisine, but its kitchen
equipment is outdated; and its charges are 'modern' for its 'traditional' clients. Deliberate analysis requires (according to Gellerman) five
steps to be taken: identifying the pace-setters (the people whose attitudes count); defining their goals, tactics and blind spots; locating
the economic challenges; and reviewing its history (through the careers
of its leaders).

  Perrow's association of an organisation's goals with its behaviour is
even more pronounced. For him, goals are the key to an organisations's
character, and thus to its conduct. Whilst not directly dependent on
the structure and technology of service-giving, goals do provide a quick
conceptual route into a hotel system, reflecting its uniqueness and the
part played by specific influences, which may be either transient or enduring. Examples of such influences are the personality of the top executives; the hotel's history; its community environment; structure and
technical ability; norms and values of significant other systems the
hotel has associations with; and the ultimate cultural setting. Vision
is important also. If it is of the 'tunnel' kind, the organisation sees
just a narrow bit of the world; but, if expansion of that vision were
possible, goals may still provide highlights and blinders or constrain
change. This may occur through the action of staff. Hotel people identify with goals, erect checks and balances to guard against risks and
such action may then become accepted as a justification for caution or
conservatism. If, on the other hand, risks are expected, communication
is simplified, but the analysis of the action harder. If staff can adapt, they recruit like-minded people and if staff cannot adapt, it may
block their advance. As often as not, change may be resisted by the
'mechanics' of the relationships, rather than by the actors themselves.
Instances of that are such inter-actional patterns as the striking of
bargains or the handling of negotiations.

  Without the concerted effort that goals require, an organisation may
still prosper, but it has neither a firm anchor within the structure,
nor direction of purpose and may be vulnerable to pressures from within
and without, so that the organisation will be shaped by the opportunist-
ic environmental forces in the struggle to achieve its feeble goals.
Although goals represent a positive resource, this does not mean that
all are viable or desirable. Indeed, says Perrow, the problem is often
that past appropriateness prevents executives from seeing their present
inappropriateness. It should be noted also that all hotel units will
pursue a variety of goals, in sequence or simultaneously, multiple or
conflicting, and that this militates against the promotion of a stability
of character. The tension that conflicting goals can generate may often
be healthy if it does emphasise the need for change. Finally, an important point to be made is that successful hotels need not have identical
goals. A hotel may be both innovative and conservative, emphasise quality or utility, or both, in the manner in which it operates its organisational elements. Thus, goals, although not as obvious and given as generally assumed, do provide the best clue to the distinctive character of

an organisation. This is where we must leave it, but we hope to have indicated its relevance to our study of the organisational structure of the hotel world and what goes on there.

The Hotel and its Principal Sub-Systems

Although we are here discussing hotels as abstract types and not specifically selected hotels in the empirical sense, the presentation of a figurative version of the diverse and all-permeating facets of the hotel and catering industrial structure will facilitate an understanding why there is, as yet, no unified definition of this industry. (See Figure 6 below, showing the heterogeneous nature of the industry).

Government agencies and private bodies have defined the industry for their own purposes. A definition as such usually entails classification for the purpose of facilitating the compilation of data and describing the magnitude and characteristics of an industry's activities in some orderly manner, and in terms of manageable categories. In view of these difficulties, we consider it convenient to devise our own simplified classification.* This scheme divides hotels into three main categories: the 'functionally-practical', which tend to be large (from 400 rooms upwards); the 'luxuriously-elaborate', which tend to be medium in size (up to 400); and the 'carefully-marginal', which tend to be small (up to 50 rooms). This categorisation is purely arbitrary, to serve our own convenience of analysis and can be further simplified by referring to them simply as functional, traditional and utilitarian. We have already indicated that hotels dislike a classification by way of the services they offer (for whatever purpose that classification may be), since fewer services appear to stamp them as inferior in the eyes of the public. The sub-systems within individual hotels can be placed in a hierarchical order, although few people in the hotel world would agree on what this order might be. Colin Dix (interviewed) suggested the following, widely accepted status hierarchy: first, management, to be followed by the kitchen department; then, the head hall porters, head housekeepers, reception managers, restaurant managers and banqueting managers sections, in that order. (14)

We know of no social research which investigated organisational relationships between departments in hotels (yet another neglected area, considering the 36,000 hotels there are) and, in particular, such questions as whether it is possible to predict the structure and role relationships in kitchens and other departments, when a hotel is categorised as either functional, traditional or utilitarian (using our classification). Whether a particular category of hotel influences size, occupational status, the technological set-up and cuisine in a kitchen; and whether the traditional hotel is likely to have a charismatic chef. What we may ask is, whether the status of the kitchen department itself is contingent on the status of the hotel, on the charisma of the chef, on the existing technology and equipment available, on clients' demands for particular kinds of food or because the kitchen is simply the favourite department

* The Standard Industrial Classification, the Wages Council, Licensing Laws, the Training Board, the Tourist Board, Motoring Associations, the Egon Ronay Organisation and various other private bodies, all use different definitions of this industry to suit their own purposes.

FIGURE 6.

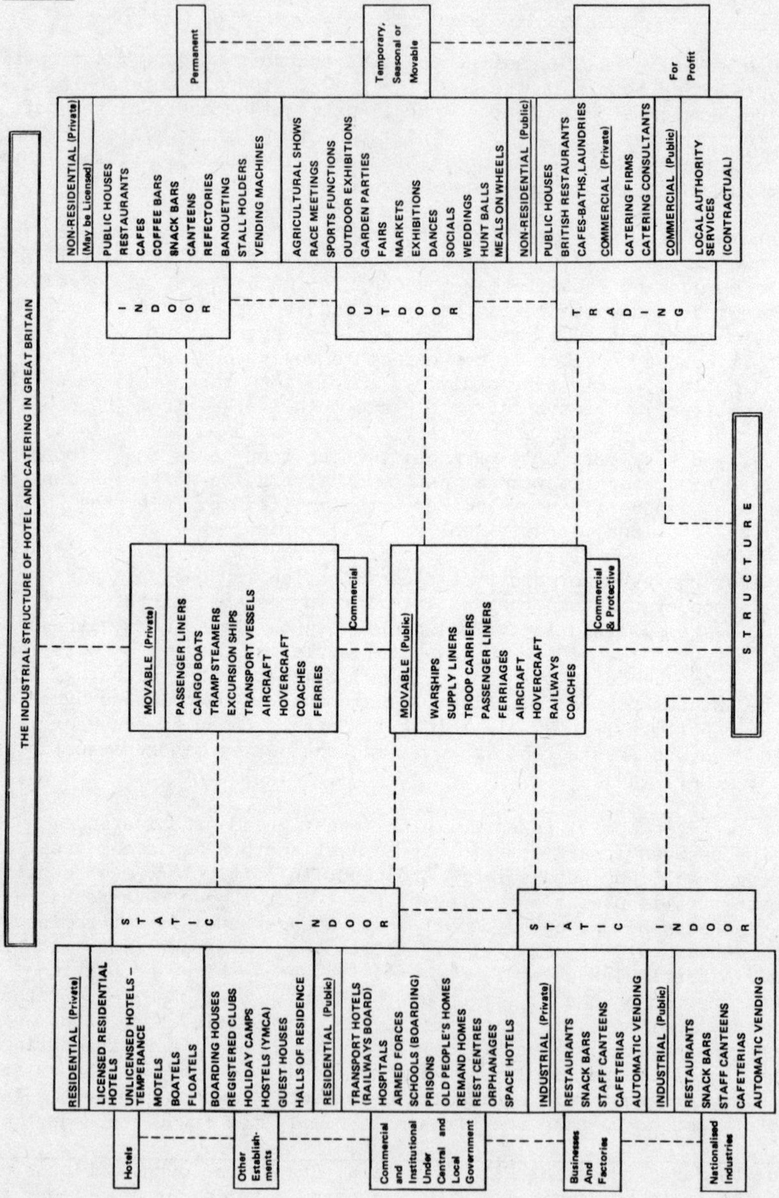

THE INDUSTRIAL STRUCTURE OF HOTEL AND CATERING IN GREAT BRITAIN

STRUCTURE

NON-RESIDENTIAL (Private) (May be Licensed)

Permanent

INDOOR:
- PUBLIC HOUSES
- RESTAURANTS
- CAFES
- COFFEE BARS
- SNACK BARS
- CANTEENS
- REFECTORIES
- BANQUETING
- STALL HOLDERS
- VENDING MACHINES

OUTDOOR:
- AGRICULTURAL SHOWS
- RACE MEETINGS
- SPORTS FUNCTIONS
- OUTDOOR EXHIBITIONS
- GARDEN PARTIES
- FAIRS
- MARKETS
- EXHIBITIONS
- DANCES
- SOCIALS
- WEDDINGS
- HUNT BALLS
- MEALS ON WHEELS

Temporary, Seasonal or Movable

NON-RESIDENTIAL (Public)

TRADING:
- PUBLIC HOUSES
- BRITISH RESTAURANTS
- CAFES-BATHS-LAUNDRIES

COMMERCIAL (Private)
- CATERING FIRMS
- CATERING CONSULTANTS

COMMERCIAL (Public)
- LOCAL AUTHORITY SERVICES (CONTRACTUAL)

For Profit

MOVABLE (Private)

STATIC / INDOOR:
- PASSENGER LINERS
- CARGO BOATS
- TRAMP STEAMERS
- EXCURSION SHIPS
- TRANSPORT VESSELS
- AIRCRAFT
- HOVERCRAFT
- COACHES
- FERRIES

Commercial

MOVABLE (Public)

STATIC / INDOOR:
- WARSHIPS
- SUPPLY LINERS
- TROOP CARRIERS
- PASSENGER LINERS
- FERRIAGES
- AIRCRAFT
- HOVERCRAFT
- RAILWAYS
- COACHES

Commercial & Protective

RESIDENTIAL (Private)

STATIC / INDOOR:
- LICENSED RESIDENTIAL HOTELS
- UNLICENSED HOTELS – TEMPERANCE
- MOTELS
- BOATELS
- FLOATELS
- BOARDING HOUSES
- REGISTERED CLUBS
- HOLIDAY CAMPS
- HOSTELS (YMCA)
- GUEST HOUSES
- HALLS OF RESIDENCE

RESIDENTIAL (Public)
- TRANSPORT HOTELS (RAILWAYS BOARD)
- HOSPITALS
- ARMED FORCES
- SCHOOLS (BOARDING)
- PRISONS
- OLD PEOPLE'S HOMES
- REMAND HOMES
- REST CENTRES
- ORPHANAGES
- SPACE HOTELS

INDUSTRIAL (Private)

STATIC / INDOOR:
- RESTAURANTS
- SNACK BARS
- STAFF CANTEENS
- CAFETERIAS
- AUTOMATIC VENDING

INDUSTRIAL (Public)
- RESTAURANTS
- SNACK BARS
- STAFF CANTEENS
- CAFETERIAS
- AUTOMATIC VENDING

Left-margin categories:
- Hotels
- Other Establishments
- Commercial and Institutional Under Central and Local Government
- Businesses And Factories
- Nationalised Industries

of the manager. Whilst, therefore, such questions, whether hotels with similar service systems (for the provision of food, drink and accommodation) may or may not evidence similar organisation structures - despite the variety of personal services offered - is beyond the scope of this project, the kitchen is very much within the ambit of our interest and will occupy us next.

THE HOTEL KITCHEN AS A SOCIAL ORGANISM

Introduction

In discussing above the institutional elements of the hotel structure, we had to select for our necessarily brief analysis only those features which appeared to us useful for gaining some idea of how the hotel system, as an ideal creation, might be seen as significant in terms of the purpose of its existence. We hope to have drawn attention to some of the less obvious factors in hotel policy planning and management by pointing to unresearched areas in the industry, and the penalties that are likely to result when there is an absence of sociological awareness of the less tangible within the operational life of the system. We express this thought for the appropriate associations, employers and educators to take up, as well they might, if they feel that this neglect should present a concern (and a gap in management education) and is deserving of deeper consideration.

Stratification by Occupation

We shall treat the kitchen as a social organism as we discern situations of relatively consistent inter-action among particular networks or occupation groupings of people in an environment of much greater departmental independence than that of the uniformed service areas of the reception, front area and accommodation side of the hotel. Whereas the departments which deal directly with the transient guest population and their personal-social needs as loosely-cohesive batches of human bodies experience a continuous cycle of sequential situations, to some extent unanticipated, the kitchen is a productive-creation, closed community, out of sight and hived off from the clients and the rest of the hotel. In this little empire, everywhere we shall find the King - le Chef de Cuisine - directing the operations of la Brigade - and the Slave - le Plongeur - immersed up to his armpits in the greasy water of his sink. In between these two reference points, we may find a status-graded hierarchy of kitchen occupations, whose rating has formal and informal aspects of role performance to interest the social interpreter, whose structural sophistication depends on the size and type of establishment and whose prestige is linked to the relative importance of the part played in the chain of creativity and to the intrinsic skills that earn them recognition from their colleagues.

Departmental Stratification

We made a point of distinguishing between the status hierarchy of hotel departments or sub-systems, because the uniformed, customer-involved service sections tend to express differential values from that of product-oriented kitchen. This traditional mutual contempt, although gradually undergoing conciliation, is still in many hotels reflected in the symbolic expression of particular customs and traditions. The

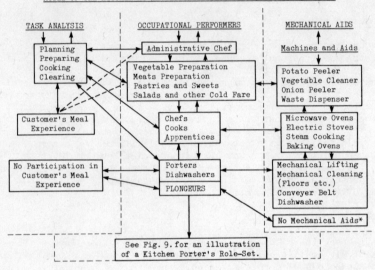

FIGURE 7.
MODEL OF THE KITCHEN AS AN ONGOING SOCIAL SYSTEM WITHIN THE HOTEL

Note: This figure demonstrates the pattern
of the interacting roles of others
with the kitchen porter in the work
situation. Machanical aids are not
normally available to plongeurs, the
potmen, although machines exist.
Figure 8. explains why these models
are not often used.

The latest piece of kitchen technology is a washing-up machine
that uses ultrasonic waves instead of soap. This model has been
produced in Japan and is of a size to fit on shelf or table-top.
The tub is filled with water, switched on, and the electronic
oscillator gives off ultrasonic frequencies that remove the
food particles and dirt. Since this novel invention will deal
only with ordinary household articles, clean jewellery, eye-
glasses and false teeth, the plongeur is not likely to derive
much benefit from this new technology.

FIGURE 8.

Model of a Potwashing Machine.

Variations of such a machine may still be found in some
catering establishments and on display at exhibitions.
They are usually heated by steam, gas or electricity.
Capital cost is high, at the time of writing in excess
of £5,000, so that only the largest undertakings can
afford it. Pots, pans and other utensils to which food
sticks have to be pre-washed before placing them in
this machine. The number sold per year are very few
and where installed, are often not used. Information
from some manufacturers is that these machines have
still to be perfected. In general, they have not replaced human labour.

prevailing tensions and conflict that often occur are not so much expressed in physical violence as in occupational consciousness, pretence of superiority, subtle action or signs of debasement, or deprecating chance remarks to brigade members. Indeed, this is traditionally a part of the role-learning process of the apprentice chef that stems from the expressed or implied attitudes displayed by the traditionally autocratic head chef and projected on to his flock. As to the internal organisations and status of the kitchen as a segment of the hotel-departmental hierarchy, this is often difficult to discern and answers to this question may, conceivably, vary in accord with the views of members of the different occupations in any particular hotel. We cannot be more scientific than that, for no workplace research has been attempted (as observed already) on the sociological side which deals with the organisational elements of hotel departments and their inter-relationships. We must, therefore, limit ourselves to indicative evidence of the climate of feeling in the trade of a possible hierarchical order, merely to gain some idea of how the kitchen rates. The assigned role of cuisine relative to the services of drink and accommodation will transmit a given weighting to the status of the occupations associated with these services. Thus, post-houses and other self-catering systems may have no chef at all, whilst in most 'better class' hotels (by whatever measuring standard), the chef and his team will play a key role on the kitchen stage, and his impact permeates the entire hotel scene.

Status Order and the Application of Skills of the Kitchen Hierarchy

The Chef de Cuisine (Head Chef)

Whether the head chef is king, or just a prince, will depend on the size, type and creative quality of his domain. He will have most of the personal attributes that people in the trade expect: a strong and healthy constitution, long experience in all branches of cooking; sound knowledge of products connected with his work, according to seasons; be a good organiser and expert in the art of cooking, with aesthetic sense and a mind for order and economy. De Boni typifies him thus:-

> ' ... he is in charge and responsible for the welfare
> of this important department, and he must know his bus-
> iness in every branch down to the smallest detail.
> Here, he must be an autocrat, and all his staff must
> feel the weight of his authority. He must enforce
> strict discipline, and exact from every subordinate
> the full measure of duty, to be carried out with zeal,
> quickness and accuracy ... (and the author goes on to
> say) ... It is by harmony and co-operation with his
> subordinate staff that he will achieve success'. (15)

Evidently, autocratic head chefs demand harmony and co-operation. We do not propose to go into his routine functions in detail, but there are certain matters of behavioural interest which should be mentioned. Most head chefs possess a certain charisma if only to their brigade. As a type, he would be of middle age, have widely travelled and is quite often a Frenchman, Italian or German when he bears all the characteristics of his cultural origin. Guests' preferences are passed to the head chef by the Maître d'hotel, so that he may have regard to this in his

planning. In the normal, functional course of events, guests do not
have contact with him, but in traditional hotel systems, it is the custom for a head chef to come out from the kitchen, in his 'whites', to
chat to the patrons who are only too eager to display their culinary
knowledge when awarding him their praise for his artistry. That is the
reward he eagerly seeks and from which he derives great joy.

The Sous Chef (Assistant Chef)

The personal attributes of the Second Chef will be similar to the head
chef and, like the head himself, will have speed and promptitude in confronting and solving any unforeseen difficulties. As no two kitchens
are alike, the variety of responsibilities will always differ according
to the locality, services provided and clientele catered for. In the
smaller establishment, the Second Chef will himself have to act as Chef
de Partie or, more usually, as Chef Saucier. In the largest kitchens,
the head chef does not wear whites at all, but carries out administrative duties only. One large London hotel collects the head chef in a
chauffeured car and takes him home each day because of his irreplaceab-
ility. The assistant will then act as a kind of operations manager in
his executive capacity and have also little direct involvement with
craft activities. He may have charge over duty rotas, attend to disciplinary matters (hygiene, dress and punctuality) and cleanliness of kitchen utensils and premises.

Chefs de Partie (Party Chefs)

Large kitchens, or kitchens catering for large numbers, are divided into
sections and party chefs have charge over the sections in which they
specialise. It is not normally possible to plan large-scale kitchen operations without such chefs. They organise their own section and dele-
gate as necessary to assistants. They are the 'backbone' of the kitchen.
Every one of these sections contributes its skill invested in the production of the menu and, should it fall below the required standard, the
whole meal may be ruined. Propensity to spoil is greatest in the production of sauces. For this reason, the chef in charge of the sauce
partie is immediately next in the status hierarchy to second chef. Also,
the larder chef is often considered to be placed higher on the status
scale than the other chefs de partie because he is responsible for perishable food, and sometimes for the whole economy of the kitchen service.
The exception among the rest of the chefs is the pastry chef, who enjoys
comparatively high status because his is the job of a specialist.

   We shall very briefly look into the activities of the various chefs de
partie that make up a kitchen porter's role relationships.

The Sauce Cook

A long apprenticeship is needed for mastering this specialism, together
with a refined palate and adequate aesthetic senses. This cook must be
able to prepare stocks of great variety and impart a special character
to the flavour of dishes. His responsibility extends also over the preparation of meat dishes served in various gravies and sauces. Some of
the creations may be his very own. He reads the menu upon starting his
duty and must know the ingredients to ask for. If the chef de cuisine
is absent and there is no second chef, the sauce cook will be in charge.

The Larder Cook

This cook also enjoys high status, since the larder in a professional kitchen holds greater significance than that of even a large household. Not only is food stored there, but all the raw materials required for cooking are prepared and dressed at that location. In the largest kitchens, larder work is broken down into sub-sections (butcher, poulterer, fishmonger, salad and hors d'oeuvre makers), which gives the cook a degree of independence. In the smaller houses, the larder cook will have charge of the sub-sections. His own work requires the preparation of cold dishes and sandwiches. Whyte (16) offers us an insight into the tension situations and status problems experienced by people working in such sections of a large and busy kitchen from his researches of human relations in the restaurant industry during the war years in America.

The Pastry Cook

In addition to knowledge of pastries and confectionery, this cook needs to possess a practical adaptation to drawings and some artistic sense for the decoration of cakes and tarts. He deals also with unsweetened pasta and generally looks after supplies, and he must be ready for any unexpected order. Such cooks need space and are sensitive to spectators getting too close or touching any of their creations, when they may fly into a temper.

The Fish Cook

He can be found in most large kitchens. With the help of his commis and apprentices, this cook will prepare all kinds of fried foods, fish dishes, fish sauces and garnishes. The hotel fishmonger will, however, attend to the basic preparation. It will be the task of the kitchen porter to clear rubbish away and take charge of all the dirty pots and pans from this section.

The Roast Cook

The work of this cook, as far as dishes go, is not as complex as that of the saucier. He roasts a wide range of poultry, game and meat, grills and deep-fries fish, potatoes and savouries. This section of the kitchen tends to be physically most demanding. The big hotels have roasting trays heavily laden with joints or birds, the handling of which needs considerable strength. The roast corner is considered one of the hottest sections of the kitchen because the cooking apparatus for roasting and deep-frying must, of necessity, be located together.

Soup and Vegetable Cook

Soup cooks are more common in the larger establishments and are the creators of the 'overture' for the main meal. They are said to enjoy a certain amount of prestige on account of this, which is further supported by the fact that the soup repertoire is very extensive. No kitchen porter will ever be kept short of work while the chef potager is performing in his section of the main kitchen.

The vegetable cook, known as the entremetier by today's kitchen brigade, is concerned in the main with all the vegetables, potatoes, egg

108

dishes and garnitures for the sauce cook's needs. Historically speaking, meat, game and poultry have been regarded as the main components in this country's menu structure, whilst vegetable cookery has not, in the past, enjoyed the same status. Hence, the vegetable cook himself has ranked at a lower level as compared with the status of other chefs de partie. Frequently, the impression is also gained that the cooking of various bulk quantities of vegetables is somewhat crude and less skilled than the smaller operations. However, this view is strongly rejected by the experts in the trade, who regard the cooking and service of vegetables of the greatest importance to the culinary reputation of an undertaking.

To complete the picture of the status order, as generally acknowledged in catering circles (although the reasons for this order will rarely be discussed in textbooks), we shall consider the remaining occupations constituting the primary relationships in the kitchen porter's role-set at work, these being the breakfast cook, the night cook and the staff cook.

The Breakfast Cook

As the name implies, that is his function. In a smaller establishment, he may not be fully occupied with breakfasts alone and may be given other duties throughout the morning. This cook is usually under orders of the roast cook and thus well down in the status scale.

The Night Cook

Known as the chef de nuit, this cook will be found mostly in the larger hotels. He will have charge of the kitchen during the night or part of the night. The reason for having a night cook is not only for late meal requirements, but also to supervise the cooking of certain foods which, for economy of space and time, can be conveniently prepared during the night. (Boiling beef, ham, etc.) He, too, is well down the scale in status, but needs to be very reliable as he is in full charge.

The Staff Cook

He also is more likely to be found in the larger hotels. Interestingly, he draws provisions not only from the stores, but uses materials left over from the entire kitchen department. He is expected to be economical so as to utilise every item of food, but is required to satisfy the staff fully, not infrequently a dilemma. The staff cook is closely supervised by the head chef at the same time as reliability is stressed for this position. It is clear why this cook is at the bottom of the status hierarchy of cooks. It appears that not the same stress is laid on culinary skills for staff as is enjoyed by patrons, and the emphasis on economy for hotel workers of a lower grade reminds one of the domestic service period in history.

We seem to have overlooked the Duty Cook, who rates in status above the breakfast cook. He fills in when there are gaps through split shifts or when most of the staff are off duty, while commis will look after some of the other stations, such as larder and pastry. Commis, or assistant, cooks help with the simpler and less important work and rank in status before apprentices.

It will be appreciated that a display of skills will enhance status among colleagues in a kitchen, but where there are several chefs de partie, of the same speciality, i.e. four roast cooks, seniority will rank some of them before the others of that particular skill. So far as experience can be equated with seniority, it will add to the prestige a cook may enjoy. This kind of horizontal status-grading is more of an informal ranking system and probably occurring when large numbers of guests have to be catered for at banquets, when (as in some American hotels) hundreds, or even thousands, of patrons may have to be satisfied by the skills of large numbers of chefs.

The Kitchen Porter's Work Routine

Uniformed porters usually rank before kitchen porters in the porter structure of hotels, but status among kitchen porters may be determined more by seniority than by the particular duties to be performed. This proposition is based on secondary information at managerial level and can only be substantiated by participant observation within a cross section of hotels for some weeks, when an insight into formal and informal role relationships may be gained and behaviourally interpreted. Limited research resources at the present time have not made this possible.

As we have selected the occupation of kitchen porter as a core around which to study a great variety of areas of sociological interest within the hotel and catering industry, it is as well that we now take a more careful look at the nature of this particular occupation's work routines.

In many organisations, the kitchen porter is identified with the scullery, nowadays mostly the wash-up area. The sculleryman or plongeur must collect, wash and return to the allocated place in the kitchen all the pots and pans. If he acts as pot washer, he will be primarily responsible for the careful cleaning of all copper and aluminium kitchen utensils (some of steel if he is lucky), usually pots, pans, frying pans, dishes, large vessels and implements used by the chefs, wash and remove grease with hot water and detergent. He will be told to keep his workplace in a hygienic condition so as to avoid objectionable smells. He is also to check utensils and draw attention to those that need repair or replacement.

As to his work area, the washing-up of pots and pans is usually separated from the crockery wash, and placed near the cooking area, where the utensils are used. Most sinks are deep, to allow for soaking of the large pots and there may be work tables large enough to hold used pots while they are scraped into waste bins before soaking. Cleaned items will be placed on rack stands, found on wheels in some places.

The kitchen porter's dress in the plunge is likely to be overalls, a big rubber apron, rubber or wooden boots, sometimes rubber gloves and occasionally goggles, to protect his eyes from steam. We shall say a great deal more about the work environment in our survey analysis later.

Now a brief look at the kitchen porter's tools. He uses nylon or bristle scrubbing brushes, pot-cleaners made of steel wool, a big wash-up cloth, soap powder, soda and detergents in liquid or powder form, which in some places are by measured quantities from a dispenser. For the very dirty pans, abrasive powder may be in use. A thermometer may sometimes be attached to the sink to measure the water temperature. The porter may stand on a duckboard, or in some kitchens with his feet in a puddle around the sink if there isn't one. Various other tools and implements may be used in the course of his duties (often provided by himself to symbolise true professionalism) or for the use of odd jobs additional or ancillary to pot washing.

The Value of Training

In view of our suggestions on training needs for kitchen porters, as reported below, the neglect of a proper recognition by employers and training officers that this is an occupation requiring a carefully thought-out and planned course of training, deserves some comment. We would recommend a certificated course of a definite duration, sufficient to impart the necessary skills so as to accord an incumbent some status and self-respect vis-a-vis the esteemed cookery skill groups he shares his work environment with. Quite apart from the sociological and psychological considerations relating to status and the way he feels about his contribution in the organisation, a kitchen porter rarely gets the benefit of even an induction course. Our later discussion on informal inter-action will evidence this. Formal recognition of a training need would undoubtedly filter through to the pool of actual and potential incumbents and influence current images of, and expectation from, such work which, together with improved conditions (about which we shall also comment later) would make for a change in work-related attitudes. Since we have been critical about the kitchen porter's training needs, we feel we must go the whole hog and take the liberty temporarily to become 'prescriptive' in identifying what these needs are. The induction interview should be 'bothered' with; a good knowledge of the casual labour market should be obtained; catering units that can meet their social obligation to train and upgrade peripheral workers should make arrangements to do so; the porter should be trained in how to use his tools efficiently and not just shown where the dirty pots are and the sink is; he should have talks on how to achieve a compatible work relationship with others (of a higher occupational status), especially during pressure periods; he should be taught how to organise his work environment, how to recognise and treat the materials from which implements are made, how to distinguish between the different kinds of detergents in terms of function, quantities, chemical effects, etc., how to operate correctly electrical or mechanical means in use and how to comply with the safety regulations, how to control and correct water temperatures, how to cope correctly with the hotel's fire drill and, finally, if he does other jobs as well, training is needed to carry those out efficiently also. It will be clear that all this cannot be acquired in the time that is normally given to it, which is sometimes minutes rather than hours, as if the latter were altogether satisfactory.

It appears to us that some employers may welcome the presence of peripheral work groups, prepared to take up such work at short notice and willing to accept termination of employment just as readily, and then complain about their instability when this actually happens. One might argue that the cost of such training is at least in part shifted on to the incumbent on account of the low pay he receives, and would be more than recouped by a trained worker and a stronger possibility of continuity of employment. Lack of training in this case would appear to constitute an under-investment in this type of human capital.

Skill, Occupational Names and Work Routines

Finally, and to revert briefly to the subject of work routines, large hotels may employ various categories of porters when the occupational designations of kitchen hand, kitchen porter, vegetable cleaner, catering worker, kitchen operative are used in addition to potman, washer-up, pot washer, kitchen assistant and plunge operation. The work will vary and may consist of lighting fires in country hotels, changing the previous day's soiled linen, preparing tools and utensils on cooks' work tables, cleaning and washing vegetables, peeling potatoes and preparing fish; and, in some places, after the service of meals, putting the kitchen in order and replacing utensils used, washing floors, tables and tiles and disposing of swill. In very large kitchens, there will be a head porter to supervise the porter brigade and in emergencies, or times of staff shortages, or sometimes on merit, a porter may be elevated to the status of assistant cook, when such tasks as preparing breadcrumbs, chopping parsley, peeling finer vegetables and transporting food from one section to another may be allocated to him.

The conclusions which may be inferred from what we have said about the kitchen porter are: that he is associated with a demographic group in society that carries low social status; that he is closely linked - in his capacity as kitchen porter - to a traditionally low-status occupation; that his social and occupational status are a function of irregular employment; and, in terms of his work environment, we may hypothesise, that the smaller the proportion of skilled to unskilled, the more insignificant the unskilled, the lower their status within the kitchen structure. What we are saying is that the evaluation of what is a skill and what is not is arbitrary. The trade, the training board, departments of employment and agencies do not generally regard the kitchen porter's work as requiring any degree of skill. As we have already suggested earlier, we do not agree that there is any kind of work that requires no skill, and from what we have said above about training needs (to which must be added 'house initiation' in a new workplace) it can hardly be maintained that kitchen porters are skill-less persons.

KITCHEN STRUCTURE AND WORK CYCLE

Whilst, for reasons of expediency, we have been able to find a convenient way of grading hotels into functional, traditional and utilitarian categories, this method cannot be adopted with kitchens in those hotels. The kitchen structure does not depend on the size of the hotel and will be more related to type of menu offered (French, A La Carte, Set Meals, Party Menu, Cold Buffet or whatever), the type of restaurant within a hotel, the skills of the staff available, the price range, kitchen equipment available and the characteristics of the Head Chef. Morel (17) holds that a kitchen is not necessarily sited, designed and equipped for the ultimate purpose it is meant to serve. Rather, kitchens are planned not only for menus and numbers, but for what kind of functional units they might become in the future. New ideas in food preparation, cooking and presentation, the use of convenience food, the onus of 'heavy' preparation now more and more upon the manufacturer and the greater speed of service demanded, all influence the changing face of the kitchen. Style of catering has, therefore, a profound influence on kitchen organisation in the back of the house. It may be possible to predict that a large hotel (which we call functional) will have an 'intra-station' structure that conforms to the production units we show on our Figure. Only large establishments will be able to afford this kind of organisation. The 'class' hotel (referred to as traditional), attracting regular, affluent clients, will have a range of specialist chefs, some of whom are nationally or internationally famous. The utilitarian hotel (of the smaller type) is likely to manage with a smaller brigade, whose members are interchangeable in the main for reasons of economy.

The status of the kitchen department vis-a-vis the other hotel departments (sub-systems) and enjoyed externally is equally difficult to predict, to determine or to measure. The external esteem will derive largely from the trading of voluntary, official bodies (as for example the Tourist Board) and privately, from commercial organisations, who, like Egon Ronay, send unannounced culinary assessors to sample the offerings, so that their evaluations may be included in the registers these bodies publish. Some registers are compiled from voluntary participants, but hotels stand to lose business from package tour operators if they are not included in the lists of recommended establishments. (18) External status is less likely to be influenced by location of the hotel, quality of the staff, size of hotel or by various other services available. It will be more a question of how important the reputation for good food is to the general image the hotel projects. If the hotel has made a name for itself in this particular specialism, the kitchen department will bathe in the halo effect transmitted from it. Sometimes, the quality of food cannot be maintained, particularly when an esteemed chef is lost and irreplaceable. External status makes an impact on the internal esteem in which the kitchen is held. That, despite the fact that this department may be a loss leader. Indeed, a financial loss may enhance its reputation on the grounds of provision of high quality fare, more than offset by highly profitable accommodation returns. The hotel accountant will tolerate the deficit with fortitude, as he enjoys this good food in the executives' dining room. We have already said something on the traditional friction between uniformed staff and kitchen brigade. When lower-status, uniformed personnel demand particular services from the chefs, they are in fact 'originating action' (using Whyte's terminology) and thus, in a sense, ordering the chefs about, which, whilst being less skilled than the latter, gives them a psychological uplift, but arouses antagonism among the chefs. (19/20)

The structural division of the specialisms employed in the kitchen depends, as we have said, on such factors as the menu structure; the sophistication of the latter on the market demand, the skills of the available staff and the technological set-up. The customary meal times in our culture, together with existing house rules, determine the daily cycle of provision for the patrons, often supplemented by special services for new arrivals, on a casual basis for non-residents and early morning/late night orders. Staff will, therefore, be on the alert from early morning to late at night, with a little free time during the post breakfast and post lunch routines, arising from the 'split shift' system. Clearly, systems differ so widely in terms of their characteristic features, that we might fare conceptionally best by typifying the continuing range of variations of activity in hotel kitchens more easily by size, features and context of inter-action. Size then refers to numbers of people, features to frequency, intensity and duration of inter-action and context to the kinds of activity which serve as the sphere of inter-action.

We wish now to develop an argument with which to show how the recipe determines strategic social action in the kitchen, and which will embrace the special characteristics mentioned above. Insofar as there is causality about patronage for cooked food, there is an unavoidable element of speculativeness about it. The weather might have changed, a plane be cancelled, an accident have occurred, or whatever the case, such uncertainty can cause waste of perishable food, although certain pre-fabricated and frozen foods help to alleviate this. But, by and large, a certain amount of planning and predictability is possible from bookings and the establishment's physical limits of accommodation. Thus, the key to production technology in the kitchen is the recipe, because it determines the whole method of work. The predominance of individuality, when it used to be a 'pinch of this' and a 'little of that', and guesswork on weights and ingredients prevailed, is largely an influence of the past. Instead of a chef being put into the kitchen and told to cook, management has taken over the planning function of what to produce. This has acted more than somewhat to undermine the chef-elite's power relative to that of other key people in the hotel, if not their authority within the kitchen itself.

The recipe standardises ingredients, mode of preparation, portions, controls quality and costs. The kitchen system develops a recipe bank of stock choices which evolve into a longitudinal cycle of routine operations for the majority of kitchen staff with tried systems often delegated downwards to semi-skilled personnel. By this means, intrinsic, creative enjoyment is drained away, to be replaced by the promotion of drill and efficiency. This trend does not augur well for the majority of incumbents that engage in the less creative specialisms, for once the creative and experimental elements are replaced by routine production, the operational cycle of tasks becomes a shop floor, where artistry gives way to motion study and measurement, speed and monotony. All this acts, therefore, to relegate the status of the erstwhile elite to a brigade of technicians, supervising semi-skilled or untrained staff, and to replace the service-link of customer-appreciation by an orientation towards routine work, with all its recognised frustrations. The recipe influence in the process of the de-skilling of this craft constitutes, therefore, an added variable to those discussed by Chivers (21) as profoundly meaningful in the trend of proletarianisation for this category of catering worker.

For a possible reversal of the 'recipe effect', there would have to occur - and be encouraged to occur - a spate of fresh excursions into culinary adventure and experiment, which has foundered on public conservatism up to now. Hence, the survival of catering units that offer dishes that transcend short-term changes of taste in food culture on the part of some sections of the clientele (we suggest the middle classes are more daring here), and the frequent departure into oblivion of those catering units which audaciously tell the patrons what they must like. Cultural diffusion in the food area finds ways of change, the transmission of which even an ocean cannot bar. Already, news has reached us (by letter from the U.S.A.) that Americans are getting thoroughly tired of convenience food and are beginning to insist on the restitution of taste and flavour that had apparently left the scene.

114

Standardised work routines also filter through to the scullery. This allows the alert kitchen hand to estimate quantity, size, condition of pots and pans and the time it takes for these to arrive, and so prepare for the deluge. As this mechanism in the work cycle facilitates initiative and organisation of the work flow, it suggests for the (trained!) kitchen porter a definite, identifiable link in the productivity chain, which offers an extended scope for initiative and, therefore, tends to operate as a status-enhancing function. The dismantling and reassembly after washing and cleaning of implements and equipment for the mechanically-minded porter is a duty that will augment his enhanced rating and possibly set him on the road to occupational mobility if he is so minded. Chivers found such occupations as kitchen porters, washers-up and kitchen hands to constitute an important source of recruitment for cooking. At least ten per cent of his whole sample came to cooking from kitchen portering, when it would have become apparent to them through their contact with food and the kitchen that a chef or cook enjoys the highest status in this domain.

In other respects, standardised production techniques will inversely affect all but the most skilled cookery occupations (as the chef saucier) and also tend to depress their status relative to the other skill-craft positions in the hotel. If chefs and cooks come to terms with this trend, the narrowed status gap may have a socially-harmonising effect. If they don't - and this is very much on the cards - diminished authority, together with frustrated ambitions and the stifling of intrinsic satisfaction from their work, may lead them to test out on subordinates what authority remains in the new situation and even lead to militancy (as Chivers suggests) because attention is now diverted from the work itself (such as commitment to craft) to matters linked to the work (economic factors and frustrated aspirations) and the less tangible, associated with the diminished esteem.

Now a brief look at the size effect. We have already noted the variables that are associated with, on the one hand, the offer of simpler, and on the other the more elaborate, menu structures. (Demand, skills, technological set-up and loss leader). Size is one of the important characteristics that we have previously said delineate a social organisation. Since there is such a considerable range of variation possible we are forced once more to simplify by using some mode of classification on which to base our propositions. In the simplest of terms, small enterprises generally refer to relatively small and closely-knit groups of catering staff, where inter-action is likely to be intense. The larger kitchens will staff a sizeable number (often exceeding a hundred cooks) where one can assume that the more persons there are who make up the constituent parts, the less will be the overall pattern of intensity of relationships. (22) The duration of inter-action may be longer or shorter, as observable from the work routines. Duration of the department itself may be regarded as long-term, since the kitchen is a permanent feature in the hotel.

Chivers (23) has obtained some empirically-tested conclusions on the size effect. A younger element was found in the larger kitchens, who felt also more acutely the interference of working hours on family and social life, and showed a more favourable attitude towards trade unions. The larger kitchen was also associated with diminished work satisfaction and an ambition on the part of employees to set up their own businesses.

(The latter often an unattainable or frustrated goal). There has been
some difficulty in separating the direct effects of size (work satisfaction) from the indirect effects (formulated ambitions on account of
working in small or large size units). Older respondents tended to get
less restless and smaller places registered more job satisfaction.
These findings are not unlike Ingham's, who researched in the engineering industry and provided evidence which suggests that as size increases member-commitment (however measured) tends to decline. (24) Chivers
did not arrive at any clear-cut conclusions regarding the nature of
size influence. Broadly speaking, he found that if specialisation of
tasks increases, the cook does not see the dish through all its stages,
is subjected to more monotonous tasks and obtains less satisfaction;
also, that division of labour modifies the inter-actional pattern between individuals, because it becomes sectionalised, resulting in a
cut-off feeling from the larger organisation and, finally, that with
increased size, communications, supervision and relationships between
grades of chef and cook have become more structured, more formal and
less satisfying. Chivers also applied Burns'and Stalker's organismic/
mechanistic concept to kitchen organisation. The first, characterised
by more change, frequent consultation and overlap or responsibilities.
The second, indicative of a complete reversal of these trends. He con-
cluded that, in the case of kitchens, they are partly mechanistic and
partly organic. Mechanistic in terms of planned action - menu structure and preparation, for ready availability to customers; cooks performing allotted tasks (except in very small kitchens) and a high degree
of work co-ordination. But, there is also a built-in organicism about
cooking, in the sense that the unexpected may frequently happen (changes in the number of covers, run on a particular dish or unforeseen
party, for example), as is quite common in this trade. A good deal of
overlap of responsibilities also occurs and there has to be some consultation, made imperative because of the contingency element of the unexpected.

We have attempted to show, partly on the basis of our own propositions, partly from interviews of experienced people in the trade, and
partly from empirical evidence derived from past research, how the
kinds of work routine and the size effect influence the organisation,
and the nature of acting out roles in hotel kitchens. In the last part
of our discussion concerning the kitchen as a social organism, we shall
demonstrate the application of Merton's role-set (discussed below) in
the context of the kitchen porter's role relations, draw attention to
some tension and conflict situations that can occur in the role performance of specific kitchen staff, and also deal with (as yet) unresearched and less-identified aspects of informal relationships in kitchens.
(25)

Roles, Tensions and Informality in Kitchens

Antecedents of role theory can be traced to the previous century, but
it was not until just prior to the last war that a language of role
concepts emerged and systematic research on role prescriptions and role
behaviour was undertaken. Role language has grown in size since and
taken on such precision as to approximate to practically a universal
language within behavioural science. Our discussion in this context
has to be strictly limited and cannot extend into probing the gaps of
a theoretical framework that even systems theory cannot yet handle.

Every individual that is gaining entry into a group is accorded a
status, a rank and a role. Any cook or kitchen porter can occupy more
than one status (wear more than one hat) and each of these will carry a
number of separate roles. Thus, we may think of all the statuses that
an individual can occupy as a status-set and of all the roles pertaining to a given status as its occupant's role-set. Some of the rules
that make up a person's status-set are probably not yet fully understood. Some of these statuses cannot be acted out in roles at the same
time; others would draw society's sanctions if their mutual exclusive-
ness were transgressed, as when a man tries to occupy, say, the status
of husband and bachelor. But, whilst we still lack a precise language
for social science purposes, and rules that can help to describe how a
reasonable status-set is established, Merton's notion of the role-set
eased the difficulties. He postulated that each status involves not
one associated role, but a whole array of roles, each relating the incumbent of the status to a whole variety of other persons with whom he
associates. Figure 9 shows how the kitchen porter's status in his work
situation and the alternative status during his extra-work time relates
to the distinct categories of the other social actors he associates
with.

Robert Merton recognised that whenever occupants of two (or more) statuses share a common concern that makes their inter-action necessary,
role relationships will develop; but he was much concerned with how conflicting demands and expectation of role-set members could be reconciled
To begin with, certain of the relationships for some members of the
role-set may not be of equal importance. For a kitchen porter, the
working relationship with a dining room porter may be peripheral as to
the cleanliness of the floor, but he will not hide his irritation when
burnt food sticks to the pots. Other persons in a role-set may be more
powerful than the status incumbent. If a plongeur wanted the cooks to
take more care with the pots, he might prefer to do it by coalescing
with other plongeurs. Inconsistency in relationships may arise when
role behaviour differs towards different members of the role-set. The
porter will express his feelings differently to an order from a cook-
apprentice than one from the head chef. In some situations, conflicting
demands made on the porter may lead those others who want his jobs done
all at the same time to compromise. Finally, if the power and authority
attached to certain groups of cooks is fairly equal, a code of conduct
may evolve to sort out priorities, or the cooks in combination may form
a counter-vailing power to cope with too autocratic a head chef. But,
a discontented party may also take the course of withdrawing from the
role-set and departing from the work place altogether. These then are
an outline of Merton's social mechanisms that can come into role play,
but this is not always an inevitable consequence as in many situations
conflicting role expectations are put up with as ongoing aspects of social life.

Erving Goffman explains how people in social encounters act out a
'line' that can express many qualities: subordination, superiority,
friendliness or social distance, but some encounters are so stylised
and conventional that they offer little scope for a choice of line.
Merton's six significant postulations go some way at least to help explain friction, conflict, stress, disharmony and tension in human inter-
action, or indeed the opposite, as when expectations are being met.

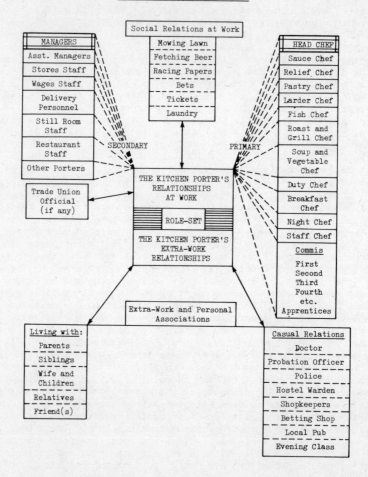

FIGURE 9.
THE KITCHEN PORTER'S ROLE-SET

Note: Role-set is a term used to signify the variety
and degree of relationships of an incumbent with
other role-players with whom he is in contact.
Such relationships at work may be primary or
secondary, all supplemented by extra-work and
more casual associations.

The nature of the hotel and catering industry is such that tension and stress do frequently arise. The impatient customer sets of a chain re-action at rush periods which permeates the entire line of the food and service provision: waiting staff, pantry workers, chefs and cooks, kitchen workers, bartenders, in fact anyone helping to get the great variety of orders out at speed. There is impatience, friction, holdups, priorities, lower-status people ordering higher-status people about, shouting, tears, protests, abuse in the back of the house, all on acc-ount of the anxiety to please the customer and (for some staff) to earn a direct reward. The only empirical evidence, repeatedly quoted in so-ciological texts with any relevance to catering, dates back to the war years, when Prof. Whyte and his team observed life in American restaur-ants and documented descriptively some of his findings. We have al-ready made reference to this study in a previous chapter. At the risk of repetition, we point once more to an urgent need for more social re-search based on an action frame of reference and participant-observer studies in the arena of the hotel, when inter-personal intimacy in de-partmental settings may be looked at (for the first time) in Britain, with the key objective of identifying the variables that hinder indust-rial harmony, of which massive labour turnover is only one of several indicators.

Turning from what Herzberg (26) has coined 'hygiene factors' to his 'motivators', we should like briefly to hypothesise on the 'formality' aspect of kitchen systems. We treated in our analysis things, people and events, and therefore the system of the kitchen, as an ideal type or typification of a social institution. In the formal organisational sense, legitimacy of conduct is usually backed by written rules such as job specifications, manuals of procedure, disciplinary codes, hygiene regulations, and sometimes policy directives, which the chef must foll-ow. But, deviations from ideal types, which are actually mixtures of different ideal types, help to identify a persistent problem faced by every formal organisation: how to keep staff reasonably satisfied while at the same time achieving its own goals effectively. We may hypothes-ise that such changes in a cook's or other occupational member's work routine, as we have discussed, can shift the aspirations of individuals from a more intrinsic to a more extrinsic reference point (in a contin-uum), when the individual's needs and the organisation's needs can only be co-ordinated (in the absence of a normative commitment to the employ-er, i.e. vested interest) by the application of the cash nexus. This point might constitute an additional variable in explaining partly at least Chivers' hint of a possible increase of militancy in the catering field.

Specific Influences on Occupational Role Performance in the Kitchen

These influences are two-fold: they derive from learned occupational behaviour and the cultural influences of the work setting itself. The workshop of the kitchen has few other purposes than cooking, unlike many othersettings, useable for a variety of purposes. Not only has a work setting its own informal rules and codes, which may or may not corresp-ond with the accepted occupational sentiments, but conduct in kitchens unencumbered by walls and partitions can be openly observed. This leaves some scope for the chef as social actor to perform at least in full view of his peers as an abating factor for depriving him of the audience of the patrons who sample his creations. When this occurs, personality characteristics, a particular philosophy towards his work and a special relationship with the ingredients he uses, merge to produce a professional identity. The example of Chef Breithaupt comes to mind for the illustration of our point. He terms his life-long interest in cooking as one in 'Modern Kitchenology', and with his new concepts brought a new excitement of discovery to his students. (27) His philosophy is that natural foods, properly prepared and combined, are the key to radiant health, and his approach, that of a 'Kitchen Symphony', which, with the kitchen herbs and spices correctly blended, would result in harmonious dishes, like the play on instruments from music scores. His relationship is with the ingredients, demonstrated by the 'note' of the 'nutmeg' in the symphony; that the little nut is played sotto voce (subdued voice), an accompaniment, but never solo. A few rappings on the grater with this little corrugated solid fellow over many kinds of broth adds aroma and the most seductive flavours.

A more current revolution in La Grande Cuisine has recently been reported in the Sunday Times Review, which stamps Michael Guerard, a French chef, as a social innovator in the sphere of food culture. (28) He goes much further than simply attempting to reconcile good eating with modest calorie intake. He appears to have started a movement in culinary events that supports the approach of a lighter style of cooking, simplicity, innermost flavour, an absence of water, the blending of vegetable and fresh fruit, the use of seaweed, nettle, pine needles, chicory and grass as ingredients, at the expense of butter, oil, cream and sugar. The younger culinary artists honour him, while some protagonists of the old school accuse him of ruining the great cultural heritage of France, because he does not operate 'by the book'. The questions sociologists interested in food culture will wish to probe are these: is chef Guerard concerned with health (he claims weight loss, arthritic pains and kidney trouble gone by eating his own creations and eating well); is he concerned with flavour (a recreator motivated by an overdue renaissance of French gastronomy); or does he practise alchemy (by following no cookery book or recipe); or, indeed, are we perhaps witnessing a gimmicky reaction of cost consciousness in the present austere climate? The passing of time will evidence the impact of the man and his philosophy.

These findings might cast a line to attract researchers in this country to get hooked on a most interesting and fertile field of investigation. A start has already been made by Stephen Mennell from the University of Exeter, on the 'Development of Cuisine and Culinary Taste in England and France'. His unpublished paper at a recent B.S.A. conference traces the evolutionary elements of food culture and the social class influences on gastronomy. Useful leads for further researching the hotel and catering industry could come from the Elias Papers (Blackwell, 1978 and B.J.S. Journal, 7(3), 1956) on the 'Civilising Process' and 'Problems of Involvement and Detachment', in which he discusses cooking routines, eating habits, table manners, hygiene and nutrition.

As the head chef's traditional authority is accepted, even copied by other aspirants in the kitchen, and the specialist tasks either performed on stations or by fewer incumbents in the smaller kitchen, the emergence of informal group ties has been less pronounced than in manufacturing industries. Among chefs, at least, the occupational affinity derives from an early occupational conditioning process, when the apprentice first enters the kitchen, and this is reinforced by customs, norms and practices that emphasise professional conduct and attire, as well as possible sanctions against an offender. The elaboration of formal roles and behaviour that conform to the unwritten sub-cultural codes appears, therefore, to matter more than the oft-quoted informal groupings referred to in management theory. How such behaviour expresses itself in the work environment of the hotel kitchen is now our task to illustrate.

The formal authority pattern tends to carry over into an informal one while, at the same time, the formal, hierarchical structure is still being adhered to. Age and experience rate higher than an attempted establishment of informal leadership, which if not backed by age and experience, is likely to be treated as rebellion. Informal associations tend to give chefs a feeling of insecurity and fear of the sack. When a chef reaches a position of authority, he will be expected, by the 'significant others', (his flock) to act in the traditional authoritative manner. The head chef is recognised as the principal social actor from whom the general attitude towards restaurant people derives. He feels that his department has made the customers' meal experience possible. But, no sooner is the food cooked (an effort of skill and several hours of preparation), than it is whipped away by the waiter, who then prepares the stage and receives all the glory. Another bone of contention is that the chef has had to undergo long training, but may earn less than the waiter, to him a mere servile plate carrier, whose knowledge of food and drink is highly questionable. Nor, in the chef's view, will the working waiter be a trained person. Thus, the battle of the hotplate goes on between chefs and waiters as all the kitchen brigade take their cue from the master. Were he not to give such a lead, the others of the brigade might even mistrust him. Were these others not to participate in open or symbolic abuse, it would be looked upon as an unforgiveable weakness. Of course, not all members of these occupational groups will wish to see this feud perpetuated.

The head chef is a supreme being, who will act out his role in an expected, traditional manner. If he is English, he may as likely as not gesticulate with his hands and put on a foreign accent, as he has seen it done before he was promoted. Young commis will do likewise and so adopt the customary socialisation pattern in the trade. The head chef may well be a tyrant, but the brigade members will work with him and show him deference, because the accepted sub-culture associates aggressiveness with expertise. Enter a new chef and he is viewed with suspicion until the group has seen the quantity and quality of his knives and other tools, seen his monogrammed whites and his well-laundered hats; and, above all, seen his degree of skill, exhibited by the speed of cutting and slicing, by his understanding of a French service and French phrases, the mispronounciation of which is quite acceptable. This testing period may take some time, when signs and signals of acceptance into the group will gradually emerge. If, however, the newcomer is well-known in the trade, or has worked in a famous hotel, or indeed, if he has some known culinary association (perhaps written a book), rapport is much more easily established, although name-dropping must eventually be supported by the display of skill. To be observed using a cookery book is not common, but acceptable, when engaging in discussion of a classical dish. Reference books on the shelves may be seen

and used for checking on the finer culinary points, but not be otherwise used if professional competence is not to come into question.

The status distinction between chef and cook will be well known. But
the social order in the kitchen also symbolically distinguishes variations in the form of dress. White trousers are immediately associated
with H.M. Forces or Hospital catering and not acceptable. Cloth butt-
ons are held in higher esteem than metal or bone. The height of a
chef's hat indicates his rank in the social order, while small, sensible
paper or cloth hats are associated with 'cowboys'. Aprons must be of a
length just below the knee as if worn above the knee they are associated with the worst American cookery, or a lack of feeling for food.
Neckerchiefs are white, of best Irish linen, but tend to become burned
during work, so chefs are forced to change them frequently and use up
a lot of these. To economise, the chefs of one well-known West End
hotel, for example, were issued with pink and white serviettes to be
used as neck scarves. This wear was at first considered objectionable
and greatly resisted. Notwithstanding this early disfavour, other establishments have adopted this practice and a number of chefs can be
seen wearing similar neckerchiefs, which by now have assumed the status
symbol of merit through association with the class hotel. Pencils or
pens in a chef's hat appear to denote a person in authority, but are
otherwise the only sign of an academic association, administrative
activity or paperwork. It is also the custom for a chef to have a
number of kitchen cloths swirling from his apron, although needed for
functional reasons, but this conveys the impression that he is very
busy and it registers an atmosphere of service-giving. The wearing of
keys is associated with responsibility. These are usually tucked just
inside the apron, with one or two of the keys just showing. Collar and
tie is worn only by the head chef, who also wears shoes when other
staff wear clogs or boots.

Although we end our discussion on chefs and cooks here, the subject
is by no means exhausted. However, we must now briefly return to our
humblest role player - the kitchen porter. On the evidence, he is
never accepted into the informal group of the cooking staff and if
allowed into the same staff room at all, a corner will be allocated to
him. Chefs do not think of the kitchen porter with any degree of compassion, but see and accept him as a stereotype with low intelligence,
who is there to do the dirty work. In times of acute staff shortage,
but rarely so in the bigger hotels, the ambitious porter may be called
upon to assume one or more of the roles of fish filleter, salad hand,
vegetable or breakfast cook, or even be trained as a butcher's assistant, and in this sense influence his work routine. Many porters have
been found not to seek responsibility, but will perform such jobs as
cleaning the chef's office, his knives, fetch coffee or beer, see to
his laundry or place bets for the chef if he trusts him with money.
Recruitment is mostly on a casual basis. In London's Soho, the so-
called 'winos' congregate in a particular area to await the chef's call
to do some kitchen portering for payment by the hour; and as the true
story goes, a Jamaican porter was recently awarded chocolate medals as
payment for overtime work, with which he was highly delighted. Clearly,
there lingers a question mark on the representativeness of these findings which justified our later in-depth investigation of this particular stigmatised occupational group. (29)

Trade Union Membership

This highly relevant problem deserves some, if only too brief, attention. We have seen that there prevails a caste system in low-grade occupations, without any compensatory provision for dirty or demeaning work. Job dissatisfaction and boredom also occur, but at different points of time in certain of the occupations, additionally influenced by the variable of personal attitudes.

On financial rewards, our survey revealed that 95% of the kitchen porters in some of the West and East Midlands towns and cities covered, earned below the average of a manual worker's wages, this confirming the Hotels and Catering E.D.C. findings (as per Manpower Policy Report, 1975) and the information from the N.E.S. (New Earnings Survey) that the average earnings of full-time manual catering workers were the lowest of all industrial orders included in the N.E.S. However, the position has since somewhat improved by revised legislation. The question why unions have found it so difficult to achieve a measure of organisation in this industry is therefore relevant to our discussion.

Organising the Unorganisable

Dr. Gerald Mars (30) has recently completed a project on trade union membership in this industry and, in discussing the difficulties of establishing a negotiating machinery, traced a close relationship to the heterogeneity of the produce and labour markets. Three main problems for any union intent to organise hotel workers are identified: the great variety of staff grades and their differing commitments to the industry; the geographical scatter of the various catering and hotel units; and the range of sizes of establishments where we find a high preponderance of small units. Three main concerns arise out of the foregoing three problems: firstly, how a union can succeed in organising a work force in view of the high labour turnover; secondly, how it can do it in view of the concentration of a fairly small number of workers within individual units; and how it can do so in view of the problems of geographical dispersal.

If unions had an infinite number of organisers and ample resources themselves, they could probably overcome these problems. Dr. Mars goes on to say: it is, for example, rather difficult to service a membership that may extend over many thousands of smaller catering units in such diverse industrial settings in Great Britain, as can be seen in Figure 10. Or, how with a labour turnover as it is, a union might keep track of its members and collect regular payments of dues? But, those are not the only problems. Unions may see little incentive in using up manpower and finance for recruitment in hotels if the return in membership achieved does not warrant the effort. The mature union with a stable membership would probably look to other industries for recruitment. Another question for a union is also whether it should confine its interests to areas more adjacent to its current grades and industries, or break new ground in an area of potential membership. As we have already said, the advent of statutory wage regulation has, to some extent, alleviated the poor conditions of employment for many hotel and catering workers who have tended to lag behind other industries and services. This, argues Prof. Medlik, has raised the status

and morale of the work force and compelled the less efficient employers
to adhere to minimum conditions. In consequence, these regulations
acted as a disincentive to unionisation in the sense that an official
body of interested parties (including the unions themselves) is in being to determine wages and conditions rather than follow the usual predominant union activity or plant bargaining, as is customary in private
industry. Trade union policy is also influenced by its membership.
It must normally be kept within the bounds of the wishes of members.
Additionally, the history and orientation of the labour force is a
further important criterion. How, for example, can foreign workers
best be recruited if they speak no English; and if, say, Spanish workers are considered, there is in their own country a history of repress-
ion of unions. Further problems arise out of the split shift practice
and unsocial working hours, which make branch meetings difficult in
what little time there is left for rest and leisure. There is also a
high proportion of casual workers, especially among the kitchen porters, which adds to the difficulties of recruitment and achieving commitment, not least on the part of women, predominant in certain categories of hotel and catering work.

The Need for Negotiating Machinery

The hotel and catering industry has more recently experienced not only
structural changes, by way of mergers and takeovers, but also a trend
towards more democratic forms of social control at the workplace, making for an increasing desire for trade union membership.   Dr. Mars
explains that where a union has no historical base, organisation of a
work force is difficult and a great deal depends on the attitudes of
officials and the policy of the union concerned. Also, maturing unions
have experienced a change in their role. Original concerns have become displaced over time, worker and union interest may differ in orientation or the talent and skills of the union official may slant more
towards negotiating than organising or recruiting. Furthermore, the
task of organising a new industry may be left to officials who have no
close knowledge of the industry, vital for strategy and tactics. All
this explains the insignificant membership among menial work groups in
this industry to date.

NOTES TO CHAPTER 5

1.   Whyte, William Foote (1948) 'Human Relations in the
        Restaurant Industry', McGraw-Hill, London

2.   Sommer, Robert (1974) 'Tight Spaces (Hard Architecture
        and How to Humanize It)', Prentice-Hall, New Jersey

3.   Buchanan-Taylor, W. (1944) 'One More Shake', Heath Cranton,
        London

4.   Green, Bryan and Johns, Edward (1966) 'An Introduction to
        Sociology', Pergamon Press

5.   Smith, Russell Gordon (1930) 'Fugitive Papers', Columbia
        University Press, New York

6.   Benedict, Ruth (1948) 'Patterns of Culture', Houghton
        Mifflin, Boston

7.   Sommer, Robert (1969) 'Personal Space (The Behavioural
        Basis of Design)', Prentice-Hall, New Jersey

8.   Etzioni, Amitai (1960) 'Two Approaches in Organizational
        Analysis: A Critique and a Suggestion', Admin. Science
        Quarterly, Vol.5,pp.257-278 Note:(as quoted in Silverman,
        see Note 9)

9.   Silverman, David (1970) 'The Theory of Organisations',
        Heinemann, London

10.   Medlik, S. (1972) 'Profile of the Hotel and Catering
        Industry', Heinemann, London

11.   Hertzler, J.O. (1961) 'American Social Institutions: A
        Sociological Analysis', Allyn & Bacon Inc., Boston

12.   Gellerman, Saul W. (1960) 'The Uses of Psychology in
        Management', Collier-Macmillan, London

13.   Perrow, Charles (1970) 'Organizational Analysis: A Sociolog-
        ical View', Tavistock Publications, London

14.   Dix, Colin. Lecturer in Reception Operations and Hotel
        Personnel Management, Middlesex Polytechnic. Interviewed
        by author July, 1973

15.   De Boni, G. and Charles, F.F. (1962) 'Hotel Organisation,
        Management and Accountancy', Pitman, London

16.   Whyte, William Foote (1948) 'Human Relations in the Restaurant
        Industry', Cornell Quarterly,1948. (Special Issue - no
        serial number)

17. Morel, J.J. (1966) 'Contemporary Catering', Barrie & Rockliff, London

18. Front page article on 'Pirate Hotels', Catering Times, 21.8.75 (Issue 611)

19. Gunn, Brian. Head of Department of Cookery, Westminster Technical College. Interviewed by author, July, 1975

20. Lyons, Dale. Senior Lecturer in Hotel Management, Middlesex Polytechnic. Interviewed by author, July, 1975

21. Chivers, T.S. (1973) 'The Proletarianisation of a Service Worker', Sociological Review, Vol.21

22. Cooley, Charles Horton (1956) 'Primary Groups and Primary Ideals', in Borgotta, E. and Meyer, H. 'Sociological Theory: Present-Day Sociology from the Past', Alfred Knopf, New York

23. Chivers, T.S. (1971) 'Study of Chefs and Cooks', Report on Findings of a Survey, Hotel and Catering Industry Training Board. , London

24. Ingham, Geoffrey K. (1970) 'Size of Industrial Organisation and Worker Behaviour', Cambridge University Press, Cambridge

25. Merton, Robert K. (1956) 'The Role-Set: Problems in Sociological Theory', British Journal of Sociology, Vol.8

26. Herzberg, R.F., Pugh, D.S., Hickson, D.J. and Hinings, C.R. (1971) 'Writers on Organisation', Penguin, London

27. Breithaupt, Herman A. (Master Chef and Teacher), as told by Betty L. Herring (1972) 'Chef Herman's Story, How We Started Students on Successful Food Careers', Institutions Feeding Magazine, Chicago, Illinois

28. Wechsberg, Joseph, 'Revolution in La Grande Cuisine', Sunday Times Weekly Review, August 1975

29. Finch, Clive. Senior Lecturer in Food and Beverage Operations, Middlesex Polytechnic. Interviewed by author, July 1975

30. Mars, Gerald. Reader in Social Anthropology, Middlesex Polytechnic, Course Unit, published by Open University, 1975

6 The kitchen porter surveyed in the West Midlands

Preliminary considerations on profile, identity and method

In the context of performable skills and tasks that normally form part of the day to day work environment of the kitchen porter, our investigation of the respondents' state of health and fitness has enabled us to construct a 'physical capacities appraisal' (see exhibit on health). The more general profile of the kitchen porter representative sample is, however, contained in a whole range of personal characteristics, each exerting a specific influence on behaviour. It is this 'facesheet' data and its significance that constitute one important dimension of an incumbent's profile, while another is his identity. If the experiences of integration in society are seen as a process of upgrading, whereby new roles are performed at the various developmental states, and identify representing progressively differentiated meanings of the 'self' (acquired from the successive stages in life of learning the norms and values of a society), then an occupational member's identity kit (such as dress, tools or other symbols) will project a meaningful self-identification to those others who are important in an incumbent's life.

What we intend here is to give sufficient biographical information to build up a viable profile and to offer an aid in the tentative discovery of positive or negative (or, if it be the case, amorphous) characteristics and orientations of our respondents in comparison with some broad, generalised findings from such other research in this country or empirical work elsewhere, as may be meaningful for the discovery of particular tendencies that give substance and validity to specific types of behaviour. In this respect, and despite the limitation of research resources, valuable spade work has been done. It is generally accepted that managements and public base phenomena on casual observation rather than an attempt at an orderly, scientific approach to facts. But what this has in common with our more methodical investigation is the awareness that there is a social problem that needs to be tackled. The propositions of a social scientist in the explanation of events have, however, to be more tentative than those of the natural scientist as the latter has access to highly developed theoretical structures by way of sharp hypothesis-testing of empirical work that the social scientist, dealing with the less predictable human in exploratory terms, cannot match.

Success if nevertheless still attainable in a more general assessment of the stigma concept and in the development of some theoretical formulations. It will also be noted that the ingredients of a number of our propositions find frequest support in more than one of the exhibits. This is unavoidable, not only because these basically constitute a family cluster to project the kitchen porter's stigmatising condition which the data is designed to verify or test, but also on account of the correlational empirical information itself as presented in our method of classifying exhibits that aim to reflect the common life/work situations and hence personally experienced stigmatisation.

Terminology

The multiplicity of terms in respect of identity quoted in behavioural literature, such as personal, social, cultural, derived and occupational, would not make some agreed inter-disciplinary definitions amiss. Until these are agreed, we shall resort to some working definitions for practical use. To take identity as an umbrella term first, it can conveniently be defined as part of the self and derived from one's active participation in social relationships. Cultural norms require us to present to others our most acceptable self, whilst our perceived identity is announced to the world gradually. If accepted, it becomes the root in us to help in an awareness of who we really are. Clothing and dress is used to tell the world of our social identity, enabling us to claim social group membership by gender, age, religion or marital status, as the case may be. In occupational terms, personal identity is reflected in the role one plays, and the question, 'Who am I?' is increasingly seen by many social interpreters in an occupational sense. Dress communicates social identity and in conjunction with names helps to validate status change. Manner, too, person-located as it usually is, signals the mode of acting out roles so as to mask our personal self by the presentation of the social self.

It will be noted that the nomenclature 'Exhibits' has been used for the thirteen sections into which the survey results are divided. This division has been retained from our original (unpublished) M.Phil. thesis entitled 'Occupational Stigmatisation in the British Hotel and Catering Inudstry', lodged with the University of Aston in September, 1976.

Sample Composition of the Kitchen Porters

Population of Sample Hotels in the West Midlands 161

less hotels, mostly family units and too
small to employ kitchen porters 40

establishments found to be non-residential ... 11

hotels where kitchen porters speak no English.. 3

hotels where kitchen porters could not be
made available for interviews 7

hotels where managers refused to co-operate .. 7

hotels where the interviewer could not
establish contact with management 13

hotels where various reasons for refusing
access have been given 9

hotel where a respondent had been
interviewed previously in another
geographical area 1

Total Number excluded   91
Number of Hotels where interviews have taken place   70

Note: The seventy hotels were spread over the cities and towns of Birmingham, Coventry, Derby, Leamington Spa, Leicester, Stoke-on-Trent, Shrewsbury, Stratford-upon-Avon, Wolverhampton, Worcester and Walsall.

EXHIBIT I. PERSONAL DETAILS

EX. 1.1 Age

We have adopted an age categorisation of three groups from which it is apparent that some eighty per cent of the respondents are over the age of 35, a stage in life when normal expectations in our society are seen for some degree of skill, in an occupation to have already been achieved. Reasons why respondents are at the time of interview engaged in kitchen portering will, however, emerge from subsequent parts of our analysis. Statistically calculated, the average age in the sample is 47, but just about half of all respondents are aged 50 or over. The under-35 age group contains few people under 30 and only three respondents under the age of twenty. (A backward boy of 17, an Italian who speaks no English and a 16-year-old, whose first job this is). It would seem that this work holds no popularity even in a bridging stage for the group. It is likely (as will be shown later) that specific life experience has already acted to spoil the endeavour to achieve a so-called 'respectable' occupational identity for the age group from 29-35.

General Observations concerning the Age Factor

Few surveys do not include age per se as a variable of some consequence although, made accountable on its own for differences in occupational behaviour, it will furnish us only with incomplete concepts and spurious explanations. Nevertheless, age is to be regarded as more than a background variable that reveals merely biological maturation. Indeed, it has a social meaning in the respondent's life cycle as successive phases signify the presence or absence of such matters as emotional attachments, his identity-shaping propensities, distinctive patterns of orientation towards the social environment by way of dependency (or otherwise) on public support, social isolation, obsolescence and a rejection by a society whose time-sense and culture make him 'old' at a certain chronological age and worthless as a regular, productive achiever, as is often the case with the inactive kitchen porter.

In the case of the kitchen porter, the greatest instability tends to be evident in the mid-life years, when he realises that the anticipated road in work socialisation bears no reflection to earlier ambitions and hopes as concerns his life/work pattern.

Comment: frustration is a psychological phenomenon which appears when a subject's needs and ambitions have remained unachieved and evidences itself in certain habitual reaction patterns at the workplace. Case studies in depth could throw more light on this. The lack of achievement in late middle age for most of the respondents is evidenced in the incumbency of their present 'unskilled' occupations.

The inferior behaviour pattern of the kitchen porter is likely to be a causal factor of advancing age. The older the respondent, the more precious become the remaining years and the more alarming the

FIGURE 10.
West Midland Area Sample Stratification Scheme

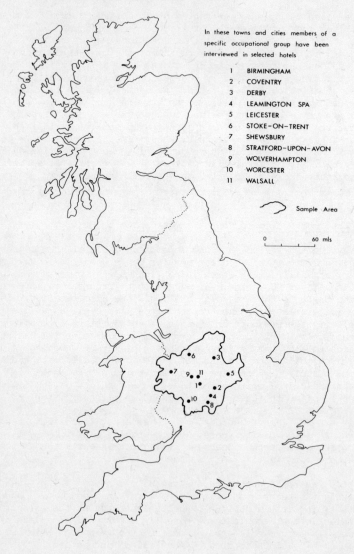

In these towns and cities members of a
specific occupational group have been
interviewed in selected hotels

1   BIRMINGHAM
2   COVENTRY
3   DERBY
4   LEAMINGTON SPA
5   LEICESTER
6   STOKE-ON-TRENT
7   SHEWSBURY
8   STRATFORD-UPON-AVON
9   WOLVERHAMPTON
10   WORCESTER
11   WALSALL

Sample Area

0   60 mls

realisation of being for long hours chained to the kitchen sink. Consequential rebellion may then take a variety of forms. However, participant observation and further managerial evidence would be needed to
support this proposition of unstableness in work and inferior behaviour
towards others in society. Exhibits 2,5 and 9 provide some evidence in
support and should be seen in conjunction with our observations in
Chapter .

EX. 1.2 Sex

It will be recalled that we are concerned with the West Midlands and
surrounding regions. Of the kitchen porters interviewed, some 90% were
men. The small number of women found were older and did the lighter
work or were not engaged full time. One Birmingham hotel employed
women only with a preference for Jamaicans. As to the reasons for this,
the manager there explained: 'Firstly, they are strong; secondly, they
need the job, are stable and do not cost too much; and thirdly, they
don't drink.'

General Observations

In the main, employers do not engage in deep study of such reference
material as exists from past research when deciding whether to employ
males or females for certain types of work. They rely more on the
cultural norms on which their personal beliefs are based than on evidence or the application of data. If they did, some divergences in
specific abilities would probably be found as concerns, at least, the
kind of work kitchen porters have to perform. Men are, in general,
more physically aggressive and likely to be praised for it. They possess greater muscular strength and, in accord with social expectations,
display such prowess in some kinds of work situation. Men appear also
to like, in general, to work with 'things' as contrasted with 'people',
and they are not averse to risk. Work for women has, in the past, not
been found instrumental to the same extent (this attitude is now changing); they are more likely to conform to rules, act in accord with expectations, have been found to be more 'service-orientated', less violent - although aggression is frequently expressed in verbal form - and
less desirous to compete. It is possible that some employers will dis-
criminate between these male/female characteristics.

Women are, therefore, less likely to become applicants for kitchen
porter jobs. Management regards them as less suitable and less available for such work. In hotel kitchens, as also in industrial kitchens,
the work may be heavy (to include large quantities of pots of all sizes)
split-shift hours, an environment of heat and steam, with a constant
flow of unpleasant, filthy and tiring chores. Institutional catering
offers lighter work, better social hours and is often local, and therefore a more likely avenue for female job seekers in the catering field.

EX. 1.3 Country of Birth and Nationality

Our random sample reveals that close on 84% of the kitchen porters were
born in Britain (assuming their mother tongue to be English) and almost
87% are of British nationality. We stress that we made no attempt to
seek out porters who could speak English. It would seem, therefore,
that respondents working in this occupation in our geographical area

of investigation are predominantly British. Some twelve per cent of
the respondents were made up of persons from British Guiana, Antigua,
Uganda, Jamaica, the Ukraine and Italy. This situation is in great
contrast to London, where some of the large West End hotels can point
to some thirty different nationals on their staff.

  Comments: by and large, nationality is a variable of a more subtle
kind. It is easy enough to code it, but its meaning to the respondent
is less easy to ascertain. Helpful as it may be to find an individual
at some point on the social map, one has to bear in mind the influence
of group differences such as age, sex, religion, class, region and the
like, all holding a perceived social importance; and exercising care
before proclaiming of global stereotypes whether they share cultural
attributes derived from inborn differences or not. The British - explains Prof. Gould - have not been so vocal or obsessed as some other
'nations' with these finer points of national identity. Since there
has not been in Britain in the past a problem to the same extent of
moulding varied characteristics into a common set of national experiences, no explicit philosophy has emerged for those that are peripheral to the majority society.(1) Leaving aside the problem of what
makes someone an English, rather than a British, national, one can say
in general that national character transcends local and regional ties,
although a sense of felt national identity can vary and seems to refer
to generalised conceptions of the presumed set of personality patterns
that typify people in entire large societies.

  The basic personality structure of our kitchen porters as a sub-
cultural unit, linked behaviourally to the work situation, need not
necessarily be an implicit or explicit guiding concept in terms of
national character for the purpose of understanding the social relationships of these respondents, although such character may affect the
'presentation of the self' in the everyday existence.

EX 1.4 Marital Status

The situation at the time of the interviews was again revealing. Nearly 72% of the kitchen porters were (for the time being) single. This
is made up by 15% of those widowed, separated and divorced; and close
to 57% single persons. Since, as we have found, respondents consist
of 90% male members, a predominant number of these are seemingly without familial support, whatever form it may take. Only 28% of the interviewees stated that they were married. Since 64% of those (we assume) that are single had no children, we may tentatively conclude that
by far the largest percentage of these porters is highly mobile and
without family 'incumbrances' that normally inhibit the high geographical mobility of manual workers. Of the widowed, separated, divorced
and married, some 36% have children. That group is made up of 43% of
the respondents, of which 22% have more than three children.

  Observations: before commenting on the marital status in our society in general terms, we mention here that we are fully aware of the
socio-economic influences that make a stable and conventional family
life possible. The marital state, in general, in our society is more
highly valued than the unmarried state. Ralph B. Turner refers to the
attractive man (or woman), with no discoverable personal deficiencies
who, failing to marry, represents a continuing puzzle to those about

him, and is likely to be plagued with questions and insinuations about his status of singleness. Dennis Marsden found that the lack of a spouse also 'throws a person out of key with married friends', while G.H. Mead, when referring to status validation, suggests that marriage remains a key mechanism for 'validating' personal adequacy, heterosexual normality and personal maturity. People become anxious about all these matters when marriage is unduly delayed, fails or breaks up. For men, in general, at least - but rarely for the kitchen porter - there are limited alternative arenas for social validation in terms of career success or positions of power in communal or government service. Bell makes reference also to the social penalties (and rewards) of being married. The prestige rating, aided by the ritual of the ceremony, is higher, financial credit rating is better and the police award more credibility and respectability to man with a wife, even if he were to be questioned at a late hour, perhaps in a hilarious state.(2) The moral implications on the 'unmarried state' are therefore considerable. The bachelor fails in his social duty, shirks family responsibilities, has his personal competence and normality questioned, is labelled as disoriented, incompetent, maladjusted and, according to Kinsey, somehow associated with homosexuality. The general implications are clear: there is still a social stigma on the unmarried and marriage is at the present time still seen as a key integrating mechanism in our society.

EX. 1.5 Religion

The survey results showed some 55% of the respondents to be Protestants, that is 7.5% Protestant and 47.5% Church of England, to be exact. The second biggest category comprised Catholics, 24.5%. Some 12% chose not to answer this question, which leaves 6% other religions and just over 1% agnostics. We have not been able to investigate the degree of religiosity of these various adherents in terms of church attendance. Other studies have, however, managed to establish the notion of a higher rate of church attendance among persons in higher status occupations.(3) Hamilton, investigating the frequency of church attendance of Catholic and Protestant workers in America, found 86% of the Catholics in clerical and sales occupations reporting church attendance once a month as compared with 73% in the operative category. Similarly, 59% of Protestants in clerical occupations report attending church once a month, while 49% of the operatives did. Thus, not only is there a lower church attendance by lower status occupations, but also by Protestant, as compared to Catholic religion.(4) What little evidence we have gleaned from the comments on the questionnaires concerning the low-status kitchen porter respondents does not induce us to dispute the above findings on church attendance.

It may be helpful to add some general comments on this aspect arising out of research. Religiosity expresses itself in various ways. The social dimension embraces mostly membership of religious organisations and church attendance. The cultural orientation may be projected by a respondent's commitment to religious beliefs and devotional matters expressed in prayer. The former involves social inter-action to express religion, the latter concerns the cognitive content of specific beliefs. The firmness of association will vary, of course, with the belief held, but the denominational inclinations as such constitute but one segment of a person's identity, as well as cutting across other aspects of his participation in society, correlational to it. Participation in

organised religious activities varies, but would primarily depend on individual need, social pressures, the availability of alternative activities
or the availability of alternative means for reinforcement of basic beliefs.
People over 50 years of age have been found to be more intense in their religion.
In Britain, regular church attendance tails off in the mid-sixties of one's age
for all religious bodies (claims Roland Robertson).(5)As is the case with all
other foregoing variables, age, sex, marital status, class and religion,
all are inter-related, while the latter may also influence work attitudes. Robertson refers to a disproportionately large number of single
people among the religiously active along social and cultural dimensions
a greater devotion on the part of widowers and many childless couples in
England. These relationships evidence the complexity of the interplay
between religious and non-religious factors.

EX. 1.6 Education and Schooling

Of our kitchen porter respondents, two-thirds or close to 66% liked
school and 30% did not. (A small number did not answer). Although this
is the case, 51% said that they had to leave school at the age of fourteen or below and some two per cent had no schooling at all. Some 69%
went either to an elementary or secondary modern school (some 26% only
to elementary school). Not one respondent went to a grammar school,
but 28% went to other schools, including schools in other countries,
denominational schools or schools in other regions. These do not include technical schools, which three per cent of the respondents attend-
ed. Nearly 96% obtained no school leaving certificate and 93% had no
other educational qualifications.

On this evidence, school is quite popular with kitchen porters. As
practically all the respondents who are of British nationality have
neither a leaving certificate, nor other educational qualifications, the
question how far this disadvantage constitutes a serious handicap for
occupational mobility needs to be looked at, although it will become
clearer later when we consider housing and physical disabilities, that
school experience is not the only factor that contributes to blocking
the mobility for improvement.

We may add by way of general observation that education is often
thought to be a crucial variable in terms of research. It is correlated
to length of schooling, to the attainment of occupational skills, to
achievement generally, to earning power and other credentials of competence. Alan Little (6), for example, refers to British evidence extracted in 1966 from the sample census and a follow-up study by the Department of Education and Science, that 40-year-old men with degrees
earned about twice the amount of the national average, and those with
an H.N.D. one third above it. Schooling and the length of it rate with
employers and, not infrequently, where such schooling was obtained also.
Little raises important questions: how far is education the determinant
of the sort of people or society we are? Or, does it merely reflect and
reinforce other more basic features of ourselves and our society? In
macro terms, are countries richer because they spend more on education,
or do rich countries spend more because they can afford it and pressure
is on them to do so? Of interest to us is undoubtedly whether education
reinforces a respondent's existing genetic and social capacities.
Little seems to share the view (with other critics) that there are more
fundamental questions about a person than his education. To begin with,
length of schooling is not to be equated with 'learning' as the latter

does not necessarily take place in school. Work performance depends on
a host of other talents also and education has, furthermore, multiple
functions, of which job preparation is but one. It is suggested by him
that compared with other forces in our society, education, as an influence on one's life chances, is limited. What broad research findings
do, however, stand out are those associated with extra-school influence and
those of particular parental interest, which make an impact in the earlier years of development of a person.

EXHIBIT II WORK EXPERIENCE

Respondents were offered the option of answering any or all of seventeen alternative questions. The popularity of the questions chosen for
answers may give us an indication of their relevance to the respondents,
while the predominance of feeling from all respondents offers an indication of what they regard as an important experience associated with
their work.

Question: What are your main reasons for working as kitchen porter?

		%
1.	Because one can make friends at the work place	79.1
2.	Because such people are always wanted	71.6
3.	Because one can get a meal when one is hungry	65.7
4.	Because it requires no training	62.7
5.	Because it is a good career to be in	61.2
6.	Because no brainwork is needed	55.2
7.	Because the place of work is near home	50.7
8.	Because it is the only job I could get	49.3
9.	Because it is warm in the winter	46.3
10.	Because there is no need to accept responsibility	43.3
11.	Because one can live-in	28.4
12.	Because one can leave at short notice	26.9
13.	Because one can avoid one's family responsibilities	19.4
14.	Because one is disabled	14.9
15.	Because one can get away from family for season	10.4
16.	Because one can work in a place where one is not known	7.5
17.	Because one can get paid the same day	0.0

Out of 17 questions asked:

3% of the respondents answered between thirteen and seventeen questions
17% of the respondents answered between one and four questions
26% of the respondents answered between nine and twelve questions
54% of the respondents answered between five and eight questions

showing a preference for answering between five and eight questions out
of seventeen.

Comments: if one may venture an interpretation of these expressed feelings, it would seem that social support on the job, the knowledge that
one is able to find work quickly to find the means to survive, and the
possibility of getting on with the job without undue formality and initiation appear to suit a high percentage of kitchen porters in the
West Midlands area.

Evidently, questions which represent a slur on their character, proficiency in occupation and implication of doubtful financial standing are

less popular. Personal needs, such as food, the convenience of proximity of the workplace to home and a comfortable work environment are sought after, but the taking of responsibility is less so, and the wish for independence does not make living-in as attractive to kitchen porters as is generally assumed in the industry.

We would suggest for the possible future researcher, intending to manipulate the statistical information in a more sophisticated way, to cluster the variables under main headings for the purposes of correlation. Thus, 'working conditions' would head training, leaving, environmental, pay and fringe benefit questions. 'Reasons for Working' would include type of work, how it can be obtained, its proximity to home, the degree of responsibility, occupational mobility and physical capacity to perform the tasks. The rest of the options would fit under some kind of head that indicates an 'evasion of personal responsibilities'. Getting away from one's family for the season or to avoid maintenance and/or seek to work in a place where one is not known, would fit under such a heading.

We have already referred to Goffman's stigma concepts as applicable to the physically disabled. (7) (See Chapter 3 above). The question of mortality and morbidity will be looked at again in Exhibit XI, in the light of our empirical data. At this point of our investigation, we merely draw attention to the seemingly low percentage of respondents (some 15%) who do not concede that disability is their main reason for working as kitchen porters, when, at the same time, 50% state that this is the only job they could get and some 60% suffer from a more serious disablement. This might well bear out Goffman's contention that those whose identity has become spoiled develop a strategy designed to hide their constant precariousness from the work-a-day world. Hence, the denial that incapacity forced them into this work, or that it is not work facilitating career progression (61%). Not being able to find another job than kitchen portering need not be due to disability. At the same time, all the interviewees did, however, work in this occupation when the survey was conducted.

A Possible Hypothesis

There is an inverse relationship between the level of occupational stigma and an individual's repertoire of possible roles.

Comments: the relevance of this exhibit to this hypothesis is only partial. The comments here should be seen in conjunction with those in Chapter 5 above and Exhibit 13 below, dealing with leisure and social roles of the incumbent. It will be noted here that close to 80% of the sample regard as one of their main reasons for working as kitchen porter the opportunity to make friends at the work place. Not only has this been shown to be fallacious, in the majority of cases, but few friendships are in fact struck. The reasons are obvious. The kitchen porter ranks at the lowest level in the kitchen hierarchy, has to wash up when the cooks and chefs have finished their work, works usually alone at the sink and is frequently the only kitchen porter on duty. For good measure, noise in the part of the kitchen or scullery where he works may be such as to make conversation extremely difficult. Only a small percentage say that the work enables them to try out pastures new or discard accepted family roles or responsibilities for the time being.

EXHIBIT III WORK ATTITUDES

In this part of the questionnaire also respondents could opt to answer
any or all of the twenty attitude possibilities offered. We have once
more arranged the data in such a manner as to reveal the number of
questions chosen and the predominant attitudes on matters uppermost in
the minds of the respondents. Attitude questions often embrace Herzberg's 'hygiene' and 'motivating' factors, where hygiene conditions
are a necessary but not a sufficient condition for a porter's willingness to continue working and where they, by themselves, are not considered to be motivating the worker. We have ourselves already made reference to the instrumentality of the kitchen porter's work values
(Chapters 2,5 and 7 in this study) and his awareness of the scant regard employers pay to the need for an element of intrinsity or appropriate extrinsic needs for that matter. Hence, the bewilderment of employers in the industry to comprehend the 'reluctant robot'.

Question: What is your general opinion about the work of kitchen portering?

%

1. That training is not given for this work   86.6
2. That the job requires a good deal of initiative   59.7
3. That chances of promotion are not good   58.2
4. That working in a hotel is better for a kitchen porter than
    working in a restaurant   58.2
5. That the job is badly paid   55.2
6. That work in a high-class hotel is better for a kitchen porter   55.2
7. That work in a good area in any hotel is better than work
    in a poorer area and a good hotel   55.2
8. That one never does anything creative to satisfy customer
    or hotel guest   46.3
9. That no one ever takes notice of a kitchen porter's
    ideas and suggestions   43.3
10. That work mates judge one by the work one does rather
    than by the sort of person one is   41.8
11. That the work is a drudge   38.8
12. That the job carries no security   35.8
13. That the job requires no initiative   32.8
14. That one's prestige at the work place is low because of
    the type of work one does   20.9
15. That one is the target for abuse by other kitchen staff   20.9
16. That it could be done by a machine   19.4
17. That training is needed for this work   19.4
18. That one's status is low because the manager never speaks
    to a kitchen porter   9.0
19. That one cannot tell people outside what work one does or
    they would look down on one   6.0
20. That one is isolated from other people   3.0

Out of twenty questions asked:

Less than two per cent of the respondents answered between sixteen
and twenty questions. Some 13% of the respondents between eleven and
fifteen questions. 28% of the respondents answered between one and

five questions and 57% of the respondents answered between six and ten questions, showing a preference for answering between six and ten questions out of twenty.

Comments: some 87% of the respondents appear to have an awareness of what possible training might entail if only it were given. A mere 19% think that training is needed and 21% that the work could be done by a machine. (We have drawn attention to the deficiences of mechanical means in Figure 7 and to training in Part 9 of Chapter 5). It seems clear that managements do not find it expedient to orient kitchen porters on such matters as proficient work flow, avoidance of breakages, treatment of implements according to composition of materials they are made of, the effective use of detergents and various other matters we have already suggested. Why it is that so few of the porters consider it necessary to be trained for operating as plongeurs is to some extent explained by their remarks upon our re-examination of the schedules. We give a few examples of their responses from a random check:-

For Training:

Standards of cleanliness must be preserved;

One has to be shown what needs to be done;

Training is needed in the beginning;

I have had a lot of previous experience, need less help.

Not appreciative of the need for training:

A child can do it;
The job is simple;
It's unskilled, just common sense;
One has to get used to it;
Training depends on the 'gaffer';
They show you and you get on with it;
One just needs an interest in tidying up;
I don't need training as long as I know my job;
No one takes any notice of what work I do;
I just do what needs to be done.

It appears to us that the need for formal training is really subject to one's philosophy on the question of the meaning of 'skill'. As this kind of work is referred to as unskilled by all parties involved, the general expectation is that one steps up to the sink and just does it. The very fact that some 60% of the respondents see a need for much initiative itself contradicts the denial for the requirement of systematic training, which appears to be seen as narrowly task-related and, in ignorance of its wider implication for the employer and the psychological needs (self actualisation is a term used by R. Blaunder in the context of alienation) of the performer. In all our endeavours to find a definition in the current sociological literature of what an 'unskilled' worker is, we can trace references only to the difficulty of attaching a 'precise meaning' to the term. (Caplow) (8). This is not surprising, as in our view there is no such animal. There are degrees of skill in all occupational tasks, which are subject to technological, attitudinal

and perceptual variations over time. We should like to see the word
'unskilled' removed from all official statistics; that would be a good
start to adjust distorted values on this question.

The association of the kitchen porter's image with low levels of
skill, low educational attainment, the absence of any formal or systematic training, low pay and instability (as defined in our Glossary) is
indicated by the expressed feelings of their perceived marginality:

My work is degrading, I get depressed at times;
It is not much of a job, I am afraid;
I would rather be called 'kitchen assistant';
I have no say at all;
The kitchen porter is an underdog;
I never mention my occupation to anyone outside;
Kitchens are all the same, it is rough work;
The manager listens, but does nothing about it;
I don't expect respect as a kitchen porter;
No promotion, it is a one-track job;
We are not in the limelight like some people in the hotel;
Management shows us chaps not enough respect;
Kitchen portering is a disease, once contaminated you can't get out.

These are comments attached to the categories of answers and taken as
random from the completed schedules. The various responses to the
question are not all negative and ego-depressing. 39% of the answers
do not consider the work a drudge (which it obviously is). A mere 21%
consider their prestige at the work place to be low and themselves to be
a target for abuse, whilst only six per cent would not disclose their
occupation to outsiders. One would also have thought that the number
who considered the job to carry no security might have been larger than
36% having regard to the average length of stay in a job. (See Exhibit
IV later on Work History). The answers towards the non-negative orientation could be seen as ego-defensive, that is, the expressed attitudes
may serve as a function designed to protect a respondent from the ack-
nowledgment of unpleasant truths about himself or the harshness of the
work environment. It is also likely that fear of losing their jobs
would constrain the incumbents to comment unfavourably upon their work
situation. Only three per cent feel isolated from other people. It is
somewhat doubtful whether this question has been understood in social
status terms or role distance. The kitchen porter is, as we shall see
from work histories, an intermittent worker, due to market vicissitudes
and/or personal disposition. He does not readily fit into the categories of traditional-deferential, traditional-proletarian or privatised
kind, erected by Goldthorpe and Lockwood in their affluence worker
studies. He is already under sentence by society: character doubtful,
social contribution marginal, general status peripheral. Isolation refers less to conditions of diminished social visibility or not working
with others than to the absence of more permanent local and social ties,
which the 'Yo-Yo' effect of job rotation undermines.

A Possible Hypothesis

The kitchen porter is one of the lowest participants in the power structure of the organisation for which he is working. His involvement tends
therefore to be alienative rather than moral.

Comments: our evidence lends support to this proposition, although incumbents in the main fail to grasp the implications. However, the expressed feelings of their marginality are not total, showing surprisingly that nearly 40% do not consider the work a drudge, whilst in excess
of 40% agree that nothing creative is done to satisfy hotel guests and
that no one takes notice of a kitchen porter's ideas and suggestions.
Nearly 60% do not value their promotion chances very highly and well
over half the sample think that the job is badly paid. In general, the
answers do not point to an affinity with the employer or strong involvement but a definite alienative expression of social action can be established only by observation at the work place.

EXHIBIT IV WORK HISTORY

Ex. 4.1   In choosing an appropriate sampling method, due allowances
have been made for both the characteristics of town or city itself
(industrial , cultural, business, spa) and the density of concentration
of hotels in the area.

Ex. 4.2 Total Number of Jobs Held

Taken to the nearest whole number (and having regard to average age of
the respondents at interviewing time when it was 47 years), 6% held between fourteen and thirty eight jobs. A convenient categorisations
shows that:

21% held between eleven and thirty eight jobs
41% held between six and ten jobs
39% held between one and five jobs

   It does not seem, for the West Midlands at least, that instability is
as excessive as the hotel industry's image projects, when 80% of all
the sample have had no more than a maximum of ten jobs during a working
life time; and, if we were to take the numbers as evenly spread (with
the percentages 39 to 41 not far apart in any case), the average number
would amount to only some five jobs, which is very similar to most and
better than in some other industries. Having said this, we did, however, have to rely on the frank (and occasionally suspect) memories of
the kitchen porters for their responses. Here, two safeguards were
adopted: one, the intermingling our in-depth questionnaire with some
repeating questions for the purpose of a counter-check; and two, the
enlistment of the services of a highly-trained interviewer, with the
dual advantage of minimising the risk of inaccurate or unrepresentative
data for analysis.

Ex. 4.3 Number of Jobs Held in the Catering Industry

Some 67% stated that they had only two jobs in the catering industry,
while only 10% held between seven and nine jobs. This, and specific
comments recorded on the schedules of the respondents themselves, leads
one strongly to assume that there has been, during the average working
life of the interviewees, considerable movement into and out of the catering field.

Ex. 4.4   Total Amount of Time spent in the Last Three Jobs

We intend presently to offer ideas and a discussion in depth on the subject of job stability. Very few, if any, researchers have found it possible to tackle it before, owing to the complexity of variables that have to be drawn into this problem. For the present, and deferring our definition of the concept for later, we simply accept the opinion of a Department of Employment officer with experience in the catering trades (formerly known as the 'Denmark Street Exchange') who does not wish to be quoted by name, that one year in a kitchen porter's job with the same employer is to be considered reasonably stable. Using this criterion as a standard for the moment, a tentative evaluation can be placed on the survey results. 75% spent three years in the last three jobs. Of these, 43% held the last three jobs for only one year. 20%, however, spent between four and eleven years in the last three jobs.

Ex. 4.5   Of the last Three Jobs, How Many in Catering?

For some 28% only were the last three jobs in catering, while 20% had two jobs in catering. 52% had come into the catering industry from other work, that is, kitchen portering being their first job in catering. In Part B, we shall produce information on what alternative employment had been considered by kitchen porters and why they eventually accepted this particular work. At this point, it is of interest to know of the kinds of occupation from which the drift into menial catering work occurs. Following a thorough, manual scan through the entire sample schedules, we discover a mere handful of 'career' kitchen porters.

Occupations from which Movement into the Catering Industry occurred

Miner, tube slinger, dispatch clerk, steel worker, car assembler, crane operator, market gardener, general labourer, technician, checker, driver, metal dealer, railway porters, welder, toolroom labourer, paper seller, engineer's attendant, farmhand, dustman, brickmaker, electric maintenance man, assembler, scaffolder, soldier, security officer, gas board worker, blacksmith, TV and radio repairer, printer, enamel worker, painter, coalman, packer, time clerk, store keeper, odd job man, foundry worker, salesman, plumber's mate, grinder, ice cream seller, dairyman, press worker, shoes and boots operative, assistant nurse, machinist, building labourer, digger, bricklayer, driller, bottler, window cleaner, weaver, tram driver, sprayer, stockman on farm.

It appears that the occupation of kitchen porter absorbs those who need work, want to work, require it at short notice and frequently require it temporarily. In few cases is there any similarity between old and new occupation. Kitchen portering seems to serve as a reservoir to take up the slack of those who suffered either from the vicissitudes of local industries or some personal reason for which they had to leave their work.

Ex. 4.6   Brief Details of any Period Unemployed

18% of the respondents admitted to being regularly out of work and 31% to being occasionally out of work. 51% claimed to be rarely out of work. This information does not tell us how long a worker remains in any one job. The interesting question here arises whether a worker is

more stable when he works intermittently and stays with the same employer for longer periods or changes jobs frequently without ever being
out of work.

Ex. 4.7 Average Time in Job

The time refers not just to catering jobs. By itself, it is not a
reliable indicator of the stability of an employee.

> 80% of the sample remained in the same job from one to five years
> 15% remained for one year
> 25% remained for two years
> 16% remained for three years
> 18% remained for four years
> 6% remained for five years
> 15% of the sample remained in the same job from six to ten years
> 6% remained from eleven to thirteen years

We have searched and scoured through a mass of documented material
concerned with labour problems to locate - if it exists - some research
on the question of employee stability indicators for an entire industry.
Ample literature referring to labour turnover, employee wastage, absenteeism, induction crises and such in individual undertakings is,
indeed, available, but that is not what we seek. We see the 'stability'
question in terms of the whole of a worker's working lifetime, and its
causes, when that has presented the sort of problem it has in this occupation. Why the question has apparently not been tackled before might
become clearer from our (as yet) unpublished research paper referred to in (9).

Ex. 4.8 Reasons for Being Out of Work

We may conveniently group the respondents under:-

Group A:	in the process of looking for work	25%
	could not find work	23%
	labour exchange could not find work for the respondent	2%
		50%

Group B:	did not want to work	7%
	could not find the job desired	2%
	want to work only when the money runs out	2%
	did not want regular work	3%
		64%

Group C:	suffered from accident or illness	10%
	was unable to accept work (prison, H.M. Forces, etc.)	9%
	had difficulty in finding accommodation	5%
	in receipt of a pension	2%
	language difficulties	1%
	interrupted work to go home abroad	1%
	incapacitated from drink to perform regular work	8%
		100%

It appears that only 14% had no desire
for regular work. 36% were either disabled or encountered other personal
problems while 50% endeavoured to obtain
work, but were not successful at the time.

Hypothesis

Working conditions for the kitchen porter rarely differ with the type
or size of particular establishments, which is a contributory factor
to high turnover of such staff.

Comments: the industry acknowledges its problems in the retention of
staff, particularly so among the lower grades, where labour turnover
has long reached proportions in excess of other industries. The Hotel
and Catering E.D.C. Report confirms this situation in the manpower
field and established a variation of turnover up to 282% and an average
of 83%. This Manpower Report established further that labour stability
(defined by the report as the percentage of full time adults remaining
with their employers for more than welve months) is significantly lower
than that of any other industrial group. (See Summary Report, p.9.).
Turnover among kitchen porter grades in London has been found to considerably exceed the average of 83%, while the E.D.C. definition of
stability of twelve months is well-supported by our findings in the
West Midlands, where 80% of our sample remained in the same job from
one to five years.

We have posed in this Exhibit the question whether a worker is more
stable when he works intermittently, but remains with the same employer
for longer periods when he works than when he changes jobs more frequently without ever being out of work. This stability/mobility question has not, in the past, received the sort of attention from researchers it really deserves and we have, in a pioneering sort of way, looked
into the implications of measuring the stability factor, having regard
to the inter-relationships of a number of key variables. (9)

As to the actual working conditions in the different establishments
of our sample, respondents' attitudes and pay are documented in Exhibit
5, but we had not the resources as part of this particular project to
look at the conditions under which the respondents worked. What is
more, we felt that this endeavour would possibly have been encouraged
by only a few of the hotels. We have not, therefore, established that
working conditions rarely differ with the type and size of the establishments (as well they might), but we did find that, in the main, conditions were not so favourable for kitchen porters as to encourage a
long stay in the job, which supports the contention that the absence of
a congenial work environment is a contributory factor to high turnover
of such staff.

Attention is now also drawn to the information in Exhibit X, which
deals with the most and least satisfying aspects of the kitchen porters
work in the context of their influence on worker stability in the job.

EXHIBIT V   WORKING CONDITIONS

This exhibit deals with respondents' attitudes towards the conditions of work and take-home pay at the time of the interviews.

Ex 5.1 The exhibit asks which of the following conditions of work would be most important to them in encouraging them to work as kitchen porters more permanently

---

A nice, clean workplace rates top, with practically all the respondents (98.5%). Next in importance is for the work to be respected by people (92.5%). Proper tools and working with a team are equally valued (85%). Job security and better pay is regarded as important by close to 84% of the sample, while a chance to become a member of a trade union is also highly regarded (79%). Next in line is the desire for mechanical aids (67%) and wearing a uniform (66%). Getting a share of the tips is desired by 61%. Nearly one half of the respondents (48%) do not favour shift work. Living-in is of interest to 43% and only 33% would like more say in the way the kitchen is run. A small number offered other reasons as to amenities that should be provided by an employer, such as showers, better ventilation, waterproof clothing and a better waste disposal system (10%).

How far the preferred conditions are actually present within the majority of undertakings would make the subject of an interesting investigation. One would hazard the proposition that the more a condition is stressed as strongly desirable, the less it is likely to be present. In terms of Herzberg's theory, most of the desired conditions fall into the 'hygiene' category, which makes them basic more to willingness to continue working than to act as actual motivators. (10) Generally, there is much scope for improving the state of the work environment in line with the Tavistock concept of the 'Socio-technical System', which emphasises the need in job design for both technical system efficiency and the psycho-sociological needs assocated with the work. (11). That a satisfactory working environment and good tools correlate with performance has been confirmed by the researches of Victor Vroom. (12) He found what a worker can do will strongly influence what he will do, and his perceptions of what he is supposed to do. So that kitchen porters who can do their job well are most likely to be more disposed towards wanting to do it. Vroom makes another interesting point, that a given level of performance will lead to certain consequences. There may, in fact, be a definite relationship between performance and 'desired' consequences and if, say, a kitchen porter does not perceive this relationship to exist, it is unlikely to positively influence him in doing a good job.

Ex. 5.2 Earnings in Previous Jobs

The bulk of our interviews took place during the last six months of 1973. The question on earnings referred to the weekly take-home pay in the previous job. The following picture emerged:-

Up to £10	22.4%
From £11 to £14	23.9%
From £15 to £20	19.4%
Above £20	22.4%
Not answered	11.9%

Note: Over 65% of the sample earned £20 or less in the previous job
and the percentage could be higher, as some 12% have not answered the question.

Ex. 5.3 Starting Wage in present job

Up to £10	13.4%
From £11 to £14	43.3%
From £15 to £20	35.8%
Above £20	3.0%
Not answered	4.5%

Note: Close to 93% earned £20 or less when starting the present job.
The predominant earnings, near 80%, fell between £11 and £20.

Ex. 5.4 Earnings at interviewing time

Up to £10	4.5%
From £11 to £14	34.3%
From £15 to £20	55.2%
Above £20	4.5%

Note: 94% earned £20 or less while nearly 90% fell into the £11 to
£20 earning bracket.

Observations

One observes during the year 1973 a general trend of the percentage
earning the lowest wage (up to £10) to fall. The number of respondents
in the catering and hotel industry earning over £20 is small. We have
noted already that a large number of our respondents came into this industry from other industries, where the numbers earning £20+ appeared
to have been higher. The trend of wages to increase at that time will
also be noted. As the percentage of lower earnings is falling, the
percentage of higher earnings is rising. Those earning between £15 to
£20 have clearly increased as a percentage during the six months to
December 1973. These figures relate to rewards for a full working
week, but do not include fringe benefits or benefits in kind, as valued
in money terms. It is possible from these figures to reliably conclude
that in the latter part of 1973, the bulk of kitchen porters working
in the West Midlands area earned not less than £11 and not more than
£20.

Towards the end of 1971, problems of recruitment and high rates of
staff turnover in this industry caused much concern and the Hotels
and Catering E.D.C. undertook an objective assessment of the manpower
situation. Projects were set in motion and, during 1972, consultants
were employed to look at levels of earning and employment practices.
The E.D.C. established also a special Manpower Working Group, which in
1973 set in motion an extensive assessment of working conditions in
major firms in the hotel and restaurant sector for the periods covering April 1973 and 1974. As we have interviewed during the last six
months of 1973, comparisons are to be considered quite meaningful.(13)

As to the average manual worker (male) in hotels and catering, the
E.D.C. Manpower Report, published in 1975, found him to be in the

lowest 13% of all manual men, as regards weekly average earnings. Information was obtained by means of a postal survey addressed to unit
managers and staff. The Department of Employment's New Earnings Survey
(N.E.S.) had been taken as a hundred in 1973 and on this basis, kitchen
hands' average weekly earnings amounted to only 53%. With an average
working week of 46 hours, kitchen hands were found to be the lowest
paid occupation in all industries and services in the country, large
companies generally paying to the extent of 6% better. Since our interviews, Wages Regulation Orders have awarded increases and the percentage increase during the period June 1972 - October 1974 has amounted to some 38% for kitchen porters. The image, in terms of hours,
earnings and conditions is poor, although the industry in general is
basically attractive as an employer for other selected occupational
groups.

Not very many months later, the Low Pay Unit (14) undertook to investigate earnings and conditions in hotels and catering also, and confirmed the unfavourable picture. The Unit offers a definition of low
pay geared to what the T.U.C. and the Government have accepted as low
pay target. The figure of £30 per week for a basic 40 hour week is
taken as a 1974 cut-off point, as it coincides with the 1974 Supplem-
entary Benefit level for a two-child family, which if earning less than
that amount, will be living in poverty. Median earnings are taken as a
further criterion, which in April 1974 stood at some £44, two-thirds of
which approximates also to the £30 level. The Wages Council statutory
minimum rate (S.M.R.) during 1974 in licensed residential establishments was in the region of £14, give or take a few pence for regional
variations. The L.P.U. has made a number of case studies of kitchen
porters and discusses how excessively long hours of work - aggravated
by the requirement of split-shifts - dominate the whole lives of these
workers. It quotes the case of one kitchen porter who worked 79 hours
to earn £35.90. We mention, in passing, the most recent Wages Regulation Order (13/1975 No.1571) at the time of writing (June 1976) required that kitchen porters be paid a minimum of £29.50 for a 40-hour
week. (15) The L.P.U. Report maintains that the industry is not tackling the root cause of the casual worker problem which is the payment
of a decent wage,and it suggests that casual workers are some of the
worst situated in the·industry. Of course, successive waves of inflat-
ion have now doubled the minimum wage.

Average Gross Weekly Wage for Unskilled Manual Workers (Comparative)

Belgium	£57
Denmark	£65
France	£34
Germany (West)	£66
Holland	£71
Italy	£32
U.K.	£46
U.S.A.	£72 approx.

Source: European Communities Commission Information Office, 1974 (16).

Personal contacts in France, the Federal Republic of Germany and the
U.S.A. enable us to say that kitchen porters earned (during 1973) between £34-£48, £63-£66, £50-£65 gross, respectively, taking account of

regional variations. (17) There may be fringe benefits in addition where this is customary in an industry. Since European countries employ guest workers in certain low-status occupations, it has been suggested by the writers of these personal letters that the amounts quoted may not be what these workers actually get. Information from hotel owners and managers is difficult to come by, as the enquirers are suspected of being trade union or local government 'snoopers'. Indirect information gathered suggested that all but a very few high-class establishments employ aliens illegally in the country and sweat them for a pittance; and that no native, excepting a down-and-out, would dream of demeaning himself to do that kind of work.

Hypothesis (a)

The kitchen porter is one of the lowest participants in the power structure of the organisation for which he is working. His involvement tends, therefore, to be alienative rather than moral.

Comments: In so far as respondents' desirable conditions of work are not being met, involvement would tend to be weakened. In order to show how far the various employers satisfy these conditions is the task of a separate survey, alas not a popular one with many employers.

Hypothesis (b)

High financial rewards, where they exist, tend to minimise stigma for the individual - although not for the occupation - and evidence of income is not by others attributed to occupational earnings.

Comments: On the evidence of kitchen porters' earnings, stigma is more likely to be maximised than minimised, as earnings are alarmingly low. It is obvious that low income does not make for conspicuous consumption patterns and property ownership. In our society, social respectability being equated with style of life, ranks the kitchen porter as a person and the kitchen porter occupation in terms of low social value.

Hypothesis (c)

Catering workers of a lower grade and kitchen porters in particular are not generally members of an industrial interest group, not because, as commonly assumed, of the diversity of hotel and catering units in terms of size and location, but owing to the diverse interests between the different levels of skills.

Comments: Despite the existence of a Catering Industry National Joint Trade Union Committee, to which the eight unions with members from this industry are affiliated, we have not been able to establish the total membership of kitchen porters, but five per cent of all such grades would, we feel, constitute a generous estimate, although there is a current trend for membership to increase. 79% of our respondents would highly regard the chance to become members of a trade union as one of the factors to motivate them to do this job more permanently, as is evidenced from the replies in this exhibit. Why then membership of kitchen porters (and, indeed, that of low-grade workers in this industry generally) is not larger could undoubtedly be traced mainly to the mobile way of life, to low income and the trade unions' difficulties with recruitment procedures and more intimate knowledge of the industry. Employer attitudes as displayed to lower-grade manual workers, could, if unfavourable, cause those workers to live in fear of the sack. As has been shown in Chapter 5, para.14, the reasons for the lower membership in the private sector are diverse and while the different levels of skills make a general or industrial kind of union more suitable for the lower grades, size of the undertaking and location do influence recruitment and maintenance of membership considerably. To the extent to which the hypothesis offers fewer variables than have, in fact, a bearing on the picture, it does not merit complete and unequivocal support.

Note: Information on the new Hotel and Catering Industry Training Board Industrial Relations Guide, designed to offer enlightenment on employment legislation and on the practices that can help to bring about good employee relations, is now available. This guide should go some way to re-orientate employers and managers in the sphere of industrial relations in this industry. The resulting alleviation of fear and suspicion towards trade unions could, therefore, in the not too distant future operate to increase membership of the lower catering worker grades.

Hypothesis (d)

As individuals, members of stigmatised occupational groups usually subscribe to a basic life orientation and sub-cultural values that are characterised by a limited comprehension of the world around them, an absence of verbal, conceptual sophistication, fatalistic values with regard to patterning, controllability of the environment and of the future; and, as groups, their shape of social existence depicting a poverty sub-culture of their own.

Comments: Any specific occupational sub-culture can be determined only by the investigation in depth over periods of time of a cross section of cases. Low income groups with largely insecure abodes substantially without family and a job security that is somewhat precarious, in many cases past middle age and without educational qualifications or verbal skills, suggest the presence of a poverty sub-culture of their own. Hard evidence of poverty is apparent.

Hypothesis (e)

There is every justification on the part of those who proclaim that certain manual tasks performed (particularly in stigmatised occupations) should long have been only a traditional stage in our technological development. The work of 'plongeur' has been ignored and by-passed by modern technology.

Comments: We found little evidence of an existence and use of mechanical or technological aids that could take the drudge out of this work, although we are aware of certain claims of progress in this direction in the U.S.A. It has not been one of our specific aims to investigate the rate of progress in the employment of such aids, but established in this exhibit that no fewer than 85% of the sample highly value proper tools to do the job and 67% mechanical aids, and that these would be conditions to induce them to do this work more permanently. Our observations in Chapter 3 are relative to this hypothesis and Chapter 5

(Figure 8) focus attention on this problem also as does Exhibit 3 above
on the perceived marginality of the work attitudes of the respondents.

EXHIBIT VI   TRAINING

We have already shown (in Chapter 5 above) how our views on the question
of training needs for certain grades of worker in the hotel and catering
industry diverge from the general attitudes of the industry. Our Exhibit III further touched on this theme, when it was found from the responses that neither are the bulk of the kitchen porters appreciative of
the training need (under 20% affirmed its need), nor is training actually given. (86.6% of the sample received no training and there is no
evidence that the remaining 13.4% are actually trained for the job).

  This exhibit looks more deeply into the personal experiences of the
incumbents with reference to training and clearly reveals some general
elements of deprivation in the lives of the kitchen porters.

Ex. 6.1   Asking whether the respondent was ever trained for a skilled
          trade

          64% received no training ever for a skilled trade
          31% received non-catering training and some 3% catering training

  Of the respondents who received training (34%), only 30% actually completed it while 58% had never, in connection with any phase of their employment, obtained any specific training or special experience that
might have assisted them in finding work in any capacity other than kitchen portering. (See Ex. 6.2.).

Ex. 6.2   Asked respondents whether they would be agreeable to be train-
          ed in a number of different tasks so that they might be
          switched to other jobs in the kitchen

70% would agree to such training. Of the respondents who answered this
question, but would not agree to this type of training, some two per
cent consider themselves unable or are unwilling to accept responsibility
while 21% prefer to retain occupational mobility. (Some did not appreciate that occupational mobility might still be possible under this type
of training). It has already been shown above that large number of kitchen porters themselves do not appreciate the need for training for this
kind of work.

Comments: Enquiries with the H.C.I.T.B. concerning the idea of training
a worker in more than one skill has brought very little definite information to light, beyond the fact that, in general, all forms of training
are encouraged, but that the employers themselves are responsible for
such training as may be given. It is quite usual in this industry to recruit lower-grade staff under the name of 'catering assistant', which
does not specify the various tasks that are intended to be included in
the work routine. In consequence, an employee will be used for a variety
of tasks in the kitchen, be expected to perform them proficiently and
not receive any extra payment other than the agreed rate, together with
possible fringe benefits. The idea of a generally-trained 'catering
worker' has been discussed in the catering press for some time and would
involve the less-skilled in the training of a variety of tasks so that

they could be switched around on the job. Schemes such as these may
be seen to have obvious advantages for employers for the benefits of
which they might be willing to increase rewards. From a worker's
viewpoint, more job security, higher rewards and an end to the split-
shift system would undoubtedly be welcome, but he may deprive himself
thereby of an occupational specialism which all this entails. Where
trade union organisation is strong (which is not predominant in commercial catering units), demarcation problems may arise when specific
skills are involved, although as far as the less-skilled are concerned,
unions are more anxious to improve working conditions than to worry
overmuch about infringements of this kind. Apart from the training
need, as such, intermittency of employment on the part of kitchen porters places an attitude of reluctance on employers to arrange for more
training on-the-job.

According to the E.D.C. Manpower Report, when asked what sort of problems the question of training entailed, nearly a quarter of the managers reported that it was difficult to find the time for training. Another fifth alluded to attributes of the staff, i.e. some said that
staff themselves had no wish to be trained, while others suggested that
the low calibre of staff made training a somewhat fruitless exercise,
or that staff left as soon as they were trained. (See also our comments on the question of training in Exhibit III above on Work Attitudes)

Hypothesis

Most, if not all, employers (and others in an official capacity) and
professional experts, take the view that no training, or a small degree
of training, is required for the work of kitchen porter or plongeur.
This view is disputed by us. Instead, it is proposed that whatever the
degree of skill needed depends on the proficiency of the training received.

Comments: Our views on the 'skill argument' in connection with the kitchen porter's work routine, have been made explicit in Chapters 2 and
5. This hypothesis is amply supported by evidence from the respondents
that training is not given, and the attitudes of both employers and respondents, and possibly the H.C.I.T.B. as well (since no attempts are
made in the direction of encouraging it actively), that it is largely
not needed. Quite apart from the social,prestige and self-respect values of training for a task, however humble it may be considered to be,
the benefits in terms of worker stability and task proficiency also do
not appear to be appreciated.

EXHIBIT VII ASSOCIATIONS AT WORK AND OUTSIDE THE WORK PLACE

Ex. 7.1 Do you like making friends at the work place?

91% answered 'yes' to this question, thereby indicating a strong need
for friendship at the work place. However, the kitchen sink is a lonely spot, particularly so during the pressures of the workflow and after
meal times. Most of the other staff will, at that time, be getting
ready for their rest period, while a porter may look forward to scraping
the food remains from a seemingly endless flow of pots and pans. In
this situation, there is little opportunity to socialise or enjoy companionship.

6% claimed to have always been lone wolves, while the remaining number felt that mixing leads to friction.

Ex. 7.2 Influences of Working Life

This exhibit asks the respondent to look back over his working life to see whether he can identify any person who played a key role in influencing the direction or nature of his work. ˙40% of the respondents were not aware of any such influence. Where familial support was given, (13%) it took the form of a wife's religious influence or relative's influence to learn a trade, or similar sentiments. We shall look at non-family influences in the next exhibit.

Ex. 7.3 Support from Outsiders for the Kitchen Porter

This kind of support refers to all kinds of help, to build a career, to learn a trade or find work. Some 47% fall into this category, of which 9% have the sympathetic ear of the chef and 6% the benefit of help from friends. Some 32% refer to a variety of personal kinds of relationships: the foreman in the factory helped me; I was offered money to start a business; I have mates all over the country; the boss on the farm where I worked gave me a cockerel as a present every Christmas; the hotel owner treated me like one of the family; the manager at the grocer's helped me to decide about the Army; the foreman in the shoe factory gave me clothes.

In addition to this extra-familial support, 18% received also institutions' support. In the main, respondents referred to help from the War Pensions people; the British Council; H.M. Services; the Disabled Persons Officer and the like.

Comments: We know, from Exhibit I, that some 72% were single and predominantly male. This means that only 28% of the respondents had the benefit of close familial support to the extent of 13%, from which one must conclude that such support was negligible in the main. The need for companionship and friendship is obvious, and of those who actually received support, this rarely amounted to more than sympathetic treatment at work, or casual socialising with those higher up in the hierarchy. We have suggested in Exhibit 13.4 a possible isolation, home-centredness and retreatist style of life when engaging in leisure activities to the extent of 67% of the respondents. The lack of closer social relationships does not appear to be offset by any dominating mass cultural influence on the social side, nor does a kitchen porter's income permit any kind of extravagance in the consumption of leisure services that may be available.

Hypothesis

The working environment of the kitchen porter hinders, and often prevents, colleague relationships found in other occupations. Diversity of location and lack of unionisation, plus the fact that the majority of catering units employ only one or two plongeurs, works against the promotion of affinity and then establishes the loosest of relationships in the 'trade'. This leaves the kitchen porter on a psychological limb for the alleviation of which he seeks, but rarely finds, a 'caretaker'.

Comments: Over 70% of the respondents feel the need for friendly association and psychological·support, from whatever source, which they are
either not able to obtain at all, or experience mainly on a casual basis
in the form of incidental kindnesses, rather than the sort of friendships they really seek. We may, therefore, observe that our survey data
lends substantial validity to the hypothesis, which finds support also
in Exhibit 13, in which we touch on the incidence of isolation.

EXHIBIT VIII PRACTICAL ADAPTATIONS

Ex. 8.1 Factors considered most important to the respondents in their
         work

This question tests how respondents feel towards their work environment.
42% prefer to work in a high class hotel, while 30% regard a high class
area as important. 28% would like to work in a large hotel and 18% in
a small one. Undoubtedly, these sentiments are based on previous experience. It is not possible to conclude that working conditions are necessarily different, according to area, but there is a likelihood that
high class hotels are owned by groups when stricter compliance with legal provisions may be followed. Also, managers are less likely to enjoy
full autonomy when head office imposes a unified policy and minimum
standards of conditions and service. The responses are not mutually
exclusive.

Ex. 8.2. Attitudes towards task performance and social rewards

The respondents were asked to say what are the most important considerations before they would accept a job as kitchen porter anywhere. We
shall tabulate the responses in order of importance to the sample:

Good hours of work	14.9%
Happy working atmosphere	14.9%
The way the hotel is run	13.4%
Cleanliness	10.4%
A good superior	7.5%
Making friends	7.5%
Enough staff in the kitchen	6.0%
Safety against accidents	6.0%
Proper equipment	4.5%
Being able to settle in	1.5%
Want people to show one respect	1.5%
Chance to cook	1.5%
Classy hotel with serene environment	0.0%

   It seems pretty evident that working conditions on the job matter more
to the respondents than the class of the hotel itself, or the environment. It shows also that there is little, if any, identification with
the employer, as such. This lack of affinity is certainly a contributory factor to the large staff turnover in this grade and should long
have alerted managers to look into it. A small number of the respondents may not have the mental equipment to evaluate priorities, but the
bulk of the sample had a good conception of what they valued as important. If work is physically hard and involves long hours, then it seems
sensible enough to want these hours reduced. If there is tension at the
work place, it makes good sense to desire a happy working atmosphere.
It would appear that where congenial working conditions are lacking, the

kitchen porters would opt for having these improved.

Ex. 8.3 Attitudes towards subsistence and economic rewards

This part extends the question asked in Ex. 8.2 to determine the economic priorities of the sample. Some 20% did not answer the following
questions, while to the rest of the percentage, economistic-instrumental
matters did not rank significantly before they would accept a job as
kitchen porter.

Money the most important	34.3%
Living-in accommodation	13.4%
Secure employment	4.5%
Needed the job	3.0%
Decent food	1.5%
Don't know	1.5%

It looks strongly like a denial by most of the sample that materialistic needs alone prompted them in the acceptance of the job.

Ex. 8.4 Asks why the respondent has accepted this job and why in this
particular hotel

There would appear to be a strong indication that respondents really
wanted to work and needed the job.

Taken this job as a last resort	38.8%
Needed a job	26.9%
Personal contact	20.9%
Official channels helped to find the job	17.9%
Location prompted acceptance in this hotel	16.4%
Money	6.0%
Promotion	1.5%

In a number of cases, more than one of the reasons applied as to why
they had accepted the job in this particular hotel, and some 12% offered
additional reasons to those categorised above, some vague, i.e. the job
was handy; I thought I would try kitchen portering; tried this new hotel
in case there is a vacancy; the job is not far from home; I have always
done this work; that job just came along; stepping stone to chef; it is
the sort of work my disablement allows me to do; manager seemed nice
when I was interviewed. The first three of the above categories (near
87%) point strongly to need and desire to work.

Ex. 8.5 How long respondents expect to remain in the present job

The answers are necessarily somewhat speculative, as the length of stay
is merely an expressed intention. It does, however, offer clues as to
intended stability/stableness in circumstances where the industry's image of the kitchen porter is an expectation of only short-term employment.

(1)	Less than one month	7.5%
(2)	One month to six months	0.0%

         (3) Six months to twelve months   1.5%
         (4) One year or longer   40.3%
         (5) Answers indefinite   50.7%

   There is a slight overlap in expressed intentions. The indefinite
answers were either 'don't know'; 'God knows'; 'time will tell';'depends
on when I get fed up'; 'till I retire' or 'if promoted, I will stay'.
If, say, we take just one half of the indefinite answers to point to a
stay of about one year, then some 66% can be taken to intend to work in
the same hotel for a year or more.

Ex. 8.6 Why a respondent would wish to leave his present employer, and
         alternative employment considered before the present job was
         accepted.

         14.9% would leave for better money
         11.9% would leave to improve conditions of work
          9.0% would leave to find a better location
          4.5% would change to another industry

   Just under 60% would not leave the job for any of the reasons mentioned above. The majority of these respondents might well have felt constrained in answering such a question, despite our assurances that the
answers will be treated in the strictest confidence.

   It will be of interest to look at the kinds of alternative employment
respondents have considered when accepting this job,as these indicate
an absence of affiliation to the hotel and catering industry, although
76% of those questioned say that they, had not considered alternative
employment to kitchen portering. The motive for such a claim could be
associated with the information given to the present employer as to experience in the hotel and catering industry and/or concern about the
security of present employment.

Alternative employment considered - respondents' answers

         Looked for a machinist's job
         Considered factory work
         Could have worked in another hotel
         Gardening - but not in winter time
         Work for an electrical contractor - but pensioner not wanted
         Considered Butlin's, but they had no vacancies
         Pottery industry - but could not get in
         Hospital - but failed my medical
         Sweeping up or something similar
         Wanted something in the catering trade
         Wanted a job as a stepping stone to better things
         Illness prevented consideration of other jobs
         Considered becoming a prison officer
         Wanted an outdoor job because of chest trouble
Hypothesis (a)

The isolated kitchen porter from group affiliation in the kitchen is excluded from becoming part of the group culture pattern which binds those
together who will eventually be credited with the rewards of their

creations.

Comments: The group culture in the kitchen, projected mainly by the chefs and cooks, who are the ones to practise skills, tends to reject that low-status human appendage to kitchen implements in social terms. We have already discussed the enormous influence an autocratic head chef may exert upon other staff who emulate him, which not infrequently finds expression in torment of a kitchen hand by the entire brigade quite beyond the normal joking relationships at work places, when any particular characteristic of disablement or handicap becomes so conspicuous as to hamper the performance of certain tasks to the head chef's satisfaction. (See Chapter 5 above on kitchens). Isolation and friendlessness as experienced by the kitchen porter have evidenced themselves repeatedly in this exhibit, as also in exhibits 2,5,7,12 and 13.

Hypothesis (b)

The indeterminate occupational role of the kitchen porter in the performance of his tasks stamps him as 'unskilled' and prejudices his chances for applying or acquiring for application (if he does not already possess them) certain extra-functional skills, the possession of which would enhance his job security under present conditions within the industry.

Comments: Extra-functional skills (sometimes referred to as social skills) must be distinguished from the informal - status-enhancing - role discussed in exhibit 9. Also, exhibit 6 has shown how little attention is given to the improvement of skill while in this one, poor conditions at work emphasise the kitchen porter's indeterminate role and make the achievement of good conditions an uppermost objective in his mind.

Hypothesis (c)

An alternative to the hypothesis of an inculcated pattern of a socially stigmatising tradition (perpetuating sub-culture) attaching certain low-grade occupations and spilling over to form a lower-class design for living, is the proposition that occupational stigma is a condition to which the actors must adapt through whatever socio-cultural resources they may control; to regard such stigma as phenomena of the environment in which the stigmatised live, determined more by the structure of the total system than by behaviours and values that they hold.

Comments: While respondents cannot be expected to enter into philosophical argument about the causal elements of stigma and its relationship to the environment or the structural-functional implications of the social system, few have questioned openly or expressed recriminations why they are in their present position. Where thoughts had been given to this aspect, incumbents tended to blame their disability more than their constraining circumstances, thereby implying that they could have been more successful had they but put their mind to it. Respondents had either given little thought to stigmatisation as such, or tried to adapt to it as best they could. 87% needed the job and wanted to work (as evidenced in this exhibit) and, although badly paid, money was not by two thirds of the subjects regarded as the key motivation, but the 'illusion' of giving service to customers was. For obvious reasons, these claims have to be accepted with reservations on account of concern about job

security at interviewing time. (Exhibit 10 refers). In our observations on this hypothesis in Chapter 4, we pose the problem whether a sub-
existence in work and life is to be understood as a problem or a solution to it. Some validity has been given in research to the culture of
poverty, but less so to the function of it. How far the environment
produced or shaped our respondents in the way they are, or whether they
are the product of a perpetuating sub-cultural pattern is difficult to
establish without case studies in depth, relative to the conditions under which they lived over time. Reference should, however, be made to
our discussion on the 'vagrancy hypothesis' in Chapter 4 above, 'working
conditions in kitchens', and Orwell's impressionistic documentaries, all
in the same chapter.

Arguably, the hotel industry holds that it provides the kind of work
that particular groups of people want and can perform without responsibility or worry. Even that assumption presents the greatest of difficulties to establish reliably from our empirical data.

EXHIBIT IX   OCCUPATIONAL PRESTIGE AND STATUS

Ex. 9.1   Kitchen Porter Image - Other Kitchen Staff and Public

Society at large and people in the kitchen porter's work environment,
where the respondent plays out his role, have preconceived ideas and
expectations of his behaviour which is often debasive of character; that
quality of performance at work is low; that his conduct is unpredictable
and his remaining in the same job of very short duration. In our sample
at least 60% did not have a normal working life in the sense that a
number of years were spent either in H.M. Forces, institutions or hospitals. It is natural that they care about public and work place images
of the occupation they, for the time being belong to and the esteem in
which they evaluate their job vis-a-vis some other occupations.

In answer to the question whether they would regard kitchen portering
as a more worthwhile job if other kitchen staff were to consider it as
such, 66% affirmed this as so. Similarly, 54% would consider the work
more worthwhile if the general public were to regard it as such.

Ex. 9.2   Respectability of Job compared with Other Occupations

Respondents tended to attach a moralistic evaluation to the word 'respectable', although the question was designed to test felt prestige in
comparison with other occupations. Hence, a large number declined to
answer the question, but those who did answer correctly understood the
meaning it was to elicit. We consider it useful to include the comput-
erised responses in full:-

	Yes	No	N/A	H-G Scale *
Teacher	28.4	13.4	58.2	61.14
Doctor	26.9	14.9	58.2	82.05
Chef	25.4	16.4	58.2	37.44
Clerk	25.4	16.4	58.2	39.85

*
More will be said about the mechanics of the new Hope-Goldthorpe Scale
(18) for classifying occupational prestige in the next section. 82.05
is the highest rating the scale provides and 18.95 is the lowest for

persons in employment. We have applied the scale to our occupations
above which appears fairly accurately to reflect societal images,
although there are some minor ambiguities, to be discussed under the
heading of observations-

	Yes	No	N/A	H-G Scale
Judge	25.4	16.4	58.2	76.29
Cook	23.9	17.9	58.2	37.44
Janitor	22.4	19.4	58.2	27.10
Toolmaker	20.9	20.9	58.2	45.57
Hospital Porter	16.4	25.4	58.2	22.95
Liftman	14.9	23.9	61.2	32.42
Hall Porter	13.4	28.4	58.2	32.42
Night-Watchman	10.4	31.3	58.2	27.10
Road Sweeper	9.0	32.8	58.2	18.36
Shoe Shiner	6.0	35.8	58.2	22.95

It will be noted that some 58% did not venture to give an opinion on
the question,but those that did regarded themselves as progressively
less inferior as (in their view) professionalism and skills are reducing
down the line of occupations. About one quarter of those that did express an opinion did not see themselves as lower in prestige on average
than the first six professions and occupations in the scale above.

Observations

The Hope-Goldthorpe Scale came into being because of a widely-held view
that the existing means of classifying and grading occupations are somewhat unsatisfactory. The scale affords the kitchen porter the lowest
grading it has for persons in employment (18.36) and thus confirms the
existing stigmatisation for this particular occupation.

In order to assess the validity of this grading, we thought it prudent
to take a closer look at this approach, particularly so as it is new,
novel, a coherent system for grouping occupations, geared to the British
census and making it possible to exercise a greater degree of comparab-
ility in social investigations. The scale is also compatible with
official statistics, and in the opinion of the authors widely applicable
to social research.

Our purpose is two-fold: to compare the H-G Scale values with those
of our respondents (see Exhibit 9.2) and to offer a new and authoritative social grading method from which the status of kitchen porters can
be seen relative to other occupations. We refer to the scale as 'authoritative' because it appears so accurately to reflect societal images
of the selected occupations we are considering. Having accorded the
scale this recognition, it appears necessary briefly to explain how it
works and what underlying rationale there is.

Application of the Scale to Occupations in our Research

Goldthorpe and Hope based their scale on the social standing of occupations and use the four criteria of standard of living, power and influence over others, the level of qualifications and value to society of the work involved. These four criteria can be gained by most people by way of personal achievement, while birth and personal qualities, said to be inborn and unconferable on others by the possessor, have been excluded. As a result, only those occupations which can be 'achieved' through personal effort have been graded in the scale and, incidentally, include the vast majority, but exclude such extremes as accumulated wealth over several generations, in any case most likely to affect only a minute segment of the population. (Shipping magnates, oil tycoons and the like). These writers doubt the Embourgeoisement Thesis of the working classes and suggest that higher earnings and increased trade union backing have decreased the status gap.

Thus, the social evaluation of an individual or the degree of honour bestowed on him by society are the main ideas behind the H-G grading system. The order of grading is obtained not from the authors, but from interviewing 600 people from all walks of life, who were given forty selected occupational titles to rank in the order in which the interviewers thought they ought to rate. The result of the findings was then divided into clusters of some 860 related occupational titles. Occupational grouping included also a division on the basis of authority of incumbents (seven groups), i.e. the self-employed and those managing larger numbers of employees, normally given higher grades. Accurate job descriptions for placement in one of the seven groups is essential, while titles such as 'engineer' are not useful. Another point made is that the scale is devised for comparing occupations in Britain and may not also hold for different social structures or political systems.

Measures obtained from the H-G Scale for Low-Status Occupations as used in Exhibit II (Health Matters)

1.	Head Hall Porters	48.15	Note:
2.	Chefs and Cooks	37.44	Highest rating
3.	Clothing Workers	35.55	83.05
4.	Building Operatives	30.00	Lowest rating
5.	Caretakers	27.10	for Employees
6.	Nightwatchmen	27.10	18.36
7.	Waiters	22.95	
8.	Hospital Porters	22.95	
9.	Service Workers (and Domestics)	22.95	
10.	Kitchen Porters	18.36	

Note: the scientifically devised occupational prestige scale, assessing the social evaluation of an individual as member of a particular occupation (the degree of honour bestowed on him by society) shows unmistakeably how our society rates the kitchen porter. It could be fairly claimed that neither a head hall porter nor a chef belong among low-status occupations, but these have been included, together with waiters, to reveal societal rating of other hotel and catering occupations, to compare with the kitchen porter rating.

Scale Ambiguities

We have already praised the merits of the scale, but some ambiguous matters might also be mentioned. Although accurate job descriptions are recommended, the skill distinctions of certain types of work are not always catered for. A general cook, to be distinguished from a chef,would clearly have to rate somewhat lower in the scale. If cook is excluded on the grounds that it is too general a term, then so is chef, for there are different kinds of chef with distinctively-rated skills. Chef and pastry chef are included in the scale, but sauce chef or vegetable cook are not. It can be argued that these may be included in the same cluster of occupations on the grounds of similarity, but precise job descriptions would undoubtedly weaken this contention. Another point noted is that some occupations may not easily fit into the categories provided for. Household servants are not listed under the 860 representative titles, nor are nurses, while professional gamblers and mole catchers are included. For certain occupational titles, we also noticed the scale produces lower ratings when the incumbents are self-employed. The barrow boy and ice cream seller have attracted the lowest measure available on the scale (17.52), although these are ranked as self-employed and are, in a sense, small-scale entrepreneurs, while the kitchen porter (an employee) performing less congenial work, ranks next-lowest with a measure of 18.36, the lowest possible among the employed category. However, there may be good reasons for the lower public esteem of street vendors.

Hypothesis

The kitchen porter has little motive or opportunity to use his occupational identity as a device for status improvement, or to elaborate his work role beyond the kitchen environment. This situation will adversely affect also his non-obligatory (leisure) preferences.

Comment: The leisure aspect has been dealt with already in Exhibit 13. The reality of his status is strongly supported by the scale and the feelings of the incumbents themselves. There is, however, an ingredient in this hypothesis which is worthy of further exploration. We refer here to opportunities to elaborate his role at work beyond his environment. The discovery how the stigmatised might be able to adjust to their low occupational status and prestige, possibly by way of adding to their formal role some concomitant ones that either promise the achievement of indispensability through the performance of specific services, or participation in an informal network engaged in profitable or unprofitable exchange of 'fiddles', or favours with non-market social side or spin-off, or the creation of social obligation and participation. Where such a situation exists, and the kitchen porter then becomes part of an informal reward structure - however successful - he is part of a team and, thereby, enhances his formal occupational role, or at least makes it bearable. Although such a situation has been aligned with pilfering, the benefits are often more social than material in creating social relations and obligations and contain, for the kitchen porter, propensities which make his low formal occupational role more bearable.

Reference should also be made to other observations in this Chapter, especially Exhibits 3,8 and 13, as well as to our introductory comments in this Chapter on profile and identity

EXHIBIT X   ASPIRATIONS AND ORIENTATIONS

Ex. 10.1   Least and Most Satisfying Aspects of Work

When a respondent is asked what he considers to be the least satisfying aspect of his work, one needs always to remember his fear that any adverse answer may incriminate him vis-a-vis his employer, or cost him his job. Not infrequently, managers hovered about when the interviews took place, which tended to inhibit a more unrestrained response. We recall interviewing a respondent in one kitchen while he was peeling potatoes and another while he was scouring pots at the kitchen sink. If, in addition, managers busy themselves in the vicinity during that time, considerable interviewing skill is required to make the best of this situation. We categorised the responses under four heads, indicating least satisfaction.

(1)	Conditions of work other than money	16.4%
(2)	Money rewards	6.0%
(3)	Human relations	13.4%
(4)	Other factors	62.7%

Exhibits 8,3,4 and 6 have already given an indication that for two thirds of the sample, money is not the key motivator for working as a kitchen porter. Under other least-liked factors at the work place, a random check of the schedules produced the following information: when everything happens at once, kitchen work, grocery deliveries, laundry deliveries, very confusing; it is hard to say, I have a lot to contend with; the way they organise the kitchen; you have to depend on yourself for a meal; some days when I come in, everything is all over the place; I don't like handling wet rags or getting wet; too many chefs giving orders; I fly off the handle when they interrupt me in the work for another job; I have to do the work of three men; the water gives me rheumatism; the chef empties dirty bits in the sink and stops up the plug hole; the late time of finishing the job; I hate mopping. It seems most of the dislikes are irritations in connection with the work routine which should be capable of remedy where a kitchen porter has the ear of the manager.

Responses to the most satisfying aspects of the work are again categorised under the same four heads:-

(1)	Conditions of work other than money	43.3%
(2)	Money rewards	7.5%
(3)	Human relations	13.4%
(4)	Other factors	31.3%

A random check of the schedules will again help to assess the orientations of the respondents and offer some insight on what they like about this kind of work. The information will, in some respects, cut across item (4), other factors. The chef never bothers you; getting everything clean and tidy; I like washing up; the fact that I am fully occupied; it is pleasant to work with the opposite sex; that a man of my age has a job to do; don't have to run up and down the stairs; it is a warm place, not like scaffolding; may be a chance to become a hall porter; impressed by all the labour-saving devices in this kitchen; people will pull together in this place; atmosphere is good; the work is hard, but I must accept it; I love washing up; I can do a good job and earn some money; adjusting my hours so I can get off the premises; I am my own boss; I sometimes get the chance to learn to cook; living-in is useful; the hours are reasonable; the work is varied, I don't just do the washing up; when you have finished work here, you get a meal. The general tenor of the answers suggests that the work environment appears to be of considerable importance to the respondents. The percentages also reflect this.

Ex. 10.4   Whether money is the most important reason why a respondent works and, if not, what the main reasons are

Money	65.7%
Satisfaction	9.0%
Friends at work	7.5%
Make a living	3.0%
Other reasons	11.9%
Not answered	3.0%

Some of the comments in other reasons are vaguely related to making a living, and some of the non-responses would be expected to feel in a similar way. Hence, some three quarters of the sample treat the material side as an important reason for work. Remembering the results in Exhibit 8, the impression gained is one of contradiction, for in that section, money was shown not to be the key motivator for working as a kitchen porter.

However, on reflection, the above answers seem plausible enough. In a sense, categorised questions limit the free expression of respondents' sentiments and tend to turn them into processed products. It is inevitable that the occasional leading question is fastened on and affirmed. In this case, although the question perhaps invited agreement, it needs to be seen more as tantamount to asking whether 'survival' is the most important reason for working. Seen in this light, it would have been surprising indeed had the predominant response not been in the affirmative.

Ex. 10.3   Whether the respondent feels he is giving a personal service to the customer and, if not, whether he works to please the person in charge of him

Personal service to customer	70.1%
Please person in charge	20.9%
Neither one nor the other	6.0%
Not answered	3.0%

Giving a service to customers must be seen from this response anyhow as an important motivating factor. It is all the more pitiful if one bears in mind that kitchen porters are kept well out of sight of patrons, never see them, never receive credit for their contribution to the customer's meal experience and never, ever establish any direct contact with them. Any praise - but no tips - if it ever comes, is likely to be communicated by the chef, who himself is eager for some kind of response to his creations. Seeing the same pots and pans as on the previous day, with differing food particles sticking to them, is perhaps by itself not the best way of making the porter feel that he is giving a service to patrons.

Ex. 10.4   Whether the respondent regards the job as a stepping stone
for promotion and, if so, what position he hopes to reach

Not a stepping stone for promotion	58.2%
Porter-Supervisor	10.4%
Commis chef	4.5%
Other promotions	19.4%
Not answered	7.5%

If we take it that most of the non-respondents also hope for some
sort of promotion, in the region of 35 to 40% entertain this hope.
Other promotions named include head kitchen porter, chef, position on
the management side, job on an ocean liner, uniformed jobs in portering,
waiting and such. (One man in Leicester still wanted to make it to
Head Chef at 67 years of age!).

Ex. 10.5   Asks respondents what they expect they will be doing in ten
years from now, in twenty years from now and after retirement

In carefully contrived laboratory situations, predictions may be more
successful than with human beings in employment. No matter what a
person's intention, the longer the time period, the more speculative
the prediction becomes. Nor do all the intended outcomes of respondents' plans hinge on their intention alone. The influences are many
and varied, of which the will and dispositions to work are but two.

Respondents' future plans with reference to work

	Ten years hence	Twenty years hence	Retirement
Same work	11.9%	4.5%	1.5%
Other but catering	3.0%	3.0%	0.0%
Other than catering	7.5%	9.0%	6.0%
Don't know	76.1%	82.1%	91.0%
Not answered	1.5%	1.5%	1.5%

It is pretty evident that respondents have no inclination to think as
far ahead as ten years hence or further in the future. Given their
general circumstances, the seasonal element of the industry they are
currently working in, possibilities of other work, lack of training or
re-training, their mobility quotient (to a large extent no homes or
families) and their general state of health, it need surprise no one
that these respondents do not see a secure future for themselves, despite their will to work.

A Likely Hypothesis

In the personal service industries - particularly where such services
relate to the hotel industry - moral involvement must constitute an
important variable in the absence of a measurable productivity factor.

Comments: The inherent difficulty in catering to measure productivity is firstly the element of uncertainty of patronage and, therefore,
planning for anticipated demand of cooked food, and the type and number of implements the brigade intends to use once a customer has made a

choice. Pots and pans tend also to vary in their condition after use
and the removal of burnt food remains is known to be laborious. Hence,
measuring a kitchen porter's productivity is even more difficult than
measuring the creation of cooked food unsold. A direct involvement on
the part of a kitchen porter with services to patrons is precluded by
the very nature of his work and the structural division of labour in the
organisation. Exhibit 8 lends ample support to the contention that the
identification of the work with service-giving is illusory. Moral involvement is, therefore, low.

EXHIBIT XI HEALTH MATTERS

In view of the image of general 'instability' kitchen porters have in
the industry, (that, incidentally, through the absence of research no
one could validly explain) the health factor brings most startling empirical information to light. The statistical picture reveals some 67%
of the respondents to have been afflicted by physical or mental illness,
or injuries. 30% of these were of a longer-term duration, that is, in
excess of six months, and 50% of the respondents who suffered these
serious disabilities incurred them frequently in earlier life (before
the age of 45). We did not look into the state of health of head hall
porters.

As far as kitchen porters are concerned, we consider the health aspect
so important with reference to employability, that we decided to present
an in-depth picture here, to draw attention to the mountainous handicap
by way of social acceptability and capacity for contribution these respondents are having to overcome. Notwithstanding this particular stigma,
their contribution (if they are capable of working at all) in economic
terms can only be assessed by speculating on what would happen to this
industry if they were not doing this job. Even if the industry did not
come to a complete standstill, few people would do this work for the
meagre reward these porters get (see Exhibits 5.2,5.3 and 5.4). As a
result, either disposables would have to be used - whoever heard of dis-
posable pots and pans? - or high rewards offered to attract operatives
to it in the wake of a conspicuous absence of technological innovation.
We have already pointed to the reluctance on the part of the industry in
sponsoring improvements to alleviate the drudge that can historically be
traced back over many centuries. Another way out might be to hire kitchen porters on an agency basis, far more costly in pragmatic terms than
the arrangements presently operated.

These workers are, therefore, not quite so 'marginal', if we think of
them in those terms. They are, however, disadvantaged when competing
for jobs, they are weak in bargaining terms, have to accept part-time or
seasonal work and have to cope with spells of unemployment when medical
treatment is needed or a relapse suffered. Indeed, neither should problems of the extra-occupational existence be overlooked. As we have seen,
the kitchen porter is educationally disadvantaged, to a large extent
lacks familial support and home ownership. He has to live with the label given him by society at large, by the hotel industry as well as by
managers of individual firms, that he lacks also the social and emotional skills for finding and keeping a job.

In answer to what serious disabilities they have incurred at some time
in their lives, the respondents gave these details: pneumonia, stroke,
thrombosis, typhoid, silverplate in head (bullet in war), car accident,

nerve trouble, diabetes, cycle accident (split head), fall of scaffold, beaten up and injured, chronic bronchitis, fall down stairs (broken shoulder), hernia, rheumatic arthritis, V.D., deformed skull, T.B., ulcer, smallpox, epilepsy, broken collarbone, smashed ankle, depression, mental deficiency. These disabilities are not necessarily all due to the work they are doing or have done, but the inference is that they render the kitchen porters unfit for more exacting work or make them less consistent in this kind of work. The schedules reveal that 59% admitted serious disability.

Of those who suffered less serious disablement, the following were given: varicose veins, appendicitis, fever, drinking and an assortment of injuries. 21% of the respondents were afflicted in this way, and claimed to suffer from the effects of these. This leaves 20%, who stated that they were not suffering or had not suffered from the effects of any serious illness or injury. However, the interviewer's careful observation which she noted down at the time, made the following analysis possible: respondents appeared to suffer from nerve trouble, fading memory, mental retardation, delusions, habitual drinking, depression, hallucinations, obsessions, speech defects, felt unwanted by management, were labelled as unstable, incoherent in expression, voiced a dislike for responsibility and referred to themselves as rehabilitated.

In sum, the following picture emerges:-

> 50% admitted serious disability
> 21% suffered from minor disabilities
> 20% did not admit disability, although the majority were found by the interviewer to be incapacitated in the way we have indicated above
> Thus, over 70% suffered from some disability.

In order to make our health findings more meaningful and possibly predictive (amd reveal the plight and lack of competitiveness of the kitchen porter for the better jobs in the labour market), we delved into the best available official statistics, with a view to gaining some orientation on the incidence of diseases, deaths and suicides nationally, in some of the occupations that have been the subject of discussion at various stages of this research.

National Indicators (Incapacity)

The (then) Ministry of Pensions and National Insurance reported in 1965 on the incidence of incapacity for work in Group XXIII (Service Workers) which includes occupations of interest to us. We have extracted information compiled by the Ministry for one specific year, that ending in June 1962, and falling into years 1959-63, a time period of interest in the next part of our discussion on deaths and suicides of males employed in the specific low-grade occupations we are considering. The information set out in the table below relates to days lost through incapacity for work. We have ranked the occupations from highest to lowest number of days lost during the year ending June 1962.

164

MORBIDITY: INCIDENCE OF INCAPACITY
FOR WORK IN DIFFERENT AREAS AND
OCCUPATIONS

Occupation	Employed Males	Number of Days lost	Days lost as a % of Employed Males
1. Hospital Porters	25,910	13,003	4 hrs. for year
2. Kitchen Hands	17,870	12,061	5.4
3. Caretakers	49,460	10.359	1.7
4. Building Operatives	24,3410	10,013	0.3
5. Service Workers	96,390	8,324	0.6
6. Clothing Workers	30,640	7,813	2.0
7. Waiters	70,830	7,420	0.8
8. Cooks	37,590	7,374	1.6
9. Nightwatchmen	*	*	*
10. Head Hall Porters	*	*	*
11. Car Park Attendants	*	*	*
12. Dustmen	*	*	*

* Occupations not listed

Source: Part II, H.M.S.O. Report, 1967 pp.71-73 (19)

Observations

(a) Of the occupations considered, only hours per year are lost through absence from work from diseases if spread over all members of these
occupations. (20) In this case, the kitchen hands score 5.4, though
higher than in the other occupations, this does not compare too unfavourably with the national average, which is one third of one day per
year.

(b) We could not ascertain the absences from sickness by occupation.
The national figure for 1962 for employed males is just over thirteen
days and may be taken as a guide with reference to our occupations.
But the following considerations must be borne in mind: not all kitch-
en hands are absent from work and some may be absent for varying periods. As we have seen from the Work History B (Exhibit 4.8) in our
survey, there are many and varied reasons for being out of, or away
from, work other than sickness, disease or injury, not least in a seasonal trade such as the hospitality industry often is.

(c) The definition used for the so-called 'unskilled' occupations presents also a problem for statistical conclusions. It is the definition
on which the numbers included in a particular occupation depend. For
example, service workers or labourers might well be employed as kitchen
hands, but not referred to as such in the Reports. On the other hand,
75,000 persons have been categorised as female kitchen hands, but may
not all be performing kitchen porter work.

National Indicators (Deaths and Suicides)

At the time of writing, the Registrar General's staff were still in the
process of compiling these rates from the 1971 Census data. (21) We,

therefore, had to resort to the Decennial Supplement of 1971, giving details of deaths and suicides by occupation for the period 1959-1963. (22)
Figures on mortality by cause of death and in some places by social
class, are also available. The five-fold breakdown by social class that
had been adopted since the 1911 Census, with Group I representing professionals and Group V the unskilled, is still in use. Kitchen hands are
defined as 'persons washing crockery, pans and preparing vegetables'.
There is no classification by age groups under specific occupations, so
that the extracts below will relate to the age group 15-64. We are
aware that from the information available to us, only a tentative interpretation is possible, which may have to be qualified and at times bord-
er a little on the intuitive. We may say in defence that no similar information, giving a profile of incumbents even on this crude basis,
could be located anywhere else.

SELECTED CASES OF OCCUPATIONAL MORTALITY

Occupation	Employed Males	Deaths	Suicides as % of Deaths	Deaths as % of Employed Males	Death Rate
Kitchen Hands	17,870	915	4.0	5.1	10.3
Hospital Porters	25,910	1,340	2.9	5.1	10.3
Caretakers	49,460	2,628	1.8	5.3	10.6
Service Workers	96,390	5,025	2.9	5.2	10.4
Cooks	37,590	1,406	3.0	3.7	7.5
Clothing Workers	30,640	2,898	2.3	9.4	18.9
Building Workers	243,410	5,951	2.6	2.4	4.8
Waiters	70,830	2,848	3.3	4.0	8.0
Nightwatchmen	*	*	*	*	*
Head Hall Porters	*	*	*	*	*
Car Park Attendants	*	*	*	*	*
Dustmen	*	*	*	*	*

Source: The Registrar General's Decennial Supplement for England and
         Wales, 1961, H.M.S.O., 1971, pp. 62-63

* Occupations not listed.

As throughout this research study, however, we have been concerned with
the specific occupations, unlisted as well as listed, as in the table
above, we continue this practice for the purposes of comparison.

Observations

The above details have been put together and percentages calculated
after obtaining from the Annual Abstract of Statistics, H.M.S.O., 1961,
the total number employed in these particular occupations. To comment
briefly, we note that:-

the most common causes of death by disease for kitchen hands, ranked in
the order of the most frequent causes were:-

        Malignant neoplasms (stomach, lungs, etc.)

```
Coronary diseases
Bronchitis
Vascular lesions of central nervous system
Suicides
Pneumonia
Tuberculosis
```

Note: these may be usefully compared with diseases advised by our
sample of respondents, although we cannot comment on the likely
mortality. If it were possible to project a profile for those
working in the named occupations, then the following comments
may offer some clues:-

(a) taken in absolute terms, the number of kitchen hands who died are
fewer than in the other occupations.

(b) taken relatively to the numbers employed in that occupation during
the period under review, the death percentage of kitchen hands is only
slightly above average for the occupations considered.

(c) the death rate is the number of deaths for every thousand of the
population each year and, taken nationally for all employed males in
the age group 45-54, was found to be 7.3. Comparing this rate with our
sample of kitchen porters (average age 47), we calculated the latter at
10.3, which is over 30% higher.

(d) the findings in the Supplement show (in general terms) the mortality rate for the unskilled (Group V) to be twice that of those employed
in the professions (Group I).

(e) it will be noted that the incidence of deaths of garment workers
is unduly high. A possible explanation is that the job carries a certain amount of stress from the pressures of piecework, is normally seden-
tary and involves the handling of plastic materials (PVC) as well as
the breathing in of dust from handling fibres.

(f) as for suicides, of those who died during the period under review,
kitchen hands comprise the largest percentage of suicides among the low
grade occupations considered. Other catering occupations (see cooks and
waiters above) show the next highest number of suicides for the period.

(g) the national suicide rate of the male working population has been
calculated by us as 1.5, from which it will be noted that only one of
our occupational groups (caretakers) is to be found somewhere near this
rate.

(h) if absolute numbers of registered suicides by occupation of the recorded age groups in the Supplement are taken (15-64), kitchen hands
appear as the lowest, followed in order of increasing progression by
hospital porters, cooks, caretakers, garment workers, waiters, people in
service and building operatives the highest.

(i) in general terms, the Supplement shows that for the five years under review (1959-1964), those in Group V (the unskilled) committed five
times as many suicides as those in Group I (the professionals), whilst
the total numbers employed in the latter were only half that of the
former. This makes it ten suicides by the unskilled for every one by

professionals.

The picture that emerged was quite difficult to compile from the information available at the time of writing. What is more, it may have changed considerably during the following ten years and might be compared with the 1971 Census figures when these become available. The only definite conclusion one can draw from these tentative calculations is that death and suicide rates of unskilled workers are substantially above the national rates and considerably higher when compared to professional workers.

Hypothesis

Physical disabilities form a cause as well as an effect of the kitchen porter's activity in his particular occupational role. In the former, ill health impedes satisfactory adjustment to work and to his associates; in the latter, cultural practices (such as certain kinds of work routine) carry with them physical ill-effects.

Comments: here once more, the evidence of physical disabilities and their handicaps in the marketability of one's skills receive strong support, especially as concerns the nature of the disabilities from a kitchen porter's occupation. Stability is a crucial phenomenon in effective integration at the work place and our supporting comments throughout in respect of this proposition appear still to hold good.

As an interesting theoretical point, reference is made to a significant earlier study of suicide at the turn of the century in France, by Emile Durkheim, one of the founding fathers of sociology. When considering his data on suicide rates, he discovered a close correlation between the length of day and suicide. It was not, however, daylight or the season that mattered, as much as a person's activity. Those who have many social relationships and are actively engaged in them will be less lonesome and less prone to suicide than those who are not in that position. Split shifts at work to make the day long and isolation in or out of work could well account for what Durkheim calls the 'anomic' condition, that is one of individual and social disorganisation or crisis, uncertainties and pressured in the pattern of life. Childless persons, the widowed, single or divorced, and the rootless, are likely to experience this state of acute anomie. Indeed, researches designed to establish a possible index of 'anomic suicide' and the testing of some of Durkheim's hypotheses could well form a useful future research project in the field of occupational sociology.

EXHIBIT XII HOUSING

Our sample of kitchen porters reveals that at least 20% have spent some time in hospitals or institutions, 19% in H.M. Forces, that 10% are female and 13% of foreign extraction. Thus, some 62% have, by reason of their circumstances, an inbuilt difficulty in leading an existence in a settled home. Those in the services, hospitals or institutions would not be endowed with princely sums to enable them to purchase homes upon re-entry into communal life. We also know of the inherent difficulties for immigrants and women generally to obtain mortgages. The remaining 40%, even though seemingly not in a position of re-settlement, have suffered to a large extent from minor ailments and small incomes which

is a vital handicap in home ownership. Add to this that 72% are for the
time being single and without the same compulsion as a family man to set
up home and it can easily be seen how home ownership is linked to stability and security.

It is, therefore, interesting to see how respondents fare in terms of
accommodation and aid from public authorities.

Ex. 12.1 Type of accommodation at the time of the interview

Living-in (employer accommodation)	29.9%
Living in a private home	28.2%
Council house	19.4%
Other accommodation (relatives, etc.)	7.5%
Hostel	6.0%
Private flat	4.5%
Rented flat	3.0%
No fixed abode	1.5%

66% are definitely not home owners and it is extremely doubtful that
all those who stated that they lived in a private house or private flat
actually owned these. What actually constitutes 'homelessness' has long
been a contentious point. If we define homelessness as a state in which
the occupier for the time being does not enjoy security of tenure, at
least 45% of the above would seem to be in that position. It is also
known for some hotels to provide transport for and make liberal use of
employees who reside in mental institutions (Timothy Bullock, an infor-
med catering manager, interviewed by the author, would be tempted to say
that they lived in a private house of private flat). (23)

Ex. 12.2 Housing, health and job

Respondents were asked whether they receive help from a public authority:

1.	To find employment	31.3%
2.	To find a home	23.9%
3.	Money aid	19.4%
4.	Concerning health matters	9.0%
5.	Not answered	1.5%

It appears that some 84% of the respondents are receiving some help
from a public authority.

The National Picture

Figures from the General Household Survey, 1973, published in 1976, but
covering approximately the same period as our interviews, offer some information on a national scale. (24) However, the tenure profile in the
various tables gives either age groups and tenure or socio-economic
groups and tenure, but not correlations of age, socio-economic membership and tenure. The latter information is available in our findings,
since all our respondents belong to the so-called 'unskilled occupational groups'. The national information we shall show here from extracts
of the tables is therefore not strictly comparable in other than 60- or
60+ groups. (The average age in our sample is 47 years).

Socio-Economic groups and household by tenure:

Extracts from Tables 2.1(a) and 2.6(b) of the Household Survey, mentioned above.

	Prof.	Unsk.	16-59	60+
Owner-occupied	24	16	19	36
Owner with mortgage	58	7	14	2
Rented with job	6	1	3	1
Rented from L.A. or new town	3	56	28	36
Rented from Housing Association	1	1	1	1
Rented privately unfurnished	4	16	15	22
Rented privately furnished	5	3	21	2

If we compare the housing situation of the unskilled above with the results from our sample kitchen porters in Exhibit 12.1, we note that council house accommodation is three times as large, which indicates greater security of tenure and reflects the more mobile existence of the kitchen porters. Living-in is less common above, as compared with the hotel and catering industry, and renting more common, while hostel accommodation is not significant at all. As one might expect, ownership with professions is high (82%), as is the mortgage element, since this category is known to be fairly mobile and spiralling upwards occupationally or promotion-wise. Nationally, it would seem that the unskilled are somewhat better situated than the kitchen porters. While 66% of the latter are unlikely to be home owners, (and that percentage is probably larger) the position appears to be similar with the unskilled generally, but the degree of security of tenure by our definition is eminently better than that of the kitchen porters. (96% as against 55%).

It may be of interest to observe from the findings in the Household Survey and from our schedules, that state of health, education and housing correlate. The unskilled in age group 45-64 suffer nearly twice the volume of chronic sickness than the professional groups, while those living in rented accommodation (compared with ownership) show a substantially higher incidence of chronic sickness as do those who, in addition, have no proper heating, fixed bath and lavatory. It is also noted that, of the persons aged 16-69 who are not in full-time education, 90% of the unskilled socio-economic group (male) have no educational qualifications while 58% of the professional category have university degrees.

We would conclude that the highly mobile kitchen porter (by circumstance or by choice) does incur psychological costs when he severs friendship or family ties (or is prevented from establishing them), disrupts his normal pattern of life (if, indeed, he has one), and loses his sense of identification with people in a local community, all matters hardly capable of quantification. A vital element in a stable pattern of life is a secure and comfortable home with all the benefits this obviously entails.

Hypothesis (a)

Official agencies tend, in their treatment of individual members of a stigmatised occupation, i.e. kitchen porters, to relate respectability to the social and economic importance of that occupation exhibited by the community.

Comments: This exhibit shows only that a large number of the respondents are receiving some help from a public authority. The determination of respective public authority attitudes towards kitchen porters by way of a collective respectability-removing ceremony in which the community and its agents impose their own definitions of abnormality and moral worth as hypothesised is a subject of separate investigation. Respondents themselves were found to be sensitive on the question of respectability, evidenced by the fact that nearly 60% declined to comment on this attribute (see Exhibit 9), having most likely attached to it the sort of interpretation we proposed in our analysis of stigma in Chapter 3 above.

Hypothesis (b)

Vagrancy and transiency are to a degree attributable to the seasonality in this industry (frequently alleviated by living-in arrangements, which have their own drawbacks), but primarily a function of homelessness and rootlessness of the low crystaliser, participating intermittently in one or more of the stigmatised occupations.

Comments: How far, in quantitative terms, vagrancy and transiency can be shown to be attributable to seasonality in this industry is difficult to establish without case study in depth. Homelessness has been shown in our observations (see Chapter 4 above), to be a contributory factor to an unstable existence. There is a certain inter-relatedness about social problems of which the kitchen porter is a victim of which instrumentality we have given as indication already in various places of the survey analysis and in the theoretical sections. It may be that the image of the kitchen porter currently held in the industry could be a derivation from the internalisation of social problems on the part of the victims, who find themselves in situations and act in terms of such values as are generally decried by the rest of society. Housing is one on those problems.

EXHIBIT XIII HOBBIES AND LEISURE PURSUITS

In view of the ever-increasing significance of the leisure question, we propose to treat this exhibit at four distinct levels. Firstly, to produce the results of our field work relating to the kitchen porters in the Midlands (the principal occupational group under investigation). Then, to add some brief, comparative notes on head hall porters by way of contrast. This will be followed by an examination of some national leisure statistics and comments on the relevance of selected current leisure theories to our empirical findings.

Ex. 13.1 Whether the respondent has ever engaged in leisure activities or has had a main hobby

76% had, indeed, felt the need to engage in these activities. We have categorised these activities under type pursued:

1. Sports (Outdoor)   37%
        (Football, tennis cricket, skating,
        swimming, cycling, walking, putting,
        golf, fishing, athletics, pigeons)
         (Indoor)   12%
        (Boxing, table tennis, darts, snooker,
        weight lifting, roller-skating)

2. Recreational and Social   21%
        (Minding children, going to clubs,
        supporting football, giving blood,
        welfare work, dancing, cinema, chess,
        courting, draughts)

3. Therapeutical   28%
        (Gardening, cooking, knitting, music,
        carpentry, mechanical-tinkering,
        photography, typing, hairdressing,
        keeping goldfish, first aid, decorating,
        playing piano, washing-up, motoring,
        life saving)

4. Educational   22%
        (Studying, evening classes, stamp
        collecting, coin collecting,
        literature reading, poetry, composing,
        occult sciences, the arts)

Ex. 13.2 When the respondent first engaged in the activity, average
          time per week spent on it and whether still pursuing it

1.   When first engaged in leisure activity:

          Since childhood   15%
          Since teens   40%
          More recently   14%
          Not answered, not applicable   29%

2.   Still actively pursuing these activities:
                                      54%

3.   Average time per week spent pursuing activities:

          No time at all   12%
          Less than five hours per week   39%
          Less than twelve hours per week   8%
          More than twelve hours per week   7%
          Other   2%
          Not answered, not applicable   32%

   Although 54% of the respondents are still actively pursuing hobbies
or leisure activities, some 60% spent barely one hour per day in which
to do so, or so it would seem.

   It will also be noted that 40% are keen on vocational/educational activities and nearly that many on outdoor leisure activities. Whether

all leisure activites are hobbies, or whether all leisure activities
are recreational, is difficult to establish, partly for definitional
reasons and partly for the main constraint in this kind of research to
establish laboratory conditions. It should also be pointed out that a
good many of the respondents will engage in more than one activity for
whatever purposes or whatever the outcome in terms of benefits.

Since some 60% spent a mere hour per day on the leisure activities
and 32% did not usefully comment on the question, Parker's 'opposition
pattern' (25), which would otherwise gain legitimacy by the great variety of contrasting activities to the actual job of kitchen portering
on this evidence, cannot be completely substantiated. The next exhibit
actually specifies the reasons why the activities are undertaken.

Ex. 13.3 Reasons for undertaking leisure activities

54% pursue the activities for their enjoyment, 15% for their personal
development and 6% for career purposes. Thus, 75% appear to derive
benefit from the activity and do not feel in any way obligated to pursue it. Some 6% perform it to supplement their income, for health reasons or because it is regarded as a civic, religious, or social obligation. 15% did not comment and 10% had other reasons for such activities as they were undertaking. What these reasons are will become
apparent from the answers to our request for information on how respondents spend their time if they have no main hobby. (See Ex.13.5)

Over half the sample used the all-embracing word enjoyment to signify
their reasons for engaging in the leisure activities. It has evidently
been used in an operative sense. For our purposes, we take it to mean
a state or feeling of derived gratification; a manifestation of joy; an
experience of delight; to be amused, entertained, experience pleasure
or an advantage. Looking at such gratification psychologically, it may
be seen as play, possibly to be thought about while work goes on, allowing relaxed, congenial and gratifying relations with human beings in
contrast with work demanding order, discipline and producing tension.
The centrality of play in the life of kitchen porters is difficult to
establish without participant observation and case studies in depth.
It would seem to us to slant towards an active, rather than passive,
pattern, although we are inclined to suggest that the activities would
be undertaken if there were time for it, rather than that they have actually been undertaken. It is, therefore, more a question of attitude
towards the role of leisure in respondents' lives than the specific use
of time in contrast to market research in the leisure industries, where
the actual activity undertaken predominates in importance over attitudes
towards it. We shall return to a consideration of some existing leisure
concepts in relation to our evidence.

Ex. 13.4 Whether activities pursued alone or jointly

31% pursue the activities alone and 33% with others, while the remaining porters did not choose to comment. The percentages for the joint
activities are made up as follows: 5% join with a member of the family,
22% with friends and 6% with other people. It is within the realms of
possibility that some 67% experience considerable isolation, bearing in
mind 'familylessness' and homelessness evidenced already to a similar
extent as this figure. Again, only in-depth case research can adequately substantiate this.

We have found it convenient to categorise the activities, if any, under
five heads. It will be noted that those respondents to whom a leisure
activity is not a main hobby may still be availing themselves of it, or
any that been mentioned in Exhibit 13.1. By and large, however, the
pattern appears to differ somewhat, particularly where isolates are concerned, when the activities seem distinctly casual or spur-of-the-moment
and unpremeditate, so to speak.

Group (a) Leisure-Oriented Socialisers: 57%

This is the out-and-about group; activities
include: dancing, watching sports, cinema,
darts playing, cycling, driving, playing
bingo, visiting friends, clubs, cafes, pubs
and engaging in betting.

Group (b) Other Socialisers: 12%

Looking after children, spare-time work,
trying to make friends, going for walks,
going to concerts, all these and similar
would come under this category.

Group (c) Home-Bound Isolates: 30%

Examples of how this category spends spare
time include: resting, sitting in garden,
pottering about, cleaning brasses, flower-
arranging, housework, domestic chores,
walking dog, listening to radio.

Group (d) Isolates performing Casual Activities: 12%

We include here again activities actually
stated in the schedules by way of answers:
for example, wandering about, smoking and such.

Group (e) Other Isolates: 10%

These include activities of a more personal
kind to the respondent, or such as dreaming,
thinking or exercising.

   The percentage of the groups exceeds one hundred because a respondent
may specify a combination of activities. Over half of the sample regard themselves as isolates (52%), although it is possible that some of
the socialisers feel the need for isolation for some of their time, or
that some of the isolates wish occasionally for social companionship.
A case investigation of a representative sample would bring the variations of investment of time to light. A very small percentage (1 to 2%)
has apparently completely lost any recreational conception, if indeed
they ever had one. For example, a 59-year-old man working as kitchen
porter in Birmingham replied thus to the question how he spends his
time if he has no main hobby: 'The only job that makes me feel happy
is washing up.'

Some Comparative Information from National Figures

The Social Survey Division of the Population Census Office publishes pe-
riodically in what is known as the 'General Household Survey' information on the leisure patterns of the population. Meaningful comparisons
are, however, to be regarded as tentative, even though these coincide
with the same year, on account of the differences of sample design, definitions, adherence to regional practices and age groups, all of which
influence participation, frequency and kinds of activity pursued. Seasonal considerations also need qualification since if, say, interviews
take place in the winter, this might tempt respondents to favour winter
sports. Although the national survey gives useful information on leisure activities by region, availability of car, total household income,
urban or rural area, together with certain correlations not offered in
our research, in turn, it included details which are not to be found in
the national survey, such as why certain activities are undertaken and a
categorisation by particular personality types, among other behavioural
details.

Extract from Tables 4.5 and 4.7 of Household Survey, 1973

Activity (Males only)	Age Group 45-49	Unskilled Workers
Active outdoor sports and games	17	8
Active indoor sports and games	8	4
Watching sports and games	15	7
Open-air outings	20	13
Visits to historic buildings, zoos, etc.	8	3
Cinema, theatre, concerts, opera, shows	13	10
Amateur music or dramatics	3	1
Going out for a meal, drink, dance, bingo	64	46
Gardening, needlework, DIY, hobbies	58	40
Social and voluntary activities, going to clubs, visting, entertaining	61	58
Betting, gambling, games of skill and other activities	35	21

   Regrettably, although our kitchen porter would fit into the socio-economic category of 'unskilled', the household survey does not give activities by age correlated with socio-economic groupings. It will be noted
that keenness on outdoor and indoor sporting activities of kitchen porters is four times as great as that of the unskilled in the household
survey. On the other hand, social participation of the latter exceeds
the former by two and a half times. The explanation for such variations
may lie in the extremity of the tasks performed, that is, the kitchen
porter is keen to escape from the heat and smell of the kitchen or scullery, although not necessarily from physical activity, while on the
other hand, the stultifying effect of the work inhibits the ability and
the will for freer social mixing. Psychologists have suggested that
single people tend to prefer more energetic pursuits, partly because
they can manage to devote more time to them and partly because they need
to sublimate their sex drives. Some 72% of our kitchen porter sample
were at interviewing time for the time being single.

New Approaches to Leisure - A Topical Aside

It will have been noted from the survey findings already discussed that most of our respondents are not 'professional' kitchen porters. They are, for the time being, part of a pool of 'available' workers who are capable of immediate application to specific tasks. Indeed, a recent article in the Catering Times (June 17th, 1976, page 13) refers to a manager of a hotel who employs 64 full time staff, but has a 'bank of 30 casuals', perhaps an indicator of the emerging 'temporariness' of our society. Certainly, more research is needed before we know to what extent and with reference to which type of activity we can distinguish between casual-trained, casual-untrained, professional-trained and professional-untrained kitchen porter, where leisure pursuits are concerned. For the moment, such questions as the inter-relationship between professional hobbyists performing or practising in their leisure time and their amateur counterparts whose activities interfere more and more with their work, must also remain open. Temporary kitchen porters may well deny the occupational label to the outside world and align themselves to the leisure habits of the socio-economic group they feel they belong to. Circumstances such as these tend further to blur the picture vis-a-vis Parker's proposed leisure concepts relative to the nature of occupational demands, where an 'extension pattern' signifies a spill-over of work into leisure and a 'neutrality pattern' that central interest veers away from the job.

At the risk of being somewhat critical and destructive, we would suggest that all so-called leisure theories thus far propounded dilute themselves, when tested, from hypotheses to mere assertions, or at best propositions, until its (leisure's) central purpose has been established by exhaustive tests. For this, we still wait in eager anticipation.

For Karl Marx, time off is for labour to replenish its strength. For Nels Anderson, leisure is the focal point in people's lives. Joffre Dumazedier diagnoses this to be true to such extent that jobs will be sought which do not constrain the leisure interest regarded as central (27), while Smiegel and his contributors regard it as a potentially disruptive force in our society.(28) For Bell, work is irksome, but its unpleasantness can be minimised by leisure.* Parker sees leisure as an integrated phenomenon in a symbiotic sense, that will make work pleasurable. Many more theories exist that attempt to define what leisure is. We are more concerned here with what it is for. Hence, the brief documentation of an aggregate of concepts, by no means more than a fraction of those that exist. How far actual cooking, as a time-consuming process, will be abandoned for thawing and heating, to turn the priority of eating from pleasure to maintenance (an inferior pursuit) will probably determine the kitchen porter's leisure time. At present, it would appear that leisure to the kitchen porter is what the kitchen porter does when he can. Hardly an adventurous prologue, but one that ails from the poverty of tested research which could be applied to our occupational group.

A kitchen porter's life style is contingent on a catering industry that can offer him stable work and his disposition to accept available employment. The work cycle will determine his free time, that is, the time available to him to organise his priorities. When the kitchen porter works, he works for survival on tasks that carry low status and
*Bell,Daniel(1956)'Work and its Discontents',Beacon Press,Boston. Reference relates to entire theme in Monograph.

precious little intrinsity. Hence, for him, leisure carries frequently
more utility than work, however it may be used. At any rate, arduous
and sustained effort, as that kind of work entails (normally under split
shift conditions, which lengthen the working day considerably) would
leave only limited leisure time.

We have already referred to Parker's leisure patterns and how these
may be applicable to our occupational group. Other researchers have
also enquired into the pattern of leisure activities. Clarke (29) discovered such a pattern from an investigation of five occupational grad-
ings to which he attached the prestige ranges from N.O.R.C. scores.
He found at the lower levels of prestige groupings higher levels of
creativity and at levels above the lowest, a degree of activities of a
more passive nature. This is what one would probably expect to find,
except that these findings are not substantiated by our evidence. Clarke
asked his respondents also how they would spend an extra two hours of
leisure per day and found workers of the lower prestige levels to prefer to rest and relax. This, too, is unconfirmed by our evidence.
Gerstl's work, pointing to work situation, skills and social imagery,
considers occupational milieu crucial in non-occupational behaviour.(30)
Although he has not investigated low prestige groups, his findings are
much closer to a proposition which we support, that there are norms derived from occupational reference groups which dictate, or are conducive
to, particular patterns of behaviour. Likewise, whilst the productive
work element of the kitchen porter is prescribed for him, he exercises
some, but not complete, control over the mode in which he uses his leisure time since (unless he be a complete isolate) peer group or reference
group will require him to adhere to the internalised culture norms of
expected leisure behaviour. As a consequence, only specific activities
will be acceptable whilst deviations may be frowned upon.

There is, as yet, no sociologically-grounded theory which helps us to
predict a leisure pattern for the totality of low prestige workers across the whole range of industries, and explain its causal connections
in terms of activities. Max Kaplan, writing on the subject of leisure
currently, makes reference to the instrumentality of social action when
he says:

> '... but the fundamental point never to be lost is that
> leisure to the participant, like his religion and his
> love, is what he thinks it is, because on that kind of
> assumption he acts out his life'. (31)

If theory may prove useful, it must be to the person who is the ultimate end of our purposes, says Kaplan, but he also offers a typology of
conceptualisations ranging over humanistic, therapeutic, quantitative,
institutional, epistomological and sociological leisure models, the detailed discussion of which goes beyond the scope of our more confined
objectives. This points to a need for an integrated model for leisure,
although Kaplan regards a psychosociological construct as the most inc-
lusive and representing leisure views not just at a unitary level. The
model takes Max Weber's lead with the leisure elements as an antithesis
to work. These elements are not random, however, and require to be syn-
thesised in terms of major, dynamic and exchangeable human activities.

Hypothesis (a)

In many instances, the kitchen porter's alienation from his work becomes alienation from life and the mental stultification produced by his labour permeates his entire leisure existence.

Comments: The occupation of kitchen porter has certain peculiarities of its own which makes it different from other socio-economic groups of the same level. We have commented on these in Exhibit 2 already. Hence, kitchen porters are found to be four times as keen on outdoor sporting activities as other unskilled socio-economic groups in the country, while the latter engage two and a half times as much in social activities as do kitchen porters. This points to a probable spillover of stultification from their work and work environment. Since some 60% spend barely one hour per day on leisure activities as defined and understood by themselves, that information would reinforce the assumption that they may not be in a physical state to do so. We have already ventured the view (in Exhibit 13.3) that it is more the activities kitchen porters would engage in, were there sufficient time and energy, rather than activities actually undertaken. We suggest that the emerging profile is more a case of impression management on the part of the kitchen porters, so that they may not appear to the world just as docile work-horses without any outside interests.

Hypothesis (b)

There is an inverse relationship between the level of occupational stigma and an individual's repertoire of possible roles.

Comments: The findings do not appear to substantiate this hypothesis in the sense that kitchen porter work, on account of its physical taxation and unsocial hours, renders an incumbent incapable of cultivating extensive social activities. Time-wise, there may be some truth in that handicap, but the range of 'leisure' activities, not necessarily 'socially shared' has been unanticipated by ourselves as investigators. The activities, though of a great variety, are predominantly self-indulged, while the time allegedly spent on them must be regarded as unreliable from the information received. One third of the respondents said that they shared leisure activities with others and our estimate is that 67% at least experience considerable isolation, while over half of the sample regard themselves as isolates. Communal roles and local activities are practically non-existent, which suggests that respondents are, in the main, transient or not well integrated, or both. To the extent that social roles and scope for friendships have been shown to be very limited for the kitchen porter, the hypothesis is close to the mark, or if we had quantifiable data, we would say that there is no significant difference between the findings and a null hypothesis. Basically, the probability that the stigmatising condition severely limits the subject's repertoire of possible roles would seem to hold true.

NOTES TO CHAPTER 6

1. Gould, Julius (1972) 'Nationality and Ethnicity',in Barker, P.
    (Ed.). 'A Sociological Portrait', Penguin Books, Middx. (Chap-
    ter II).

2. Bell, Colin (1972) 'Marital Status' in Barker, P. (Ed.) 'A
    Sociological Portrait', Penguin Books, Middx.

3. Goode, Enid (1966) 'Social Class and Church Participation',
    American Journal of Sociology, Vol.72,(pp.102-111)

4. Hamilton, Richard (1964) 'The Behaviour of Skilled Workers'
    in Shostack, A. and Gomberg, W. (Eds.), 'Blue-Collar World:
    Studies of the American Worker', Prentice-Hall, New Jersey,
    (pp. 42-57)

5. Robertson, Roland (1972) 'Education' in Barker, P. (Ed.), 'A
    Sociological Portrait', Penguin Books, Middlesex,(Chapter 14)

6. Little, Alan (1972) 'Education' in Barker, P. (Ed.) 'A Socio-
    logical Portrait', Penguin Books, Middx. (Chapter 9)

7. Goffman, Erving (1968) 'Stigma: Notes on the Management of
    Spoiled Identity', Penguin Books, Middx.

8. Caplow, Theodore (1964) 'The Sociology of Work', McGraw-Hill,
    New York (pp.172-3)

9. Saunders, K.C. (1976) 'An Experimental Supplement on Stableness
    in Employment as measured by Social and Statistical Indicators',
    unpublished Research Paper.

10. Herzberg, Frederick (1966) 'Work and the Nature of Man', World
    Publishing Co., Cleveland and New York.

11. Emery, F.E. (1959) 'Characteristics of Socio-Technical Systems'
    Tavistock Institute of Human Relations, London (Doc.No.527)
    Also in Emery, F.E. (Ed) 1969 'Systems Thinking', Penguin Books,
    Middx. (pp.281-296)

12. Vroom, Victor (1964) 'Work and Motivation', John Wiley, New
    York (Chapter 7)

13. Manpower Policy in the Hotel and Restaurant Industry (Research
    Findings), Hotel and Catering E.D.C., N.E.D.O., London, 1975
    (pp.4,5,6,7,28,73,9)

14. Brown, M. and Winyard, S. (1975) 'Low Pay in Hotels and Cater-
    ing' (Low Pay Pamphlet No.2), Low Pay Unit, London (pp.4,5,22,
    26)

15. Wages Council Order, 1975, No.1571, H.M.S.O., 1975 (p.9)

16. 'Comparative Earnings, 1974-75', European Communities Commission
    Statistical and Information Offices, 23 Chesham St. London SW1

17.   Woolf, Renee, France (Personal Contact with author, 1975),
      Rogers, Randolph, U.S.A. (letters to author, 1976)
      McIntyre, John, Federal Republic of Germany (letters to author,
      1976)

18.   Goldthorpe, J.H. and Hope, K. (1974) 'The Social Grading of
      Occupations: A New Approach and Scale' (Oxford Studies in Social
      Mobility), Clarendon Press, Oxford. (Entire monograph relevant)

19.   'Incidence of Incapacity for Work in Different Areas and
      Occupations, Part II', H.M.S.O., 1967 (pp.71-73)

20.   Health and Safety Executive (Branch of Department of Health and
      Social Security, London) Dr. Fox (telephone conversation with
      author, May 1976)

21.   Office of Population Censuses and Surveys, Medical Statistics
      Division, St. Catherine's House, London (Personal interview and
      telephone conversation with offical, conducted by author)

22.   Registrar General's Decennial Supplement for England and Wales
      1961, 'Occupational Mortality', H.M.S.O., London, 1971, (pp.
      62-63)

23.   Bullock, Timothy, Lecturer in Industrial Catering Management,
      Middlesex Polytechnic at Hendon (formerly hotel manager and
      contract catering executive), interviewed by author, June 1976

24.   General Household Survey, 1973 (Leisure Patterns), H.M.S.O.,
      London, 1976,(pp. 26,32,123)

25.   Parker, Stanley (1972) 'The Future of Work and Leisure',Paladin
      London (pp.96,97,98,74)

26.   Anderson, Nels (1974) 'Man's Work and Leisure', F.J. Brill,
      Leiden

27.   Dumazedier, Joffre (1967) 'Towards A Society of Leisure', The
      Free Press, New York (pp.5 and 75-76)

28.   Smiegel, Erwin O. (Ed.) (1963) 'Work and Leisure', College and
      University Press, New Haven, Connecticut,(esp. Chapter 5,
      Faunce, Chapter 2, Bell)

29.   Clarke, A.C. (1956) 'The Use of Leisure and its Relation to
      Levels of Occupational Prestige', American Sociological Review,
      Vol.21, (pp.301-307)

30.   Gerstl, J.E. (1963) 'Leisure, Taste and Occupational Milieu',
      in Smiegel, E.O. (Ed.), College and University Press, New
      Haven, Connecticut, (pp.146-167)

31.   Kaplan, Max (1975) 'Leisure, Theory and Policy', John Wiley,
      New York (pp.50,18)

7   A re-appraisal of stigmatisation

Introductory Matters

In Chapter 3 above, we have presented schematically and discussed such
matters as the meaning, definition, anatomy, composition and the possible causal elements of occupational stigma. We also drew comparative
profiles of the expressed feelings of individuals in other (than catering) low-grade occupations. In this Chapter, we turn from the subjective experiences of incumbents to objective conceptualisation at macro
level, so as to inter-relate the stigma effect across industrial, occupational and individual boundaries.

   As a general rule, most societies count about half of their populations as members of the labour force, whilst at least in Western society
the conventional allocation of active, gainful employment of some two
thirds of an individual's life cycle shows the centrality of the role
of work itself. We have earlier considered the shift of work values in
a historical context as an illuminating base for our contemporary analysis of the hotel industry and of specific occupations within it. In
addition to our acquainting the reader with the dominant meanings of
work, our historical analysis of the domestic service and the hotel industry has attempted to show also some regard towards certain social
characteristics and emphasising such phenomena as are likely to give
rise to societal stigmata towards servile and menial occupational tasks.
What we have omitted - it being beyond the scope of this research project - is to consider in depth the sociological aspects of the changing
structure of the hotel industry; but we shall briefly sketch out what
we consider these needs are.

Stigmatised Industries

It has been noted that stigmatised persons may be labelled in accordance
with their social identity and occupational membership. But, individuals stand also in a certain relationship to their trade or employment,
and here, a classification of industrial status is of consequence.
Structurally, the size and distribution of undertakings, the nature of
the service or product and the effect of conditions of entry for various
occupational grades, may reveal its status in society. Judgment will
also derive from the conduct of an industry: how, in social terms, behaviour on such matters as pricing policy, the quality of service or
product and the promotional and profit policies, affect its patrons,
clients or customers. A third criterion will be performance, by way of
a longitudinal, national contribution within a socially beneficial context: the hotel industry's contribution to tourism and to recuperation-
al hospitality for the users and citizens.

   Certain structures may result in desirable performances and conduct
internally to the various units or segments of an industry, and externally to the world outside. What we are saying here is that it is feasible not only to recognise occupationally and socially stigmatised
elements of a country's work force, but also of whole industries, which

by image, performance, industrial unrest and problems of location, indicate characteristics of deprivation and attract a society's stigmata.

Some indicators may be suggested here, because of their high degree
of relevance in our subsequent discussion: does, for example, the industry concerned offer regular or only intermittent employment; has it
got a stable, well-trained work force, or does the greater majority consist of less-skilled, unskilled and untrained workers; does the industry
offer good working conditions and security of employment, or are the
standards taken from the minimum requirements of a wages council; does
the location of the industry allow for union representation, or does the
scatter inhibit this; does the industry employ a predominant element of
immigrants or 'guest workers', part-time workers and older workers;
does it make maximum use of available technology; do research and innovation play an important role; has the industry a long-term developmental
policy for the nation's benefit; and finally, is the product that it
offers beneficial in the nature of a direct service to the consuming
person? The answers to questions of this kind enable one to construct a
fairly objective profile in assessing what social role a particular industry may play in society at any period of time.

The Stigma Effect

The social problem of occupational stigma may be viewed purely as a phenomenon affecting large numbers of people capable of statistical analysis, or it may be visualised in its directly human proportions by the
selection and analysis of human types. In either case, the association
of stigma with an industry that attracts peripheral workers seems to us
highly relevant, because of the mutually reinforcing stigmatising propensities. Societal reaction towards occupational stigma tends to operate at three levels: towards the observable individual, towards the
occupational group and towards the entire industry. All three possess
visible, symbolic or intrinsic attributes that have long mediated to
nurture the stigmatising process.

Influential media of communication have tended to promote this influence. Daily press reports particularly can be seen to label any transgressor of the law by occupation. In the eyes of society, it therefore
does this vicariously to the weary numbers of the whole occupation, reflecting incidentally also upon the industry to which this occupation
belongs. 'Kitchen Porter accused of Arson'; 'Kitchen Porter threatens
Chef with Carving Knife'. Reports like those and similar associate the
occupation with the act committed, not because the individual is vind-
ictive, or aggressive, but because he is a kitchen porter who, in the
industry's image 'potentially does these things'. We intend to show
later in our discussion why direct social encounters are not necessary
for these societal predispositions to exist.

Clearly, the social stigma precedes the entrance into a job these occupational members take and pursues them long after they have made their
exit. They feel it, are aware of it and are degraded by it. This self-
realisation is something internal, psychological for a man. Equally,
externally - sociologically - the community exhudes it, slurs and brands
(in the social sense) the incumbent. Prestige at first derives usually
from a position held or membership of an occupation, but is later transmitted to the holder himself; prestige can shape his conduct and a person's conduct can gain esteem. But, take away his pride and contaminate

him and the likely effects will be retaliation by way of physical dest-
ruction of property, breakages, blocking up the sink, creating bottlenecks in the work flow, or even violence. We may call this the 'stigma
effect'.

The Concern of Respectability

Attitudes towards work, as such, are to be kept distinct from the work
tasks of the job itself. Work values are largely a function of cultural norms, quite separate from the work environment in which the individual performs. The moral value of carrying out particular kinds of
work has given rise to confusion with reference to the respectability
aspect of belonging to an identifiable occupational group. One question
in our survey asks the opinion of respondents whether their present job
(of kitchen portering) is less respectable than that of some specified
other occupations and professions. This has proved a thoroughly sensitive issue with some half of the number in our sample, for they attached moral value to the actual work tasks performed and the very question
of respectability as a blemish on their character. Their awareness of
the adverse image in the 'trade' and society at large tended to add sensitivity to the issue, and here comes an outsider to 'rub salt into the
wound'. The question related to membership of what might be regarded
as a socially worthy occupation. Some incumbents feared to pronounce
upon the status of their occupational role and a manifest defence of
moral worth in the display of indignation provided a rational escape
from the dilemma. Evidence of past research reveals ways in which the
respectability of an occupation may be enhanced or professionally leg-
itimised. For example, in an illegal abortion clinic, patrons have been
found to treat staff as legitimate medical personnel. (1) Police have
been found to designate their informers as 'special employees'.(2)

Pharmacists used partitions to separate spatially their professional
role of dispensing from the demeaning one of shopkeeper purveying cos-
metics and toys. (3) Some of the kitchen porters are beginning to assume a professional stance, as exemplified by such cases as carrying a
toolbox with rubber mat to keep feet dry, goggles to protect eyes from
steam, thermometers to measure temperature of water and a selection of
suitably-tested detergents. (4) All these examples involve basic prop-
erties of respectability: actors and audiences; maintaining favourable
identities; and creating improved images. Hence, sociological concern
with respectability is quite a significant factor in the analysis of
occupational devaluation.

Stereotyping and Labelling

The kitchen porter is a member of an occupational group within the hotel
and catering industry, on whom we are focusing in some depth our theoretical and, in the main, practical interest. Our survey is built upon
this group. This occupation is said to thrive on the supply of particular 'types' to a needy establishment without undue formality for short
term mutual benefit. The image that the 'trade' and society have bestowed on the kitchen porter has labelled him with the specific characteristics already discussed. Having done that, society then treats him in
terms of this undesirable ascribed status. To avoid the disadvantages
this entails, the labelled porter finds it easier to restrict his social
relationships to others like himself. He may react to the stigma in a
variety of ways, either rationally, trying to adapt to his current

environment, or adopting his own norms to adjust his relationship to a
rejecting society.

We intend, presently, to look conceptually deeper into the foundations
of stigma-generating situations. For the present, we have established
that a typical image of the kitchen porter vis-a-vis the outside world
which may be charted by, what in technical language, we may call a
'subjective socialisation pattern'. This pattern aims to identify the
phases in a person's life cycle from which the maladjustment derives.
Before presenting this conceptual scheme, we must first look at the
question of labelling.

The Labelled Kitchen Porter

In a sense, stereotypes function as a substitute for knowledge, although
the catering trade claims to have a good knowledge of particular actors
in specific situations. Objectively, this is hardly sufficient to place
collective blame upon the occupation. More illuminating is the interactionist idea which holds that breaking a norm is really the product
of a transaction between the transgressor and society and perceived by
some as a threat of which the more powerful groups in society or their
agents disapprove. Social groups are said to create the condition of
deviance by making the rules whose infraction brings it about. Thus,
the act disapproved of is held to be not a quality of deviance by the
infactor, but a consequence of the application by others of rules and
sanctions to an 'offender'. Therefore, deviance is that behaviour which
people so label. What matters is the 'meaning' attached to the disapproved conduct, the degree to which one's life is acted out in a public
arena. Indeed, responses tend to change over time and what passes un-
noticed today may be transgression tomorrow. How an act is treated depends also on who commits it, and who disapproves of it, and what may
count is not the response of 'significant others', but the consequences
of the act itself. Labelling may follow if one looks like the stereotype kitchen porter, or if one associates with those who follow the
typed behaviour pattern. Inter-actionists do not attach a finite quality to norm infringement, but make it contingent on how others in society regard such contact. (5) and (6)

The traditional view in Western society regarded social rules and
norms as absolute and obvious, independent of person and time factor,
and unchanging. Indeed, very much a derivation from an unconscious socialisation pattern. Social interactionism constitutes an important
break with this absolutist perspective. Labelling theory, which uses
the interactionist orientation, investigates the conflicts and uncertainties over social meaning, as we have seen. It shows that the stigma
phenomenon may be seen not as an instance of individual pathology, but
as a product of interaction in everyday life, where those with the power to manufacture labels can stick them on to those powerless to resist
this.

We can conceive, by looking at this process in a phenomenological sense,
how a kitchen porter is stigmatised in the everyday situation by the examples we now present. Thus agencies (such as welfare and employment) do
not regard him as competitive in the labour market, except for jobs no
one else wants. For management, he is the type that: can be used only
for short-term work; that will be pilfering if not watched; that may

abscond at busy periods; that is not in possession of any skills; that
may not be fully fit for the job; that may be violent, lazy or have a
drink problem; that is probably in need of a bed; a type to be kept out
of sight of customers, in fact.

Stigma and Mal-Socialisation

The theoretical approach which we have pursued permits of a construction
of a subjective socialisation pattern which reflects the stigmatised
actor's interactional incompetence in his relationship with society
and his occupation. This incompetence may (and in many cases does)
arise from the inability of the actor's mind to recall the past, have
proper awareness of the present and project a hypothetical future. He
has also problems of identifying, classifying, recognising and understanding particular sets of experiences. Hence the difficulties with
the construction and interpretation of social inter-action by respondents, clearly evident from the interviews conducted for our survey.

The Mal-Socialised Incumbent: Seven Suggested Categories

Social actor born into stigmatised work	Characteristics: parents poor, uneducated, no life chance, stigma almost ascribed.
Social actor socially maladjusted	Avoids responsibility, spirits blunted by failure, signs of achieved stigma.
Social actor disabled	Physically or mentally disabled, can do no other work or cannot obtain it, stigma achieved.
Social actor a refugee from moral/social responsibilities	Avoids wife and children, pays no maintenance, permanently on the move.
Social actor an economic convert	Older age group, redundancy, can find only stigmatised work.
Social actor an 'opter-out' of society	Works, eats, drinks, washes, sleeps, etc. only when no other option, has few personal possessions.
Social actor an alien or ethnic group member	Forced into stigmatised work by discrimination or economic necessity.

These categories indicate a characteristic overall social pattern for
those forced into, or willing to work in, stigmatised circumstances.
By far the largest number of kitchen porters in (or for the time being
out of) employment fall into one or more of these specified categories,
which constitute the sub-patterns of mal-socialisation.

Our previous survey analysis in Chapter 6 of the sample of kitchen
porters from the West Midlands area has furnished empirical evidence of
the validity of these categories. These may also be usefully compared
with the reasons for pauperism during the late nineteenth century, and
the categorisation of itinerant social groups among the Victorian poor
(see Chapter 4 above) for an idea of the inter-relatedness of the economic fortunes of an industry, its occupations, incumbents and society

itself relative to the generation and fermentation of social stigma.
We may note that these social groups - which do not, by the way, possess Karl Marx's stratification elements of class conflict and class
consciousness as such,* although distinct in Max Weber's terms by life
style or even occupational connections - over generations, have significantly almost acquired a kind of institutionalised legitimacy, that
is, an acceptance that the transient worker is an ever-present phenomenon.

Member and Occupation

Our next immediate task is to probe into a possible relationship between a stigmatised occupation and its members. We have suggested ways
in which stigma characteristics can give an adverse image to an entire
industry. And, we have considered the position of stigmatised incumbents, that is, the effect of diminished respectability, stereotyping
and labelling, and criteria of mal-socialisation. Quite separate from
the status considerations of the occupational role the employee plays
within a particular establishment, it is possible to discover ways in
which he interacts with his occupation and how, in turn, the occupation itself, as an abstract conceptualisation, may reflect an image of
its members as persons to fellow citizens of wider society.

   Inter-action occurs not only by how an individual represents the occupation to his public or how he acts out his occupation role. An occupational affinity is also recognised by the expression of particular
collective values, by manifest attitudes, by a specific life style, by
some kind of allegiance to a code, by recognition of certain standards
of dress, a prescribed use of tools, recognition of representatives who
speak for the occupation by trade union or interest groups, by the mode
of joining and leaving, by technical knowledge and, indeed, by specific
working conditions the member is prepared to accept. We are not even
considering formal organisation or subscription here by symbols of identity, customs and norms.

   Argued arbitrarily by the criteria we have stated, some task-identif-
ied occupations are not occupations at all, or if they are, some classification system is externally imposed. Evidently, many low-status
occupations are identified by the tasks performed rather than by their
institutionalised status and associated with a variety of arbitrary
designations. Thus, the kitchen porter is also known as pot washer,
plongeur, hotel and restaurant worker, kitchen operative and kitchen
hand (now the census classification). Few such porters display an occupational affinity, although they may admit to working on mundane tasks.
There is no sign of an occupational voice pressing for technical innovation, the invention of sophisticated tools, training or technician
status. In retrospect, industrial status as such derives also from the
status of the member occupations of an industry. The hotel and catering
industry, as represented by managements, has a low regard for the occupation of kitchen porter, as we have seen. Identified by the performance

---

* In his writings, Marx refers frequently to 'Lumpen Proletariat',
however, as a composition of social groups, consisting of the degenerate, the demoralised, the unemployable, people without a definite occupation or permanent domicile, as the lowest sediment of relative surplus population, which dwells in the world of pauperism.

of unpleasant tasks, an uncomplimentary name, and typed incumbents of
intermittent availability, the occupation should by all the laws of cultural sensibility have long ended up in fragmentation or obliteration.
Instead, it has, by means of an uncertain, ambiguous identity, without
ever enjoying some kind of formal structural organisation, preserved
its existence and continuity for at least the centuries we have cont-
oured and that is some 850 years, no less.

The Survival of an Occupation

What then, we may ask, enables a stigmatised occupation to survive? In
the case of kitchen portering, the question defies easy analysis. Loos-
ely defined, there is now at least one catering worker for every fifty
people of our population; one hotel bedroom for every 100 members of
our population; an entire hotel for every 1,500 of the population. This
gives an idea of the huge expansion of this industry that our historical chapter above has attempted to show. Nor is it merely a question of
accommodation for those away from home. Hospitality embraces cookery
and food by the very nature of this industry and so long as meals are
offered in quantities, this occupation's survival is assured. Undoubtedly, washing up and portering originated long before the advent of
hotel keeping, possibly from the time of the ancient civilisations. We
recall the sequence of the social changes in the hospitality sphere via
the Roman inns, the monasteries, the coaching inns, the railway hotels,
and then the travel revolution, with the tourist boom and the super
hotel, which carried the occupation of kitchen porter like its sidekick
through the ages in the wake of the social and economic upheavals of
the times. But, while the established need for a regular pattern of
meal provision explains a lot, more subtle matters to interest the social scientist exist which make for occupational continuity and distinct-
iveness. We shall consider these criteria further, in comparison with
the membership of other occupations and in particular the Jews in the
rag trade, cooks, building operatives and domestic service workers.

As in most of the lower-grade services of sweated occupations, there
is ample demand and a permanent reservoir of candidates for the job.
Apprenticeship for kitchen portering is unknown and the need for training is ignored by the trade. This means that a man can start at once
and is usually willing to do so for whatever reward is offered and accepted. Employers expect his stay to be of short duration and, in fact,
may welcome this in case the man is 'trouble'. Mainly physical strength
is looked for, which makes the occupation a prerogative of the male,
although hefty Jamaican women have been known to be welcomed by managements for the job. There is no discrimination on ethnic grounds (with
the kitchen porter operating behind the scenes and out of sight of the
patrons) and there is little perceived need for language or communication. As soon as a man starts work, he is a member of the occupation;
little matter that he may have drifted into it from another industry or
occupation.

Perhaps one of the most potent reasons for the survival is that capital equipment cannot replace the kitchen porter, even if it were cheaper
to do so, for there is no machine yet that has been perfected to do the
job, while only a few establishments could manage the capital cost in
any case and survive. (See Figure 8). Yet, the cooking implements must
speedily be cleaned for re-use and reasons of hygiene if conflict with

a temperamental chef is to be avoided. Indeed, the hygiene function
deserves to be stressed so as to accord the members of this occupation,
together with their other contributions, the rationale of preservers of
health of the patrons. The past had not been without its problems.
Until the advent of pottery vessels, cooked food was contaminated by
soil, ash and smoke, which hardly improved its taste. Bacterial contamination from the roughly-surfaced cooking pots might, without the benefits of soap and today's detergents, have caused serious health hazards
but for the kitchen porter's skill.

   This social usefulness reminds us of Dr. William Kitchener, M.D., a
Glasgow man who, in the early nineteenth century, wrote a most popular
book entitled 'The Cook's Oracle', of which 15,000 copies were sold and
six editions produced. For a doctor to produce a cookery book at that
time was novel and new, and for such a man to experiment in his kitchen
with recipes, an analeptic part of the art of physics. As the establish-
er of a culinary code for the rational epicure, this physician advanced
for the occupation of cook the status of preventer of disease and pro-
longer of life by food. (7) This is an interesting case where the pres-
tige-rating of one occupation is enhanced through a member of another.
Some of the low-status occupations in this trade also compete with each
other for prestige via the Hotel and Catering Industry Training Board,
which has more recently instituted machinery for the attainment of
status-enhancing qualifications, but regrettably not yet for the kitchen
porter. Will his turn ever come?

Concentration and Fragmentation - The Role of Geographical Mobility

To turn to a further criterion by which to explain the survival of this
occupation, we must mention mobility. Geographical mobility enables the
kitchen porter to work anywhere, with the only constraint that he needs
to find a bed. When the seasonal cycle moves towards its height, hotels
meet the desperate need for staff of this kind by offering living-in
accommodation, reluctantly as it may be, for it means the sacrifice of
rooms that may otherwise be hired out to guests. This provision frequently acts as a lever of instability rather than the reverse, in that
it facilitates movement and change for a slightly better reward in a
labour suppliers' market. By way of contrast to the enforced or voluntary movement during a busy season - so high in this occupation that many
firms will not include labour turnover in calculations,which evidence
low commitment to a current employer, disaffection with a work environment, or some anomic condition afflicting the incumbent - we feel that it
would add something to our discussion if we offered a glimpse at a port-
rait of other industries where occupational affliction is prevalent and
transiency a telling characteristic.

The Jews in the Clothing Trade

The East End of London has been the traditional home of the poor since
the sixteenth century. When Cromwell lifted the mediaeval ban on Jew-
ish residence in England, immigrants arrived to settle in the area
adjacent to the docks. Even before the great wave of immigration, the
clothing industry, like the area, was traditionally East European. The
first arrivals went into it to be joined later by friends and relatives,
for entry into a different industry meant problems with adult apprent-
iceships and the observance of the Sabbath. By the eighteenth and nineteenth centuries, Jews crowded into the clothing trade. Friends and

relations were already there, the amenities were there, soup kitchen, free schools, synagogues and the Jews' shelter. The seasonal character of this trade suited the elastic living standards of the Jews. The labour exchange consisted of a couple of streets where the 'sweaters'were recruited from the crowd. To learn the trade, immigrants would live on meagre diets for a time to find the money to pay the sweaters to teach them. We know inertia has preserved a still flourishing clothing trade in the same location, which is only now slowly beginning to dis-integrate.

Not unlike kitchen portering,in the catering trades the organic life of rag trade work has, in the evolutionary sense, acquired a 'personal-ity' directly from the characteristics of its composite members, but with the distinction that it is highly sectionalised in particular loc-ations, with endows it with an identity of its very own. This is evid-ent not by the organisation of strong interest groups (it is still a Wages Council industry, as is catering), but by a communal pattern with strong informal ties among the cohorts through ethnic affinities and a social network, which spills over into extra-workplace associations.

In contrast, the kitchen porter's existence is seen to function on a more individualistic pattern, devoid of colleague relationship and be-longing to a heterogeneous group in a geographically widely dispersed industry of hotel and catering units, the potential employers. If there are shared cultural values in the latter's case, these are not obvious and not necessarily derived from similar backgrounds, as may also be true of other, less distinctive, segments of the clothing industry, which weds occupations together by materials, like catering does with food. It seems to us that, on the basis of Gouldner's two types of role orientations, the 'cosmopolitan' and the 'local', we might now need two new names for our categories of stigmatised occupations. (8) For want of better terms, we shall for the moment refer to these as 'stickers' and 'mobilants'.

To qualify our proposition, we may add that the 'sticker syndrome' does not apply to all segments of the garment trade, but refers to one particular ethnic group's tradition, of which evidence is still to be found today. More recently, Asians and Indians have joined the ranks of the clothing industry in which the lower-paid sewing operations by far account for the largest number of employees.

As we have seen, the occupations of tailoring and machining in the ghetto-like pockets of the industry were almost a way of life to their members. People are bound to the trade, to the location and to their community. The kitchen porter, on the other hand, is by image an 'occ-upational minstrel', who thrives on mobility, shuns association, would as soon rest as work and does not, as a rule, seek upward social move-ment occupation-wise. He is not, therefore, a cosmopolitan in Gouldner's sense. The terms 'cosmopolitan' and 'local' originate from the American social scientist, Robert Merton, and have been adapted by Alvin Gouldner for his studies of organisations. Merton produced a division of comm-unity leaders while Gouldner attributed low organisational loyalty and a high commitment for specialised role skills to cosmopolitans and the reverse to locals. Then, along came Ronald Frankenberg (9), an English university professor who used the labels in his research to distinguish between Banbury-centred individuals as either locals or cosmopolitans, the latter for those locally-based but identifying with a national

category. We, too, have chosen to adapt the idea of the two-fold division and attached the terms to suit the circumstances of our illustration.

The Building Industry

We would now like to extend our comparative analysis to include the building industry, in our discussion, where the weather plays a key role in
the unstable job opportunities for the operatives. This makes for an
interesting comparison with the industries and occupations already considered and domestic service work, which we consider below. Reliable
estimates suggest that more than one in five workers is a labourer. The
less-skilled or unskilled do not appear to enjoy a specific occupational
name and are generally known as building or construction operatives,
which identifies them with the industry, but deprives them of an occupational identity. Mobility here comes in a different guise, which is
why we are better served by the meaningful word 'casualisation'. This
industry, unlike the catering and garment industries, manages to solve
its industrial relations problems on a voluntary basis, via a National
Joint Council, by way of wage agreements between the industrial parties,
but in other respects carries a large casual labour force for reasons
which it finds difficult to control. During winter time, the intermittent nature of building work, due to inclement weather, can shade into
the commonly known 'sea-freeze-up'. Contractors have long tried to protect the men in our more severe weather and keep the work going, but a
fall-out invariably results when conditions are really bad. Among the
more innovative employers, plastic covers that inflate themselves have
been tried, as have electrically-heated work suits.

A second problem has been created by the post-war building boom, with
which the industry has long tried to come to grips and that is sub-con-
tracting, or 'the lump'. Regarded as an anachronism in modern industry
by the trade unions, a highly motivated work group who work for themselves, with a responsibility to get a job done on contract and then
share out the rewards, has clearly something to commend it, were it not
for such side effects as the absence of holiday arrangements, social insurance contributions, payment of the appropriate taxes and leading to
bad workmanship, neglect of safety, welfare and health, as well as inhibiting organised industrial negotiations.

A third problem relates to the various types of unemployment, known as
intermittent, frictional, technological, seasonal, cyclical and general.
We need not go into all these in detail, but it will be appreciated that
the incidence of casualisation means interruptions in the work routines,
movement to various sites, flows into and out of the industry, insecurity, exposure to cold, heat and rain, setting up second homes or being
separated from family, in addition to the work itself being physically
hard and exhausting. There is, additionally, an accepted custom for men
to leave the employer when the building operations on the site are completed and take work with another. Clearly, the cosmopolitan nature of
this relationship contains an element of ambivalence, since it has neither encouraged loyalty to the organisation, nor developed a high commitment to specialised role skills or occupational identity among the grades
we have been considering. 'Casualisation' in the construction industry
is therefore not so much a function of the 'impatience of steady labour'
(as Booth referred to it) as a characteristic of the incidence of an

unstable work milieu and the Acts of God.

Occupational Afflictions

As we have been able to show, some parent industries evolved by and by
as their occupational children were born, and the mixed fortunes of the
former have nurtured the latter to either health and strength or seen
them wither away. By the very nature of its product or service, an industry may contain sectors of either fluidity or permanency. New sib-
ling occupations may appear and older ones die. Some of these may be
chronically diseased, but nonetheless live on for ever more. Our specific attention in this study has been directed at occupations: earlier,
the janitor, the nightwatchman, the catering worker and the hospital
porter. In this Chapter, the kitchen porter once more, the garment
worker, the building operative, and below another look at the life cycle
of the domestic service worker.

But, it is not just the economic kaleidoscope that will, by way of
the seasonal vicissitudes, technology or spending power, produce change;
nor the cultural attributes by the endowment of status and prestige.
An occupation may, by its very nature, be ailing from inherent causes;
like people's homes fixed in specific geographical locations, whereas
hotels, restaurants, construction sites or hospitals are to be found
anywhere. Casualisation, intermittence, itinerance, mobilance, or whatever we choose to call it, is a chronic concomitant in the patient himself. A second afflication is organically grounded in certain occupations which stifles the aspirations of incumbents by an intrinsic limitation to occupational advance. In some of the occupations, we have
been concerned with mobility, for progress rests not so much in the
work tasks and their essential skills themselves as it is to be achieved by a change of occupation or the assumption of responsibility over
others.

We shall now turn our attention briefly to domestic service once more,
but this time approach it as a case study of occupational mortality and
appraise the housemaid's (and other domestic service occupations) possible future as an exemplar for stigmatised work such as performed by the
kitchen porter. Our historical chapter has revealed the decline of
domestic service from 1½ million employees in its heyday to a number
that could easily be accommodated in Wembley Stadium, were members disposed to hold a convention there. (10) But, recovery in another guise
is within the realms of the possible as we speculate on its rebirth below under the heading of 'tradition and change'.

Household Service - Tradition and Change

At this stage of our discussion, it will be of interest also to establish the characteristics which emerged from the occupational biography
of the domestic service industry. We must, however, limit ourselves to
the lowest grade in the hierarchy, the general maid. The possibility
of comparing her experiences with those in other stigmatised occupations
and to establish a set of fundamental features peculiar to such work
(and possibly predict a likely future impact on our occupational structure), justifies an inclusion of this group in the investigations of the
evolution of specific occupational roles.

Historically, her status amounted almost to ascription (being born into it) for, as we have seen, mothers needed to place their daughters by economic necessity and only domestic service was predominantly available, however unpopular. Class distinction was a social inheritance from childhood and a young girl went into service with a resentment against a mistress she had never seen, not because she herself had suffered maltreatment, but because her mother, mother's sister and girlfriends experienced it without redress. The master and servant relationship required unquestioning obedience and when legal norms eventually appeared, conformity was lax and violation common. There were no standards of performance, no informal colleague relations and no companionship.

The rigidly enforced hierarchical structure in the household specified status and prestige ratings, while the attached diffuseness of work tasks meant an invasion of private life, since the place of work of the domestic was not separated from her home. The work itself was generally regarded as an 'unskilled calling' and such training as was obtainable in housework care came from orphanages and workhouses. (11) Middle class women were rigorous in their enforcement of occupational caste reverence. That the capacity to feel is an innate one and does not depend on education was not understood and the two vastly differing living standards under one roof aroused bitterness among the maids. Finally, there was also the problem of emotional investment: obedience, indignity, servility on the one hand; the close personal involvement with the employer's family instead of her own on the other, all showing the marginal character of the housemaid's role. At least, the saving grace in this occupational situation, says Vilheim Aubert, must be sought in a certain emotional security and opportunity for affective expression. (12) Many a housemaid did form an attachment towards children she had seen growing up in service.

Domestic service as such has undergone a radical change. New cultural attitudes towards it, a different occupational structure, offering other opportunities for employment and an increasing mechanisation of domestic chores, has practically put an end to this industry. But a resurgence in a different guise is on the horizon. Poor working conditions and low pay in work offering no intrinsic compensatory rewards (as do nursing, teaching or social work) may resolve themselves in agency work or self-employment. Nursing is moving in this direction, the intrinsic rewards not having proved compensatory enough to offset the comparatively low extrinsic benefits. Menial work, such as window cleaning, has attracted large numbers of self-employed. In the shorter future, domestic workers, kitchen porters and other menial workers will, in a situation of full employment, be available on hire for definite hourly fees. Thus, this new kind of 'professionalisation' may act to alter not only the functional image in the marginal occupations where unionisation has not succeeded, but may also do so as a status-equalising agent between a range of occupations themselves.

One further empirically varifiable tendency has recently made its entrance into some areas of domestic service. This has occurred at the professional/managerial level in households sufficiently large and affluent where the new university graduate / butler acts in a managerial capacity and the nanny as a trained psychologist. In such instances, however, servants and employer will be status-equals in terms of contractual relationships as elsewhere, and the designation of servant is probably a misnomer. Where the housemaid, in fact, survives, her occupational role may be said to depend largely on that of the house-wife herself who is not regarded as economically gainful at present,on account of the emotional content as a member of the family concerned with its welfare. In contrast to this more speculative consideration of domestic service occupations, the kitchen porter was, and is, less fortunate. He can develop no attachment to a machine he does not use, and no easy affective relationship with greasy brush and pot. The negative impact of the work environment tends, therefore, to be worse, as we shall indicate from our findings in the next chapter.

NOTES TO CHAPTER 7

1.   Ball, Donald W. (1967) 'An Abortion Clinic Ethnography', Social
        Problems, Vol.XIV (Winter)

2.   Skolnick, Jerome H. (1966) 'Justice Without Trial', John Wiley,
        New York

3.   Fasken, Joan (1963) 'Pharmacists and the Presentation of Self'
        (unpublished text)

4.   Hegarty, Joseph A., Head of Department of Hotel and Catering
        Management, Dublic College (Interview with author, 1973)

5.   Cohen, Stan (Ed.) (1971) 'Images of Deviance', Penguin, Middx.

6.   Becker, Howard S. (1963) 'Outsiders: Studies in the Sociology
        of Deviance', Free Press, New York

7.   Cooper, Charles (1929) 'The English Table (History and Liter-
        ature)', Sampson, Low, Marston & Co.

8.   Gouldner, Alvin W. 'Cosmopolitans and Locals: Towards an
        Analysis of Latent Social Roles', Administrative Science
        Quarterly, Vols.I and II, December 1957

9.   Frankenberg, Ronald (1966) 'Communities in Britain'(Social Life
        in Town and Country) , Pelican, Middx.

10.   Annual Abstract of Statistics, 1973. Table 141, p.135, Central
        Statistical Office. Estimated figures for G.B. of people in
        private domestic service is 90,000

11.   Firth, Violet M. (1925) 'The Psychology of the Servant Problem:
        (A Study of Social Relationships)', The C.W. Daniel Co., London

12.   Aubert, Vilheim 'The Housemaid - An Occupational Role in Crisis'
        Acta Sociologica, Vol.I (1955-56)

8   Survey summary, discussion and concluding evaluation

Introductory Matters

Kitchen porters have toiled from as long as a thousand years back
and do so still. Primates have been tried to do the job and failed.
Technological aids have not taken the drudge out of this work and costly machines, where installed, mostly collect rust and dust. Today, experts talk of the electronic worker, and his engineers of the bionic
man. Will it remain talk, or will these robots replace the plongeur a
few centuries hence? Meanwhile, with some twelve million tourists flooding the country and five hundred million meals per year eaten out, this
occupation is not only in no danger of extinction, but ipso facto guar-
anteed to flourish for decades to come. Why then, in view of our need
of him and his virtues, does society generally, and managements in particular, treat him as if he were an object of a lower order?

The answer points strongly to a universal and persisting tendency
(cutting even across cultures) of attaching a low social evaluation to
certain types of work and categories of incumbents themselves, associated with such work. Our project may be seen as a study in depth
which, in sequence, diagnoses the existence of occupational stigmatisation, seeks to establish its origins from an evolving work ethic,
traces the effects of its perpetuation over a number of centuries, provides a model and discusses the anatomy of the stigma concept and offers authentic empirical evidence by means of a survey of the situation,
experiences and feelings of a specific representative group of lowly
rated occupations, the kitchen porters in the British hotel industry.

The general structure of our approach has been by way of a series of
steps - the philosophical, the conceptual, the hypothetical, the evolutionary, the interpretative, the methodological and finally, the empirical. This abstract-concrete continuum, so to speak, may help to make
the stigma phenomenon and its effect upon the occupational membership
of concern more intelligible. We propose to conclude in reverse order
and portray the kitchen porter as he has emerged from the findings and
then step back from examining the 'trees' to look at the outline of the
'wood'. Or, to put it differently, we shall leave the sample and turn
our minds to the stigma concept once more and attempt to find a suitable place for it within the behavioural sciences concerned with occupations.

The Sample and the Method

Our survey has identified the kitchen porter and we now know who he is,
at least for the large area of the Midlands (and probably representative
for the country as a whole, with the exclusion of London), and this identification differs substantially from the derogatory picture presented in the industry. True, a stereotype has emerged, but not the one
variously described in the 'trade' as vagrant, scum, thief, crook, dod-
ger, alcoholic or committer of arson. This is not to disclaim that such
individuals among kitchen porters exist, but many of the beliefs do

rest on isolated experiences or encounters made explicit by reference to 'what everyone in the industry knows', or alternatively are to a large extent based on generalisations, unfounded assumptions, prejudices, distorted stories or hearsay, quite unsubstantiated by scientifically valid and reliable representative data. Thus, society at large, and managements in the work situation where the respondent plays out his role, hold preconceived expectations that his performance is likely to be low, his conduct unpredictable or eccentric and his stay at the work place of short duration.

A suitable method to project the profile of our respondents from the survey would be one that yields a measure of the central tendency equal perhaps to the most commonly occurring kitchen porter: the typical, or modal, man. This satisfies the statistical requirement of not having the findings distorted by extreme values in the distribution. As behavioural scientists, we are also interested in social types and hence the possible emergence from the survey of a stereotype of respondent to whom other individuals or groups in society assign a most frequent combination of traits - albeit a biased collection as it turned out to be, often not even acquired from first-hand experience, as already indicated above. The stereotyped individual can well come to share a stereotype of himself and, in consequence, act in accord with it. To test this and to strengthen the reliability of our findings, we have placed some emphasis on the phenomenological approach in the sense of using in our interpretations of the questions during the interviews wording and terms from the target population, the kitchen porters themselves, by making the meaning explicit in terms of their language and frame of reference. This, incidentally, helped us to understand how a respondent can contribute to the creation of his public image by his expressed self-conception, low aspirations, self-fulfilling prophecies and, therefore, negative stereotype.

The Typical Respondent

The typical kitchen porter in the Midlands is predominantly male, aged within a periphery of fifty years, born in Britain and of British nationality. He is single and largely without familial support and his denomination is either Protestant or Church of England. We have not investigated denominational involvement in terms of church attendance, but casual comments by respondents in the schedules and during interviews support previous research that church attendance is lower among low-status occupations and lower among Protestants as compared with Catholics, the latter consisting of a quarter of our sample. He liked school, but had to leave at an early age (fourteen or below) and did not get beyond elementary or secondary school. As to work experience, he is keen to make friends at the work place, but does not often succeed, feels that the work tasks are within his capacity to cope without special training, and that the job offers protection against the elements, helps with subsistence, does not demand special responsibilities and work can be started without undue formality.

The typical porter is largely ignorant of the value of training, thinks of his work as 'unskilled' and feels strongly about the marginality of his position. The work history reveals that he had up to, but no more than, ten jobs during his working life (to date of interview) and remained fairly mobile between the catering and other industries.

That is, he is not in any true sense a 'professional' kitchen porter, as the different and largely semi-skilled or unskilled occupations held previously outside catering, reveal. Rarely is there any similarity between the old and the new occupation, and to the typical respondent, kitchen portering tends to serve more as a stopgap until other work becomes available, thereby indicating a willingness of a person to take on such work as he can at short notice obtain.

Concerning working conditions, the typical worker in kitchen portering in the West Midlands area likes a nice, clean work place most of all, his work to be respected by people, proper tools, work with a team (which is rarely the case, however), wants more job security and better pay, as well as the chance for trade union membership, to wear a uniform and get a share of the tips, all in that order. Other conditions are also of consequence to him, such as living-in, the dislike of shift work and more say in the way the kitchen is run; but these latter sentiments do not appear to be predominant. Weekly take-home pay between £11 and £20 per week (at interviewing time) compared rather unfavourably with E.E.C. or U.S.A. earnings in the same occupation and the same year. The attitude of the typical respondent towards training has already been shown. We may add here that he largely never received training for any skilled trade, but would agree to be trained in a variety of catering tasks, so that he could be switched to other jobs in the kitchen. No formal training schemes for kitchen porters are known to exist (or, if indeed they do, no publicity is given to them) and the H.C.I.T.B. appears to have no plans as yet for sponsoring any training scheme for this occupation.

In respect of his associations at work, the typical kitchen porter feels a strong need for friendly relations and psychological support (colleague relationships), which the nature of the work often hinders and his low status constrains. (See manager-kitchen porter relationships under the heading of 'discussion'). How then does he adapt to the environment in the practical sense? No strong attitudes are expressed about work in high class hotels and high class areas, although these are preferred. It seems evident that working conditions on the job matter more to the respondent than hotel size, class of hotel or area, but there is little, if any, identification with the employer as such. This lack of affinity is certainly a contributory factor to the large staff turnover in this grade. On our evidence, the respondent has clearly the mental equipment to evaluate sensible priorities and shows a good conception of what he evaluates as important. Significantly, given a reasonable reward for his work, economistic-instrumental matters did not rank in predominance before he would accept a job as a kitchen porter, but this could be interpreted as a denial that materialistic needs alone prompted the acceptance of the job. Strong confirmation appears that this employment is needed, but no definite answer emerged as to how long an incumbent intended to remain in the job held at the time.

With regard to the typical kitchen porter's status and prestige, he ranks by reason of his membership of that occupation, and not infrequently, by reason of his personal make-up, low in the hotel hierarchy, where his comically-displayed symbols and idiosyncrasies may often preclude the proper integration into the social system of the kitchen, unless he displays that kind of ingenuity which allows him to elaborate his role

in a status-enhancing capacity, formally be extending responsibility in
the kitchen and informally by performing special services for those in
authority. Sociological scales place this menial occupation among the
lowest of all in terms of social prestige, while the typical respondent
himself feels most reluctant to compare himself with other occupations
and to suggest a comparative rating. Kitchen portering would, however,
be regarded as a more worthwhile job if other kitchen staff were to
consider it as such, say the respondents.

That part of the survey which deals with aspirations and orientations
confirms (by way of our counter-check-questions) from what are the
least and most satisfying aspects of the work that money, as such, is
not a key motivating force in kitchen portering. Minor irritating incidents in the day-to-day work routine do, however, generate frustrations, while similarly, in the performance of the daily tasks, good conditions and good treatment predominate in the feeling of what is appreciated most. Money is important only for survival and the typical respondent feels - amazing as this may seem - that he is giving a service
to the customer, although the job is not regarded as a stepping stone
for promotion. Finally, the reply to the question what he will do in
ten years' time is quite definite: he doesn't know!

We come now to the health factor, which brings some startling information to light. The typical respondent has been plagued by physical
disability or impairment for many years, which severely handicapped him
in the competition for jobs. He may also have had some contact with
institutional life, not always of his own choosing. The disablement
frequently originated in youth and presented a mountainous hurdle in
social acceptability, regularity of work performance and the management
of the stigma. Occupational diseases like hernia, eczema and dermatit-
is, bronchitis and arthritis, are sometimes high in incidence, but time
lost, although slightly higher than in other low-grade occupations, is
minimal when spread over the total numbers of kitchen porters employed.
Relatively to the numbers in that occupation, the percentage of deaths
is slightly above that of other low-grade occupations considered and
can be causally traced to such illnesses as malignant neoplasms, coro-
nary diseases, bronchitis, tuberculosis, among other diseases, and suicides. As for suicides, of those who died during the period under review, kitchen porters comprised the largest percentage among the low-
grade occupations we investigated.

With reference to housing, we noted that the typical porter has, by
reason of his circumstances, an inbuilt difficulty in leading an existence in a settled home. Mortgages and home ownership are, by reason of
his low and frequently irregular income, out of his reach and unattainable at a time of resettlement; also security of tenure, while homelessness too is frequently a problem. In view of his status as a
single man, without the same compulsion to set up a family home, it can
be easily appreciated how family support and home ownership are linked
to work, social stability and a feeling of security.

There is also evidence of a definite correlation between health, education and housing. People with no educational qualifications end up
in low-grade occupations and the unskilled have been found (in the
Household Survey) to suffer twice the volume of chronic sickness compared with the professional groups, while those living in rented

accommodation show high incidence of chronic sickness as additionally
they do not enjoy the basic amenities of proper heating, fixed bath,
and such. Thus, the highly mobile kitchen porter incurs the psychological cost of severed or non-existent family ties, disruption of a
normal pattern of life through the seasonal and uncertain demands for
regular work in the industry and his fitness and capacity to meet it,
without a permanent and secure base in the form of a home and a sense
of identification with the residents in a local community.

Our respondent's profile will be completed if we finally consider
his orientations and activities in the non-work situation. The general
impression we gained from the survey results is that the typical kitchen porter is only a temporary one, in that capacity, and guesting in
the hotel and catering industry so to speak. He pursues leisure activities of an enormous variety, most popularly indoor and outdoor
sports, the anomaly, however, being that he spends barely one hour per
day on all the activities undertaken. That seems hardly sufficient
time to allow the pursuance of a 'professional' hobby, but it is at any
rate difficult to establish to what extent leisure activities are
hobbies or whether, indeed, they are all recreational, without the opportunity to research this topic further under laboratory conditions.
All the activities, which we detailed under sports, recreational and
social, therapeutical and educational, are predominantly undertaken for
'enjoyment' (which we attempted to define), but the centrality of play
in the life of the typical kitchen porter is once more difficult to
assess. It would seem to slant towards an active , rather than passive,
leisure pattern, although we would suggest - in view of the alleged
time spent on them - that these are more activities he would be interested to undertake given different circumstances, than that he has
actually undertaken them.

We, therefore, believe that the preferences expressed amount more to
an attitude towards the role of leisure in his life than the specific
use of actual time. The impression was also gained - and only in-depth
case research can adequately establish this with any degree of certainty - that the kitchen porter away from the work environment experiences
considerable isolation and pursues free-time activities mostly alone,
and that these are often distinctly casual, spur-of-the-moment and un-
premeditated. In comparison with the national sample for unskilled
socio-economic groups, the kitchen porter's keenness on outdoor and indoor sporting activities is four times as great, but the national sample two and a half times more active in social participation than our
typical respondent. It is reasonable to assume that the extremity of
the menial work tasks would reduce the desire for strenuous activities,
with a consequential mode of recuperation less demanding of energy than
some leisure theories would suggest. Such theories also proclaim for
the lowest levels of occupational prestige a predominance of the 'popular' activities commensurate with their strata, (1) such as drinking,
card-playing and television viewing, which are practically unsupported
by our evidence. The picture that emerged for our typical man differs
therefore visibly from the national one, in respect of preferred activities and, by deviation from certain recognised leisure theories.
Quite possibly, the already commented upon peculiarities of this occupation, which make members different from other socio-economic groups of
the same lower-grade level, may account for this.

Discussion

This then is our typical man: no permanent home, no family, no communal links, limited education, no qualifications, mostly disabled, limited capacity to compete in the labour market, economically weak, isolated and in need of friends and carrying the label of a stigmatised occupation - but willing to work. A marginal person indeed.

The cosmopolitan kitchen porter is seen by the industry as a 'career deviant' * and stories abound that tell of his eccentricities. No doubt, a big metropolis like London has its own hazards and opportunities for the temporary job seeker in the hotel world and this image attracts a labelling process of its own that encourages unconventional and, at times, a negative execution of his role. But, in the rest of the country, of which our social actor in the West Midlands area is a most likely representative, his occupational role is more that of a peripheral worker. His work is discredited by considering it unworthy of training, and debased because it has no lasting, tangible value; his work environment, too isolated to offer social satisfaction, his rewards too meagre to provide an incentive and the prestige accorded him too low for self-respect. Apart from the ascription of a non-occupation role, he is also a person with an identity, and with a biographical sequence of experience of a socialisation process that holds inbuilt ingredients of deprivation from the very start of his working life, and all this leading almost inevitably to a low profile in society and public affirmation of a stigmatised status. **

Few studies have, as yet, correlated the means and the mode of the life of a worker with his working efficiency. We are here reminded of Holme and Rahe's interesting Social Readjustment Rating Scale, in which life crises units up to one hundred are awarded for forty-three different life events. (2) Thus, a score of 150 would indicate no serious problems, while 300 units and over is to be seen as a major life crisis with an 80% chance of illness. If then, for example, within a two year period, the kitchen porter experiences marital separation or a term in jail and trouble with the employer, gets the sack, changes his line of work, his living conditions, eating and sleeping habits, his working hours and recreation, and in addition commits a minor violation of the law, he runs up a score of 276, equivalent to a moderate life crisis and 50% chance of illness. These contingencies are not that unusual in the life of a homeless kitchen porter and if also injury should befall him (53 units), the score would amount to 329 and be indicative of an extreme susceptibility to major problems in survival management.

Stigma and Occupation/Person Inter-action

We have, in Chapter 7 above, explained that the particular structural form of an industry determines the type of conduct and its performance that will prevail, and the service or product cycle, the structure of the occupational mix. Thus, we may by our own classification identify
* Deviant from the conventional status role, displaying own sub-culture.
** Through inter-action of background, behaviour and occupation, frequently typified in the press and other media, by reference to occupation of the digressing or legally offending kitchen porter. (See Appendices I and II).

on the food preparation and cookery side in a hotel craft and ancillary
occupations, certain of which we have chosen to designate as marginal
or peripheral. Disregarding ownership concentration for the moment as
not directly relevant to our argument, we note however that the size
and structure of this industry has tended, in recent years, towards a
new pattern of concentration at the multiple organisation level of
hotel and catering groups * while various technological changes on the
mechanical and convenience food side have accompanied this trend.
Hence our previous reference to the mixed fortunes of industry-linked
occupations, some chronically diseased, but living on for ever more.

Caplow's social status indicators show how specialisation has the
effect of replacing individuality by incumbency, formal behavioural
prescriptions removing informal controls and occupational titles existing for the narrowest ranges of tasks, making frequently occupational
requirements obscure to the lay public. (3) Thus, the kitchen porter,
although earning for himself an identity, loses the credentials of be-
longing to a 'legitimate' occupation. The industry was not slow to recognise the pretence of this condition, for where, one may ask, are
the educational credentials, where is the training, where is the organisation of a collectivity or interest group and the symbols of an occupational ideology? So, a non-occupation it is!

While other occupational specialisms may mystify those outside, the
world knows what a kitchen porter is and does, since every household
has one. We have already alluded to status-enhancing and status-for-
feiting criteria above, but how do we assess general public esteem?
Here, well-documented sociological research has confirmed that stigmatising values towards certain occupations transcend the boundaries of
nations and cultures, and that these values tend to persist over time.
It will be recalled that the placement of kitchen porters by the Hope-
Goldthorpe scale (based on popular assessment of the social standing
of occupations) is the lowest the scale has as an indicator of the social evaluation of an individual, or the degree of honour bestowed by
society, as a reflection of his occupational membership. Such placement (not substantially deviating from other existing scales) is clearly an important piece of evidence to show how stigmatisation attaches
to particular types of work and how, by rejecting his occupation, one
rejects the incumbent himself as worthless when he is a member of that
occupation. So, the subjective meaning of social disgrace which attaches to an incumbent kitchen porter in the 'trade', intertwined with
the occupation as it is, constitutes undoubtedly a malignant agent that
has, thus far, shown itself impervious to neutralisation by social
means. We shall presently return to the subject of occupational prestige to demonstrate how one can, by means of historical sociology (a la
Weber and Durkheim) associate its causality with forces of fermentation
additional to the social and cultural elements that engender change in
society.

---

* H.C.I.M.A. Branch News, 13.9.1976. On the subject of the Hotel and
Catering Industry Structure: ... London Courts flooded with an unexpected wave of bankruptcies, most failures being hoteliers and caterers,
of which the majority are small businesses, with unpaid bills for tax,
V.A.T. and social security stamps. Will the industry soon be left with
large companies having a near monopoly? What is the future of the
entrepreneur ...?

Managerial and Institutional Perceptions

Managerial attitudes towards kitchen porters have never been empirically tested. What then is a kitchen porter to management? Secondary
evidence suggests that he is perceived by them as a man who 'bums'
around the kitchen; a man whom one ignores; a man who muddles through;
a man who plays the system; an appendage to the sink; an undefinable
individual without a precise place, doing an unattractive job that
must be done by someone. This absence of understanding and rapport is
not helped by the official and peculiar categorisation of similar and
casual workers on the part of public authorities (i.e. the Department
of Employment), which defines him as one 'whose previous employment
was on a casual basis', and so attaching a label addressed to all and
sundry who have contact with him that he is a permanently unstable
individual. Such an orientation might well be typical of all public
and institutional agencies a kitchen porter has contact with, and operate to produce a state of (Merton's) self-fulfilling prophecy. We
shall suggest alternative managerial attitudes later in this discussion.

The Kitchen Porter as an Ill-defined Stereotype

We have now given attention to the social imagery bearing upon the kitchen porter occupational role at the extra-institutional (wider public
and official agencies) and intra-institutional (management-perception)
level; and noted how the mutual influence of the perceived stereotype
and credential-less occupation reinforce the impressionistic social
construction placed upon the social actor, operates as a deviance-gen-
erating influence, develops a contra-culture, clouds the opportunity
structure and results in an anomic reaction and retreatism of the incumbent, where (to use again Merton's terminology), both means and
ends are rejected.

   If such values as a stable working life, the application of skill,
industry and creativity, are understood to be normative expectations
in our culture, then any actor who is seen to infringe these values
attracts the label of norm-breaker and hence becomes a candidate for
public disgrace, regardless of the circumstances which earned him that
ascription. In the public eye, he has assumed the role of a 'free-
loader', who contributes nothing to the tangible utilities of the nation, misguidedly a common evaluation widely attached to service occupations. That, however, is an ill-defined stereotype which our evidence
does not seem to support. What has led to its formation is probably a
general public 'missverstehen' * that the representative member of this
social group is a creature of circumstance; an ignorance that, hopefully, such as our empirical work will help to correct.

---

* The word 'missverstehen' translated from the German means to mis-
understand (as individuals) in the allied sense in which Weber uses
'verstehen'. We are suggesting that the wider public has difficulty
in identifying with the plongeur as an occupation (although, in the
subjective sense, there is plunging at mealtimes in every household),
by way of re-living the meaning of actions as experienced by him.

Crucial career decisions are normally made and work orientations acquired early in life, when at the same time, other demanding challenges confront a person. Some social actors do not manage to find a niche in the prevailing system of their time and become an element carried by the currents of circumstance over which they have lost control. We have, in this context, already drawn attention to the eternal presence of the weaker and less competitive social groups throughout the phases of modern history, who are not equipped to cope with the provision of their basic needs in a society where the ethic demands sustained partipation in the world of work. (See Chapter 4 above). Additionally, defining social types more narrowly, in the terms in which they express their 'self', life styles may be subject to variations in accordance with their individualistic or social value orientation. Various questions in our survey were specifically designed to establish how our incumbent experiences and feels about his exposure to stigmatisation. This kind of qualitative research, emanating from the philosopher, Edmund Husserl, has in recent years been illuminated by the intervention of phenomenological thinking into sociology, upon which we should now like to comment briefly in the context of our work.

Phenomenological thinking has already helped us to an awareness that the typical kitchen porter, as he has been presented to us by the hotel industry and by society at large, cannot be taken for granted. Seen in retrospect, this justified our somewhat qualitative (but not exclusively so) orientation in this research. In Weber's sociological thinking, functional interpretations alone were not enough and he resorted to the 'verstehen' approach to human behaviour, not to substitute it for observation or empirical evidence, but as a preferable tool of analysis to the introspective experiences the erstwhile philosophers then accorded validity. If phenomenological thinking attempts to determine and describe the actual, everyday life experiences of the social actor in the way in which he himself sees these by participation and in the field, then our work is the more complete, for the endeavour to comply, although we cannot be certain that one or the other responses in our sample did not arise from the desire to match what incumbents thought were our (or management-oriented) expectations, a plausibility already commented upon in the exhibits.

While phenomenology comes in various guises, * is now being resurrected and in the process of bloom, one cannot, as yet, hope for systematised and standardised meanings to emerge; but one can (and we did) enlist for our discussion of stigma some of the conceptual tools emanating from Erving Goffman, the American impressionistic artist, who probes into the hidden spaces of human everyday life, and whose perceptive treatment accepts the part macro-social phenomena has to play in the interpretations of the social order. (4) We recall, in the context of our discussion, his waiter in a luxury restaurant - on stage as it were - to satisfy the fastidious demands of the guests and doing his best to disguise his innermost feelings of contempt. No sooner protected from their view backstage in the adjoining kitchen, restraint is replaced by a fit of aggressive behaviour, reflecting not the 'real man', but another manifestation of the same thing, where the very collapse of the social order is itself a precondition for order in society.

---

* Reflexive, dramaturgical, labelling theory, ethnomethodological and symbolic inter-actionism, to mention some.

Neither of the two behavioural manifestations is intrinsic, but both
are social and balance out two contradictory needs: that of social
order and that of the individual (Goffman). In the work-a-day world
of the kitchen porter, the kitchen or scullery is the stage, his clients the chef and his brigade, but no backstage to escape their torment unless it be the loo, to have a smoke or crush a plate in frustration, or resort to violence if this be his disposition, to redress
the social balance of order by some expression of his needs.

A Framework for Occupational Stigmatisation

Any framework for occupational stigmatisation and its social effects
needs essentially to take account of the historical fortunes of an
occupation under review and the biographical experiences of the members themselves,and hence the stigmatising characteristics of an occupation in its dynamic social setting of the 'lebenswelt' of the incumbents, and thereby achieving a mode of analysis which does not divorce
the objective impersonal phenomena of structure, system and role from
the subjective reality and immediacy of the personal experience of
role occupants. Such analysis is facilitated by the employment of the
social process concept, which imbues the social framework with the
dynamics of change. One of the key ingredients of processes in social
relations, where human inter-action in occupational life is concerned
is the social feature of 'RESPECT' by means of which we may connect
objective reality and subjective experience. We shall attempt to demonstrate by way of two examples, involving the idea of 'respect' (de-
finable for our purposes as the supreme worth attached to an individual and fundamental to the moral, political and religious ideals of
our society), how this may be done by employing a macroscopic perspective for the first and a microscopic for the second of our examples.

The first illustration concerns a country (Israel) that has already
passed certain stages of historical development and, in the course of
it, experienced a change in the rating of particular occupations. The
highly respected occupation of bus driver (elsewhere usually to be
found lower down in social status scales) has a direct connection with
the rebirth of that country from the old Palestine, when immigrants
could not find jobs except in the communes, known as 'kibbutzim'.
Communications between the widely scattered settlements were poor and
journeys dangerous on account of Arab attacks. To cope with the problem, the Jews founded a bus corporation and used their best and most
carefully selected young people as drivers who were, at the same time,
also capable of defending themselves, passengers and cargo, when the
frequent skirmishes took place. The characteristics of driving skill,
courage and the ability to defend and protect, plus secure pay, operated in combination to accord incumbents the highest of occupational
prestige.

On the other hand, doctors, engineers and other immigrants in the
professions, mostly from highly-developed central European society,
could not be absorbed in the then Palestine and were diverted to jobs
on farms and other manual work of lesser skills, while occupations
such as carpenters and similar crafts rated highly in status and prestige. This historical account permits the advancement of the proposition that occupational status, esteem and respect are closely bound
up with such objective macroscopic influences as the economic and
political climate and industrial change, additional to the social,

cultural and ideological processes that go in in a society.

We now turn to our second illustration and transfer our projection from the status of an occupation to the occupational status of an individual. We would call this the 'Downward Spiral Respect Effect'. We have previously considered the meaning to our respondents of their occupation relative to certain others, and their arousal of sensitive reaction to such evaluations. (See Exhibit 9, Chapter 6 above). An extension of the phenomenological perspective and a derivation from the 'respectability' of an occupation is the criterion of 'respect' to be regarded as a central factor in the maintenance of a stable work force among the lower-grade catering workers.* Extreme specialisation in the kitchen has defined the work at the plunge as an occupation in which managements have dramatically failed to demonstrate to incumbents the importance of it. But, the job, to the kitchen porter himself, is important only if the 'immediate others' (his co-workers) support this definition. Further difficulties arise when 'remote others' (society-at-large) emphasise occupational status as the primary basis for self-respect and rank occupations in a hierarchy of prestige. Occupational status defines esteem of the self and if an occupation lacks prestige, there is no escape from the stigma and its punitive sanctions, negative self-image, feeling of inadequacy and not infrequently, guilt, remorse and shame. The incumbent then labours merely to exist and the benefits of industrialisation are inconsequential to him.

Finally, the level of proficiency expected - and hence the level the incumbents expect of themselves - depends on how worthy the job must be in order to be worthy enough for self-respect, and in turn depends upon a man's non-occupational identity. The problem is that the surviving, non-rational, preconceptions of the traditional society are not compatible with the rational performance and status-oriented industrialism of today, where market and firm accord statuses on the basis of competence (and less so on the basis of personal qualities), and extends to the job-holder prestige-income rewards on the basis of relative scarcity of that competence. As a result, the weaker, less competent, less competitive, less physically capable, less socially attractive members become the 'untouchables' of society. And so, the kitchen porter lacks respect, comes cheap, is always available, his status obligation unmotivated by reward, devoid of a sense of pride, commitment or ego-gratification; escape only to be found in deviant adjustment or by recourse to compensatory satisfaction.

The spiral effect therefore begins when the public fail to give respect to the occupational and social statuses, and thereby endow the occupant of the statuses with an unfavourable self-image. If he cannot then obtain a self-respect from conscientious performance of his role, he loses the vital incentive to perform competently; and when he fails to carry out his obligation conscientiously, the public (and the 'immediate others') become dissatisfied with the services it receives, and when this occurs, the public is still less willing to accord respect to statuses, which increases the difficulty of the status-occupant to find a favourable self-image, which makes it less likely that he will take his work seriously, which, in turn, accelerates the spiral downwards or at best produces an orientation of a circular flow. Our

* Verified by the empirical work in restaurants of Angela Bowey,
Sociology of Organisations, Hodder and Stoughton, 1976

central hypothesis (in Chapter 3 above) is thus a highly probably reality.

Stigmatisation - Incumbent Adjustment and Managerial Re-orientation

We have already established that the origins of stigma are derived from
the impurities attached to task and person, and its perpetuation sustained through such functions of occupational specialisation as are associated with dirt and servility. This state is likely to persist until
technological application removes these occupations from the structure.
Paradoxically, in times of affluence, when an organisation could afford
the extra cost, higher productivity also creates a surplus of workers
at the periphery which tends to swell the service occupations, for such
deprived groups then come cheap and will accept any work that comes to
hand. This, in turn, discourages the development of technical aids and
human power in unorganised form will continue to work for the rewards
it is prepared to accept. If interest group organisation of kitchen
porters achieves compensatory rewards at a level at which employers find
the cost too high at the margin, their thoughts will once more return
to machines. On present trends, that time is far distant still. It
thus appears that managements justify the hitherto poor rewards by a
claim that the industry gives work to an otherwise unemployable category
by pretence of a social benevolence when the underlying rationale appears to be really economic. But, even more alienating to the job holder than poor financial rewards is the feeling of low esteem on the job.
It is here that a reappraisal of attitudes, along the lines we shall
suggest, may have a vital and beneficial effect.

   In social terms, it is possible to think of stigma in its impact upon
an individual as a process of completeness or incompleteness. When
there is still hope for upward mobility or occupational progression, or
performance of the occupational role to expectations, stigmatisation is
not yet complete. But, once that hope is lost to the socially handicapped - and the stigmatisation process, as interpreted by him, is complete - he must come to terms with it and manage the stigma by way of
some kind of adjustment. How can this be accomplished and how can management help? If respect has initially been forfeited through occupational membership, all is not lost for the plongeur or other marginal
occupational member, if some mechanism can be found to break the circular flow we have identified and procure respect. One way to achieve
this is to structure status and role-sets in cross-cutting ties, so
that, say, a kitchen porter's opponent in one contest becomes his ally
in another. It would, for example, be feasible for chef and porter to
have a shared religious identity and so bridge the status differential
which causes disequilibrium in the kitchen. Proficiency in, or manifest
enthusiasm for, a mutual sporting interest (fencing or rugger?) or a
shared affinity to horticulture or photography can make allies of status
opponents (manager and kitchen porter) and make the contestants appreciative and tolerant of each other's occupational identity. Any 'inbred'
sub-group with homogeneous identities (like a group of middle management) may be less likely to understand a kitchen porter's feelings or
the meanings, intentions and purposes behind his actions, than occupational peers, but it is equally fallacious to suggest that simple contact
alone is sufficient to breed understanding and respect.

   A second mechanism that may function as an enhancement of role identification is the potentially powerful influence of the mass media. In

this context, selected occupational roles are so attractively presented as to carry an individual beyond his own circumscribed experiences and identify, at least temporarily, with that role.* Lauda, the racing driver's terrible facial disfigurement, incurred when his car exploded at the Nurnbergring, is apparently impervious to the public effect his temporary face projects, and at least in the short run carries lightly the stigma of physical brand his occupation presented him with. But, occupational stigma it is not; the world champion performs, spectators identify with the sport, cameras witness the act and the media pays reverence to a hero returned from the dead. Lauda manages to accept the risks of his chosen profession and to trade off the physical presentation of the self against the preserved driving skills, the then leadership in the stakes, an attractive and loyal wife and the respect of the world as communicated by a media that has not yet favoured the likes of kitchen porter with its interest.

At a further level of analysis, if lowly-evaluated occupations aim to attract respect, conscientious role performance is essential. This is our third point. Peter Blau (5) discovered in his researches that people tend to do what the structure of their situation rewards and avoid doing what the structure penalises. Ingenuity in productive and conscientious role-playing is therefore contingent on an appreciation of their efforts and appropriate rewards. To play the role this way, a kitchen porter needs both maximum proficiency - itself an independent status elevator - to be adjudged a 'professional' in his own right, and commitment to the employer. Since, however, the job is seen as the worst in the industry and the porter as 'general dogsbody' in any kitchen, no sooner does he join, managements tend to expect less and less while the better man can do the work in a shorter time. The time so gained can then be used to perform some other tasks he is asked to do, which takes him to various parts in the food production area to which he would not otherwise have access: the cellar, the stores, the refrigerator, indeed a passport to 'anywhere', in fact. If it be that the unpleasant work is not adequately rewarded or if the porter is not properly fed, ingenuity will come into play and he will take what he can get to barter for what he needs. Such fluid situations restore the imbalance to equilibrium of a sort. (6)

Devotion to status obligation (and commitment to firm) is not easy to achieve when the occupational handicap is that of kitchen porter and the social handicap a deprived background. If commitment to occupation is difficult and proficiency in work routines not encouraged (training not given), motivation is, at best, only subsistence-related and therefore unlikely to encourage any degree of permanency.

A recent visitor to the U.S.A., to study catering operations and the orientation of various grades of worker in the industry, reported interestingly on American occupational socialisation practices designed to achieve maximum commitment to and loyalty for the employing firm. (7) Some of the catering and hotel organisations there conduct a number of courses for what are known as 'hourly-paid' staff, including such grades as porters, room maids and waiters. No previous knowledge is

* Particularly conspicuous in television presentation are the occupations of detective, surgeon, nurse, bus driver, waitress, shop-keeper, inmate of a total institution, tailor, etc.

expected when joining the company and all induction periods share the following common characteristics: newcomers are made 'company persons', talks are given on the company's history, aims, achievements and success trends; incumbents are told how they can progress in the company, when they can expect their first promotion, what to do when they get it and how the company can help them. Employees are made welcome and the company bends over backwards to show they are wanted, needed and part of a team, so that even before newcomers finish their intitial training, they are already proud of 'their' company. This feeling for a particular company exists at all levels and grades of staff, everyone convinced that their company is best, great to work for and it is there that their future lies. Modern methods of training are employed (including competitions among various grades) and trainees of any age have to pass an examination, following their induction period, to earn a certificate of proficiency.

As against these seemingly enlightened methods (critics refer to them as 'indoctrination'), training for the less skilled appears to be emphasised on the Pavlovian conditioning principle of reinforcement, that is strict rote-learning according to the firm's manual of operations. The likely end result of this method is that what has been learnt is so highly specialised and applicable to only one particular firm that it cannot be utilised elsewhere.

One further point that managements tend to neglect is to take care to keep the kitchen porter in a sane environment. Day in and day out, he is surrounded by a world of steam, grease, wrappers, cigarette ash, melon skins, slops and scraps of food, containers with dirty dishes, glasses, cutlery and bins for swill, and broken glass. To be motivated towards a relationship with these elements requires compensatory measures on a fairly wide front, to keep a man in this work for any length of time. Chefs, restaurant managers and head waiters have, in the past, been blamed for their stigmatising attitudes and inhuman treatment, particularly during pressure periods. Instead, genuine interest in the man and his background, a caretaker role and psychological support, perhaps even sincere paternalism, together with a tangible recognition of his contribution, would, we feel, go some way towards achieving a hoped-for stability in this grade.

It is taken as given that managements are aware of the usually prescribed methods of job satisfaction, and we have tried, in our analysis, to look beyond such remedies as part of a deeper behavioural perspective, in the consideration of the marginal worker. It has been noted (Introduction above) that work as such holds a centrality in most adults' lives and contributes to identity and self-esteem, and that it has the utility to bring order and meaning to life. In terms of national policy, our empirical and theoretical formulations strongly suggest that the more than can be done for the peripheral work groups on the lines we advocate, the less might have to be done in the field of medical care, public aid and social measures for the deprived.

Despite the multi-dimensional definition attached to work (in its social and economic context), the personal meaning of it is crucial in the phenomenological sense. The work place is one of the major foci of personal evaluation (write Kahn and French)(8) and it is a place where one finds out whether one is 'making the grade'; where one's esteem is constantly on the line, and where every effort will be made to avoid reduction in self-evaluation and its attending sense of failure. If job withdrawal is to be avoided, unpleasant work must be made tolerable and oppressive features of the work removed; more autonomy allowed in tackling tasks, more opportunity offered to increase skills and the rewards more directly related to the intrinsic contribution of the work. It is, therefore, likely that what we shall see in the future is a shift in the perspective from public support to an extension of corporate responsibility on the lines of what might be referred to as a 'social efficiency model', where firms in an industry enlarge on their narrower interest of producing goods and services to the broader one that relates their activities also to other social concerns.

Contributions to New Knowledge

1. The concept of stigmatisation has hitherto not been related to occupations. We have shown how this can be done, by selecting a group of low-status occupations and unfolding their peculiarities and characteristics in order to identify a common denominator for the discovery of the stigma.

2. We attempted a definition of occupational stigma and offered a theoretical framework, supported by a model which depicts its anatomy and possible causal influences, not previously attempted in social researches of occupations.

3. We have delved into some 800 years of history and reconstructed the relevant data to yield a coherent picture of the occupational history of the kitchen porter, about which little was previously gathered together and shown how the stigmatising influence works its way through all stages of historical development, as an attachment upon an incumbent in the 'wrong' occupation, static in its location, and transcending in time, events, social settings and culture.

4. We traced the historical fortunes of some industries in order to identify the social forces which gave rise to the preservation and perpetuation of stigma and established that the decline of one industry can aid the ascent of another. (Household Service/Hotel and Catering).

5. We managed to discover a correlation between poverty, vagrancy, workshyness, employability, the stigma phenomenon and the specific patterns of historical events, and venture to propose as a historical truth that human response and resilience between individuals and groups vary under adverse conditions of life.

6. We produced a social view of the institutional components of a hotel structure and considered specific levels of behaviour in the kitchen as a social unit, not as far as we ascertained previously researched. Explanatory models and a chart, presenting the entire structure of the British hotel and catering industry, have also been constructed.

7. We investigated some stigmatised industries, criteria of survival and fragmentation, and relative thereto conceptualised upon such social concerns as respectability, stereotyping, labelling, mal-socialisation and occupational afflictions, as a contrasting treatment to the previously discussed subjective experiences of incumbents and so to

objectively relate at macro-level the stigma effect across industrial, occupational and individual boundaries.

8. We have constructed a TYPOLOGY of subjective socialisation patterns for occupational stigma, which can be used as a valid scheme to categorise other low-grade occupations, such as railway porters, lavatory attendants, road sweepers, drainage workers, shoe-shiners and garbage collectors, among others.

9. We have conducted an exhaustive survey in eleven Midland cities and towns and interviewed kitchen porters in seventy hotels to obtain important empirical information in thirteen areas of their life/work experiences and attitudes, which produced a hitherto unsuspected stereotype and validated a number of our propositions.

10. And we have finally produced an experimental scheme for the quantitative measurement of worker stability in employment, by means of a statistical and social indicator, not so far suggested elsewhere. *

---

* Saunders, K.C., April 1977, 'Measuring Stability in Employment: An Experimental Analysis based on Life/Work Histories of Lower-grade Workers in the Hotel and Catering Industry' (unpublished Research Paper).

NOTES TO CHAPTER 8

1.   Clarke, A.C. (1956)'The Use of Leisure and its Relation to
    Levels of Occupational Prestige', American Sociological
    Review, Vol.21, pp.301-307

2.   Holme T.H. and Rahe, R.H. (1967) 'The Social Readjustment
    Rating Scale', Journal of Psychosomatic Research, Vol.II,No.2,
    pp.213-218

3.   Caplow, Theodore (1964) 'The Sociology of Work', McGraw-Hill,
    New York, pp.19-24

4.   Goffman, Erving (1956) 'The Presentation of Self in Everyday
    Life', University of Edinburgh Social Research Centre, pp.
    104-105

5.   Blau, Peter (1954) 'Competition and Co-operation in Bureaucracy',
    American Journal of Sociology, Vol.59, pp.530-535

6.   Lyons, Dale, now Head of Department, Hotel and Catering Studies,
    Birmingham College of Food and Domestic Arts (formerly industrial
    catering manager).Interviewed by author, September 1976

7.   Pesek, John, Senior Lecturer in Food and Beverage Operations,
    Middlesex Polytechnic (formerly hotel manager), Interviewed by
    author, September, 1976

8.   Kahn, Harry and French, J.R.P. (1962) 'A Programmatic Approach
    to Studying the Industrial Environment and Mental Health',
    Journal of Social Issues, Vol.3,(July), pp.1-47

A CAR worker was being
detained at Luton today

ARSON CHARGE

Kitchen porter David Sim-
mons, 30, was again re-
manded at Chichester, Sussex,
yesterday, accused of arson
at the Bishop of Chichester's
Palace.

KITCHEN porter
Michael Charles-
worth deliberately
left his four-year-old
son on the Penzance
express.

He told police that the
boy had been bad-tem-
pered and this had got
on top of him, a court
was told yesterday.

The statement went on : 'I
was drunk and I decided the
best thing to do was to walk

Driver's anger 'led to murder'

Hospital nurses accused of swindles

Hotel fires:
man remanded

A 22-year-old kitchen porter
was remanded in custody for a
week by magistrates at Brighton today on two charges of
arson at a sea-front hotel last
Friday.

Charles Michael Fisher, of
no fixed address, was charged
with unlawfully and mali-
ciously setting fire to five
chairs and a carpet at the
Hotel Metropole and starting
another fire in the hotel.

<u>References to Transgressors by Occupation.</u>

Occupation is so important a criterion for
the Registrar-General's Standard Industrial
Classification because it so closely links
to an individual's economic status educational background and his whole pattern of
living. Viewed in human proportions, occupation confers an identity upon an incumbent or job holder. The illustrations also
demonstrate the centrality of work in our
lives, as seen by the media at least. Chapter 7. under the heading of 'The Stigma
Effect' explains how a media label upon a
transgressor by occupation reinforces stigmatising propensities and mediates to nor-
ture these, and in the eyes of society presents the occupation itself in bad light.

One of many. He is representative of one of the several categories in the trade.

This kitchen porter has been asked to record his work routine for one day. This sample reflects in general the literacy of porters who have had a modest schooling experience.

Brief personal details:

He is known as 'Harry', has no relatives, looks 65 years of age but is younger. He has no home of his own, works 17 hrs per day throughout the year at various race meetings, sleeps in a dormitory if at Ascot, or in a caravan provided at other race tracks. Most tracks have staff eating facilities but kitchens are used only at race meetings.

According to the kitchen staff he works with, he is generally regarded as having assumed the role of a workhorse.

Note: Chapter 7. identifies seven likely categories of mal-socialisation into which it is possible to place an individual. These groupings indicate a characteristic overall social pattern for those forced into or willing to work in stigmatised circumstances.

KITCHEN PORTER

Goodwood

Outyp

6-OC get up make Tea fore Staff and Cell Staff Then open Kitchen Lite ovens and Stove fore Breakfast Set Table fore Same get Boilers ready to Boil make Tea with Teapots fore all Breakfast after Breakfast help cheef to get Things ready

~oc Clean Toilets rans and Doormatrys Each Day Change Tea Cloths fore Kitchen Each day Then work in Kitch Whasing up Class Salud bowls and Silver Flats Each day Same rooteen Each Day Saterday Colect sheets from Bedroom and Turn up Maltes ready fore Colecting by Lerry Clean Kitchen Claning ovens Be Emptying Boalers and Gas on.

Glossary of terms

Action Frame of Reference: seen as an atomistic approach which attempts to explain social phenomena in terms of individual actions and interactions rather than in holistic terms that look upon society as an integrated whole. Max Weber is the best-known exponent of this view.

Alienation: first used by Marx in the context of man's involvement in impersonal and dehumanising work. The term has come to mean a state of social isolation, especially in modern industrial society.

Analeptic Part: of a science, i.e. analeptic medicines, which help to strengthen, restore, repair the body, nerves or renew the spirits. Restoration may occur also by analeptic and pleasant diet.

Anomic Condition: first used by the French sociologist, Durkheim, to indicate a condition of normlessness in society; hence a loss of function or role, feeling of confusion of values and identity.

Arteriosclerosis: used here in the institutional sense and means that an organisation - like a man - can contract stiffness and hardening of the arteries in later life, lose its elasticity to events and eventually degenerate. The disease is said to cause more deaths in the Western world than do all the other diseases combined. Could be true of many organisations also.

Conceptual Liquidation: in the context used here, an outsider (pauper or vagrant) perceived by society as incapable of making any intellectual contribution by reason of an inferior social status and position.

Confucian Principles: derive from Confucius the Chinese philosopher, and teacher of history and ethics. He spent many years of his life in developing the principles of 'right living' and ideal human relations, which were to form the core of his philosophy. Has many living descendants and followers in China today.

Control Occupation: the term relates to an experimental rather than to a natural setting in a research situation. The function of the control occupation is to show us what would have happened to an experimental occupation if it had not been exposed to the experimental influences.

Crystalliser: is a term used by the American Gerhard Lenski in his writings on social class and status and how individual rankings are to be determined. Low status crystallisers are seen as those who rate low in terms of education, occupation, income and ethnic status.

Culture: may be defined as the total way of life of a society, that has been (a) lived, (b) organised and (c) handed down from generation to generation. Culture includes language, ethical values, social and economic aspirations, political ideals, style of clothes and religions of the members of a society.

Deviant: in sociological terms, a person whose behaviour is outside the limits of tolerance or counter to societal norms, or to the values of his own group. Erving Goffman refers to 'disaffiliates' in corporate life as one type of deviance.

Embourgeoisement: is a term traceable to F. Zweig, who researched work
people in Sheffield in the 1950's. His hypothesis proclaimed that class
differences are disappearing in this country as the more affluent of
the working class are beginning to assume middle class life styles and
values. Current research does not support this view.

Empirical Research: is a tool that social scientists employ to obtain
data that are based on evidence or proof from experiment or observation,
at times also reasoning but never purely speculation or supernatural re-
velation.

Epistemology: studies questions associated with the sources, limits,
nature and possibility of knowledge. Relative to the epistomological
concept of leisure, activities and meanings are connected with aesthetic
and analytical views of the world, that is, those that transform the
world like painting a picture; examine the world like a political text;
or confirm the world like playing some familiar game.

Extension Pattern: (see also Opposition and Neutrality Patterns),
according to Stanley Parker's definition, indicates a close relationship
between work and leisure; that is, a spillover of work into leisure time.
Professionals, crafts people, shop-keepers or people working on farms
would fall into this category.

Folkway: is a term originally suggested by W.G. Sumner. It is a standard of behaviour that is socially approved but not accompanied by deep,
or moral, implications. Dress or eating habits of customary standards
are examples. Social sanctions like gossip exist as an informal control
mechanism to make people conform.

Heterodoxy: this word is used to convey that conflicting religious views
and values were held at the historical time under review. Holding other
opinions than the right one is not in accord with those generally established and recognised as right or orthodox, mainly in a religious or
theological sense.

Ideal-type: a term used by Max Weber in his book on the methodology for
social sciences. It refers to the construction of sociological models
linked to, but not exact representations of, concrete data. It could be
seen as a standard, hypothetical idea or abstraction of a phenomenon
with exaggerated characteristic features against which to measure reality.

Infra dignitate: really means that something is below one's dignity. In
the context used refers to the desire of some job holders to conceal to
the wider public or friends the kind of work they are doing on the
grounds that it will do their social status no credit.

Institution: (Social Institution) is not to be understood in sociology
as a building or an organised body of people, but as a form of social
organisation where a traditionally accepted pattern of behaviour with
clear rules and norms prevails. Examples from our society are religion,
marriage, family, class and education.

Instrumental Pattern: in context expresses an attitude towards work by
individuals or groups that is treating the job strictly as a means to an

215

end, namely in terms of material rewards that will be gained from it, rather than the fulfilment of intrinsic satisfaction or the self-actualising kind of need.

Institutional Sanctions: are generally understood to mean the informal (or sometimes formal) control mechanism that is applied if the deviant or non-conformist behaves counter to expectations. Formal punishment may occur by operation of law and informal by violence, shaming a person or ostracising him, among other methods.

Internalising: is a process whereby an individual incorporates the values and norms of his community so as to make them his own. In the social sciences, the term is often used synonymously with learning, where the user wishes to emphasise the imparting of meaning or experience upon a personality.

Joking Relationships: is a term derived from Social Anthropology and prescribing that particular kin must maintain familiarity with one another. Such rituals often take the form of teasing that by convention must be accepted with apparent equanimity by those subjected to it. This kind of relationship is also evident in work and tends to avoid conflict situations by making, for example, a deviant conform to the norms of the group.

Lebenswelt: is a term derived from the German language which philosophers often popularly use to paint a panorama of the times, one's milieu or environment. It is really the world in which a person functions.

Legitimacy: in the sociological sense beliefs about who is rightfully entitled to exercise authority. Also the extent to which an act or behaviour is approved socially; it means as well that the act or behaviour is lawful.

Marginality: is often explained culturally as the person who grows up in one culture and then participates in another, so that the individual does not feel completely at home in either. In our example, the kitchen worker perceives himself through his low-status work as a sub-person to whom society accords little or no respect, a marginal man.

Mores: (singular: mos) are behaviour patterns that are strongly backed by community rewards or punishments. They are cultural expectations in a society that matter. Examples are the observance of standards of morality, or care of children, and controls against cannibalism or murder. Mores are much stricter norms than folkways and a breach attracts severe punishment.

Neutrality Pattern: (see also Extension and Opposition Patterns), in Stanley Parker's researches used to show that family interests and leisure pursuits take precedence in the lives of those people where their job is not of central interest although otherwise bearable. Routine and some non-manual work would come into this category.

Normative Aspirations: in our context, generally accepted work-related aspirations shared by the individual concerned in his occupation of a particular status in the organisation, e.g. the incumbent's expectations of what type of work merits upgrading may be at variance with that considered justifiable by the organisation.

Norms: are rules of behaviour which guide and regulate relationships
among people. Some basic norms apply to all (be polite to tourists);
some to few and these may be written (fouls on the football pitch).
Norms can be weak or strong (see folkways and mores).

Occupational Mobility: in general means change which may be horizontal,
that is a job change involving no status change; or vertical, which is
up or down a hierarchy and hence improvement or decline in status. Such
change need not necessarily be within the same organisation.

Opposition Pattern: (see also Extension and Neutrality Patterns), in
Stanley Parker's definition suggests that arduous, demanding or unattractive work attracts completely contrasting leisure activities, designed
to facilitate recuperation or in some cases escapism. (Kitchen Portering and some occupations discussed in our study, as well as such work as
mining and fishing, would come into this category).

Oganicism: is a term used to explain reality by constructing a picture
of the world as an organic model. Hence, segments of society like, say,
kitchen organisation and the tasks chefs and cooks perform, may be seen
as the kind of organicism which has built-in characteristics where the
unexpected may happen as a contingency not provided for, i.e. cooked
food not for some reason consumed.

Phenomenal World: is the world seen by a theoretical stance which
stresses the meanings of phenomena to the individuals involved in the
natural settings of everyday life. To discover such meanings, field research methods are more useful than laboratory or questionnaire methods.

Plongeur (Plonge): low-status worker washing up in a kitchen or restaurant. Could be bottle washer. The plonge would indicate a job requiring immersion in water.

Polar Occupational Types: if there is an occupational continuum from
high to low in terms of status and prestige, then polarisation towards
the former or the latter would depend on whether (in Raymond Mack's interpretation) the occupation belongs to the 'determinate' or the 'indeterminate' group. The first consists of high-status and the second of
low-status type occupations.

Role-Set: is a term coined by the American social writer Robert Merton
and signifies simply the array of roles associated with a given position.
Our visual presentation of the kitchen porter's role-set gives a good
illustration of the concept.

Role Theory: social scientists have adopted this concept from the theatre. In life, a person's role is what he is expected to do; it is the
dynamic or functional aspect of status. A role also specifies an individual's rights and obligations towards other actors in a given situation.
The associated theory relates to interrelated testable propositions which
specify conditions under which certain forms of role behaviour will occur.

Self-actualisation: the need to develop one's abilities to the full extent, to realise one's full potential for doing or creating and become

everything one is capable of becoming.

Social Actor: is one who as an individual (or in groups) as a prime agent of change in any given situation becomes the focal point for the study of modes of orientation towards a situation or in interaction. The image of the individual is that he is not just a 'behaver' or 'actor' but an 'interactor'.

Social Distance: the extent to which members of a group or individuals are willing to interact with varying degrees of intimacy with members of another group. It is also the degree of understanding existing between persons or groups relative to one another.

Social Identity: is explained by Goffman as follows: 'When a stranger comes into our presence, first appearances are likely to enable us to anticipate his category and attributes, his social identity - to use a term that is better than social status because personal attributes such as honesty are involved, as well as structural ones, like occupation.'

Socialisation: is the process of learning (or teaching) the shared values, attitudes, behaviour and/or beliefs of some group. Learning how to fit into society.

Social Mobility: is the movement from one social class to another as the social scientist understands it.

Social Structure: signifies a network of relationships among the members of a group or society. The term has also been defined as consisting of factors that persist over time, are external to the individual (like urbanisation, technology or social norms, for example) and are assumed to influence behaviour and thought.

Status (Social Status): indicates a position in society (Son, Doctor, Councillor, etc.) Prestige evaluation or other ranking of an individual or group by society may be attached to the term. Each status has also a dynamic aspect, that is, a prescribed action or behaviour, known as 'role'.

Status-set: (see also status), constitutes a particular individual's statuses as a group, that is, a complex of statuses occupied by an individual.

Stereotype: is held to be a fixed belief, usually resistant to evidence, that a given group or occupation possesses certain social traits, most frequently negative ones. Not only do stereotypes often represent misinformation, distorted information and caricatured ideas, but also have a profound influence on the formation of attitudes pertaining to these areas of experience.

Stigma: (see also Occupational Stigma in Chapter 3), defined by Goffman as a blemish, defect or sign as such, which as a serious negative effect on an individual's social acceptance.

Stigmatising Symbols: may be physical, abominations of the body - the various visible deformities; may be blemishes of character expressed in

218

behaviour - weak willed, domineering, treacherous, dishonest and such; may be evident also by stigmatising tools used in work - rags, brushes, brooms, dustcart or bin and similar; may also be reflected in the materials handled in work - corpses, smelly materials as in a slaughterhouse or kitchen.

Stultification: is to render someone ineffective or to exhibit him in a ridiculous light. If the word is used in the context of an occupational experience, that is, the mental stultification engendered by the nature of the work itself, it is the dulling effect that is thereby produced which permeates the entire existence of that person, including his leisure.

Sub-Culture: is a distinctive cultural group within the larger culture. Refers to norms that set a group apart from the total society. Example - punkrockers, rastafarians, Gaelic speakers, as a regional sub-culture.

Substantive Model: a model is usually a representation in either abstract, simplified or miniature form of an aspect of reality or simplified system of variables. In substantive form, a model specifies the whole or a major part of the area under review, or a comprehensive view of the model in focus.

Sub-system: (see also System), simply a system that is part of a larger system. If one looks at the world as a social system, then nation-states may be seen as sub-systems. The latter may also exist within a state, say a parish council, or it may be a club, association like a trade union, or even a department of a business.

Symbiotic Situation: symbiosis in a general sense comes from biology and denotes a situation where organisms live together to their mutual advantage. In the behavioural sciences a situation of this kind denotes some kind of economic interdependence which is a consequence of the division of labour. A human community is usually composed of symbiotic and cultural relationships.

System (Social System): is basically an entity made up of interrelated structural parts. Social systems are thought of as abstractions of social groups in terms of shared expectations, symbolic definitions and statistics. Examples of structural parts may be kinship, economic or political, each including also the cultural elements of values, norms, beliefs and knowledge. All these parts interrelate and so make up the social system.

Trucking: is a term that originated during the 19th Century when the coming of new industries and the idea of 'selling one's labour' produced debate on how such labour should be paid. Apart from coin of the realm, employers also paid in goods or tokens to be used in their shops, known as truck or 'tommy shop system'. Successive Truck Acts from 1831 onwards endeavoured to ensure that payment to workmen in cash and the prohibition of unwarrantable deductions from wages in respect of food, fuel and such.

Typology: is a method of organising data in sociological studies and research. It is a set of categories for comparing empirical data so that a researcher can see how closely the empirical phenomena correspond to his type. It is thus no more than a classification which may be ad hoc such as the division of kitchen porters who are socialisers and those who are isolates, following an analysis of the elements implicit in the concept of, say, social personality.

Variable: commonly known as a social feature which varies, as for example age, class, sex or race. Statisticians and researchers distinguish between dependent variables or quantities and independent ones. The former appears to be explained by one or more other phenomena (a causal relationship), while the latter has an apparent causal relationship with one or more of these other phenomena.

Values: are criteria or standards by which beliefs, actions and various social objects are evaluated. The characteristics of goodness, virtue, rightness, ritual purity, or indeed aesthetic excellence as an imposed measure by a particular social group. It is a wider and more general concept than 'norm' and thus more difficult to apply to specific behaviour. In the case of work values, however, one specific orientation would be a belief in the adherence to the Protestant Ethic.

Vertical Mobility: is a change of status which can be upward or downward. Thus, if in a job change status and role are altered by way of a more permanent movement from one rank to another in a status hierarchy, it would constitute such a mobility. If the job change involves no status change, the term horizontal mobility is used. Other kinds of vertical mobility may relate to income groups, classes or years of education, for example.

Virtual Stigmatisation: (see also Stigma and Stigmatising Symbols), distinguishes imputed from actual stigmatisation where the former, in Goffman's argument, is only a potential characterisation while the latter can be shown to exist by means of factual evidence.

Index

232